W9-BIA-810

INTRODUCING:
THE LAKE ERIE QUADRANGLE SHIPWRECK SERIES

# Kiss of the Devil Wind:

## THE SINKING

## OF THE

## STEAMSHIP *GERKEN*

David R. Frew

Erie County
& Museums
Historical Society

*Address all correspondence to:*
Erie County Historical Society & Museums
417 State Street
Erie, Pennsylvania 16501


*Publishing Management:*
Meridian Creative Group,
a Division of Larson Texts, Inc.
1762 Norcross Road
Erie, Pennsylvania 16510


Cover illustration: Brian Altman

Cover design: Eric Armbruster

Copyright ©2000 by the Erie County Historical Society &
Museums. All rights reserved. No part of this publication may
be reproduced or transmitted in any form or by any means,
electronic or mechanical, including photocopy, recording, or any
information storage or retrieval system, without prior written
permission of the Erie County Historical Society & Museums.

Printed in the United States of America

ISBN No. 1–883658–38–1

1   2   3   4   5   6   7   8   9   0

**FOR FURTHER READING ON CENTRAL LAKE ERIE** you might try the following publications which are available at bookstores throughout the region and may be obtained at the Museum Shop (814-454-1813) or by mail order from the Erie County Historical Society & Museums, 419 State Street, Erie, PA 16501. Please add 15% shipping. Pennsylvania residents: add 6% sales tax on the cost of the book and the shipping.

*Home Port Erie: Voices of Silent Images.* Robert J. MacDonald and David Frew. Erie: Erie County Historical Society, 1997. 334 pp., 408 photographs, $31.95. ISBN No. 1-883658-33-0.

Erie is and has always been a port town. Its central Lake Erie location, canal linkage to Pittsburgh and natural harbor were critical to its development. Bob MacDonald spent his life collecting stories and photos of the harbor and the people who worked and played there. David Frew has helped to make these silent voices speak to the reader in a way that renews interest in our maritime heritage.

*The Lake Erie Quadrangle: Waters of Repose.* David Stone and David Frew. Erie: Erie County Historical Society, 1993. 304 pp., 125 illustrations. $16.95 soft cover, ISBN No. 1-883658-19-5; $22.95 hard cover, ISBN No. 1-883658-20-9.

By statistical comparison, The Lake Erie Quadrangle between Presque Isle and Long Point is 21 times more dangerous than the infamous Bermuda Triangle. Dave Stone, the beachcomber from Long Point, and David Frew, a Gannon University Professor, have combined to tell the saga of shipwrecks, pirates, rum running, ice walking, lore and legend on Lake Erie. The book includes a table of the 429 maritime disasters in the quadrangle.

"Ghostships of the South Shore Quadrangle." David Frew. Erie: Erie County Historical Society, 1993. 22" x 38" chart. $5.00, ISBN No. 1-883658-16-0.

A chart of the south shore of Lake Erie from Conneaut, OH to Barcelona, NY showing the approximate locations of 200 shipwrecks recorded since the eighteenth century.

"The Ghost Fleet of Long Point: Graveyard of the Great Lakes." Dave Stone. Ingersoll, Ontario, 1978. 21" x 38" chart. $7.50, ISBN No. 1-883658-22-5.

This popular chart is now available in the Erie area showing the approximate locations of recorded shipwrecks on and off Long Point, Ontario since the eighteenth century.

# Overview

On Friday, August 20, 1926, a ferocious gale suddenly struck Central Lake Erie, placing several commercial ships and a sailing yacht in peril. Such a storm might have been expected in March or November. In fact, the treacherous waters of Central Lake Erie have been named the Lake Erie Quadrangle as a result of the 458 shipwrecks recorded there since the 1800s. But the unexpected nature of this particular summer storm, coupled with its incredible ferocity, wreaked such havoc that locals referred to it as "The August Gale" for decades thereafter. In the predawn hours of Saturday, August 21, a number of sailors were left fighting for their lives as eighty-mile-per-hour winds and breaking twenty-five-foot waves totally devastated two vessels. By dawn, the 241-foot steamship *Gerken* was gone with only two of her three lifeboats recovered, and the sailing yacht *Pterodactyl* had broken up and foundered. Six men were left swimming in the maelstrom of breaking waves that night as a railroad car ferry, two U.S. Coast Guard vessels and a luxury passenger liner searched for them. *Kiss of the Devil Wind* is a story of lives that collided in the storm. It is an account of tragedy, transformation and the ultimate survival of the human spirit.

# Author's Note

*Kiss of the Devil Wind* is based upon actual events that occurred during August, 1926 and the people that experienced them. I took great lengths to research the characters and to base the dialogue upon newspaper interviews. Subplots are based upon oral history—stories that I heard as a youngster prowling the commercial docks. I owe them to Bill Beckman, the yard crew at the Cascade Docks and conversations with Mary Howard. It is my hope that this story will honor the memory of the story's main characters and the contributions that they and their fellow sailors made to Lake Erie's maritime history.

David R. Frew
August 31, 2000

# The Author

Dr. David Frew is a full professor of organizational behavior at Gannon University in Erie, Pennsylvania, where he has served on the faculty and held a number of administrative posts since 1970. He has written 20 books and more than 100 articles and technical papers. His publications run the gamut from scholarly works to articles in popular magazines such as *Cruising World* and *Sail*. An avid sailor, he has raced and cruised his auxiliary sailboat extensively with his wife Mary Ann, three now-grown children and six grandchildren. His books on the maritime history of Central Lake Erie have won regional and national awards.

# Acknowledgements

I can't believe how long this project has taken! The research, writing and manuscript re-engineering process seemed endless. Now that the book is finished, I fully realize and truly appreciate the impact of contributions made by so many important people along the way.

I'll begin with my wife, Mary Ann. So much more than a marriage partner of thirty-five years, she is my long-time friend, professional colleague and favorite co-author. She knows my writing and never hesitates to tell me the truth. Thanks also to my children Kristin, Cheryl and David, who were my sailing partners for many years, crewing on adventures through the nooks and crannies of Central Lake Erie. And a special appreciation to my newest sailing buddies, my grandchildren: Noah, Abigail, Jordi, Eden, Phineas and Colin. Their hopefulness and youth inspires me to keep Lake Erie's maritime adventures alive. As I toiled at the manuscript I could see them as adults reading this story to their own children.

I must have spent thousands of hours, reading source documents in libraries from Cleveland to Buffalo. I owe a great debt of gratitude to the patience of librarians who helped me dredge up the original newspaper articles and operate microfilm readers. Reading the many accounts of the August 1926 storm reminded me of my obligation to friends and families of the sailors who were involved in this story. I hope that my work serves as a lasting tribute to the contribution they made to our maritime heritage.

My friend and colleague, Robert Wall (who died just before the publication of the book) made a very special contribution to the manuscript. He read it critically from his perspective as an accomplished historical novelist and made invaluable suggestions. I miss you Robert. I also owe special thanks to Robert "Bob" MacDonald (also deceased), co-author of *Home Port Erie*. It was Bob who taught me the nuances of local maritime history. Mary Howard read the first draft with a fine-toothed diver's comb. And Father Homer DeWalt! One day when I was stuck on a bit of history relating to the Gerken family, there was a sudden knock on my office door. I opened it and found Father DeWalt holding a file folder filled with photographs and newspaper articles. As it turned out, he is related to the Gerken family and had found his way to my office at the most amazing moment to ask if I was interested in his records. Steve Blasko, chief scientist on the Titanic Project, helped coach me on the geology.

Armed with a rough manuscript, I coerced several graduate students into reading it. To Peggy DiMattio, Fred Popeski and Rick Stoczinski, I owe profound thanks. Peggy and Fred developed a book club; reading, then arguing the merits and weaknesses of each chapter. Rick read the early manuscript with pencil in hand and made many valuable edits. Lots of friends and colleagues helped, as well. Judi Alex, Harry Barrett, Bill Burke, Chet Czynowski, Bob Kaczenski, John Mitchell, Scott O'Neil, and Terry Walsh all made valuable suggestions. Thanks are due to Lee Belovarac who toiled over the editing of the manuscript. And special appreciation is owed to Don Muller of the Erie County Historical Society and Museums, whose continued faith in my writing projects has been invaluable.

When I added the adventures of the sailing yacht *Pterodactyl* to the manuscript, I couldn't stop thinking about my lifelong friend and sailing companion, Tom Leonardi, who died five years ago. Tom and I experienced Long Point's waves many times, and every time I sail, I am reminded of how much I miss his friendship. Your spirit lives within the manuscript, Tom!

Finally, without the inspiration and guidance of Dave Stone, "The Beachcomber of Long Point," this manuscript would never have become a reality. It was Dave who first took me to Long Point, where he shared his passion for Great Lakes history and shipwrecks. He walked the forbidden, mysterious beaches with me many times, pointing out Long Point's sandy monuments to history. It was Dave Stone, co-author of *Waters of Repose* who started me on this maritime writing quest. I am unbelievably fortunate to have Dave as a friend and forever grateful for the time he has spent acting as my wizard.

Thank you, Dave Stone, your protégé has finally produced something!

# Contents

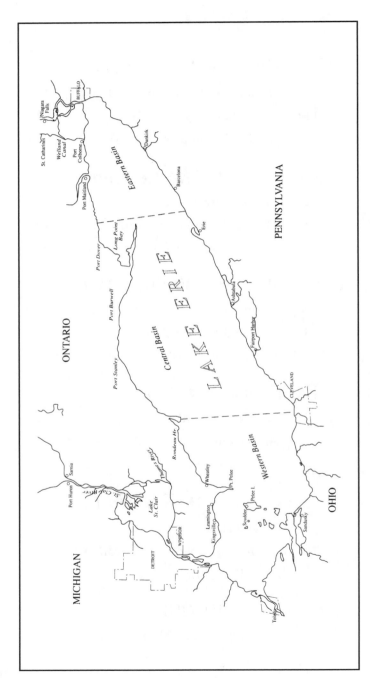

*Chart of Lake Erie depicting the three primary basins.*

*The steamship Gerken, prior to the addition of deck equipment and steam shovel.*

# PRELUDE
# Iroquois Fishing Party at Presque Isle

## [EARLY APRIL, 1626]

Hayano had celebrated a birthday earlier that winter. At 14, he was not quite old enough to join the men from the longhouse on their spring fishing expedition. But the youngster was anxious to become a brave, and true to his Indian name (Iroquois for runner) he was fast and tireless. Hayano's father, a chief, had convinced the elder women that he should be allowed to join the men on their fishing trip to the great sand spit. And so far, his decision seemed sound.

It was an all day trek from the village to the fishing beach and already Hayano had been sent ahead three times to confirm the best trails, check for and clear obstructions. As the youngster raced back and forth reporting conditions ahead, the main party of twenty ponderously dragged a canoe, tents and equipment along a trail that had been ravaged by winter. Much of the ground was still snow covered, but the men were confident that when they reached the sand spit, the warm waters would have created a thaw. They hoped to find exposed sand beaches where they could set up camp and gather fish. With luck, fishing would take only a few days but the men realized that early spring waters could be treacherous. They were prepared to stay as long as necessary, waiting for good fishing

---

conditions. To prepare for this eventuality, they carried dried food, blankets and supplies in the baskets that they brought to store the fish.

The sheer weight of equipment and supplies slowed them to a pace that was frustrating to Hayano. The youngster was anxious to demonstrate his abilities to his father and the rest of the braves. But he was also eager to return to life at the longhouse. He had heard the men talk of past fishing trips which had taken weeks rather than days, and he hoped that his skills would help make this year's expedition go faster than usual. But then Hayano was always in a hurry. His mother often joked that he should have been named "impetuous one" rather than "runner."

The sun was dropping toward the horizon when Hayano made his fourth scouting run. As he streaked through stands of cottonwood trees he listened intently for sounds of the great waves that his father had told him would herald their arrival at the beach. The sound of rustling branches above him was almost deafening but he heard no waves. Hayano was growing concerned that the party would not even make it to the water that day when suddenly an opening in the trees revealed a panorama of water that nearly took his breath away. Soft, white snowless sand traced a path to a deep brown ribbon of hard-packed sand. Then an endless expanse of brilliant blue. Hayano couldn't believe how beautiful it was. The descriptions of his father had long been branded into his brain, but childhood visions of azure could not compare with the massive spectacle of water confronting him. Still confused by the absence of the pounding waves that his father had described so vividly, he joyously ran through sand until he was ankle deep in water. The blue turned almost white as his feet stirred the icy cold water. And fish, thousands of them, skimmed away as he splashed. Hayano knew instantly that fishing would be exceptional this season. With a whoop of joy, he turned toward the trees again and sprinted back to tell his father and the rest of the fishing party the good news.

"Father," he blurted out excitedly as he approached, "the water is only steps away. We can make it today, easily."

With that, he enthusiastically pitched in, helping the men who were dragging the fishing canoe filled with nets and baskets; a ponderous appendage propped atop a traditional Indian travois. With his energetic assistance the canoe suddenly became the caravan's lead item, pressing ahead of the rest of the party.

"We can begin fishing immediately," he shouted over his shoulder to his father. "I will launch the canoe while you and the others set up camp. We'll be finished and headed home in just a few days," he added.

Hayano's father muttered something in a stern tone, but the exact nature of the words were lost in the din created by the overhead rustling of the trees.

"There are no waves," Hayano shouted gleefully, to no one in particular, as he and three young braves continued to put distance between themselves and the rest of the party. "It is a perfect time to begin fishing."

Even though the other canoe carriers put up a mild objection, Hayano pulled the canoe to the water's edge as soon as they reached the sand. There he began unlashing it from its carrier. In an instant he was in the small boat floating away from shore. Hayano's dreams of more than a year were about to come true. He dipped a paddle into the blue water, slowly turning the boat away from the beach. Two strokes, then three. He was finally paddling a canoe through water rather than pretending as he had often done sitting in the dust behind the longhouse. Hayano didn't exactly know how to begin fishing so he slowed the canoe's progress and stopped to gaze just below the surface of the clear water at the teaming schools of fish. Playfully, he tried to touch the fish with his paddle.

At that very moment a shrill shriek pierced the quiet of the beach. Hayano looked up from the fish and followed the sound toward shore where he saw his father sprinting toward the water and running faster than Hayano had ever seen him move. Frozen in place in the canoe, Hayano slowly began to realize that it was his father who was making the shrill sound. As he watched, his father rushed headlong into chest-deep water, stopped next to him and gripped the canoe violently. With one deft motion, his father turned the canoe upside down, spilling Hayano into the chilly water. Then he grabbed his son by the hair and dragged him to shore, towing the canoe with his other hand. With the rest of the fishing party laughing uncontrollably, Hayano's father deposited his son and the canoe on the beach and began a deriding lecture on youth and irresponsibility.

"How could you have been so foolish?" he growled. "You dared to launch our only canoe in a Devil Wind without supervision?" he asked. "You could have drowned. But more important, we could have lost the canoe!"

At that, the men in the fishing party fell into further peels of mirth. Several laughed so hard that they had to sit on the sand to collect themselves. Hayano was devastated. He had been humiliated in front of the very men he had hoped to impress. Feeling more like a child than a man, he quietly helped set up camp, subjugating himself to the instructions of the older braves. Then long before sunset, he crawled into his tent and despondently fell into a deep sleep.

Hours later, a hand tugged at Hayano's blanket. It was his father motioning him to be silent and to follow. The two walked to the beach a few hundred yards from the encampment.

"I'm afraid that your mother was right," his father said in a quiet tone. "Perhaps you are too young and impetuous to be with the men. You tempted the God of the sea tonight, and you very well could have been killed," he continued. "What were you thinking when you launched the canoe by yourself?"

"There were no waves, Father, and I was anxious to begin the fishing," Hayano answered.

"Your mother was right," his father answered, "we should have named you impetuous! There was indeed a wind, and a very strong one. But you were in a hurry and greedy to fish, so you did not sense it. You were almost kissed by the Devil Wind and you didn't even realize it. You have much to learn," Hayano's father chided.

"What is the Devil Wind?" asked Hayano. For the first time since he had been humiliated in front of the braves, he was beginning to understand that his father had actually been trying to protect him, and that his father may, in fact, have actually saved him from a terrible fate. Slowly his father gathered himself and began to teach Hayano the Iroquois theology of the winds that lived on the water.

"My son," he began, "there are many different winds living on this water. Some are good winds and others are frightening, even evil. The winds which blow back and forth across the water," he noted, gesturing from right to left as he faced the beach, "are the good winds. Even when they blow their hardest, they announce themselves and act in predictable ways. We have learned to use them to move up and down the long shores, traveling to meet other tribes or to hunt. But the two contrary winds are the troublesome ones. The first is called the Cold Wind. It blows in our face as we stand facing the water. It warns of great changes in weather, storms and an angered God. The harder it blows, the greater and faster the change. Sometimes it brings the snows of winter!"

"But what of the Devil Wind?" asked Hayano, growing impatient for an answer. "Tell me more about that one," he begged.

"Still the impetuous one," his father chuckled as he put his arm around him. "The Devil Wind blows on your back when you face the water. She seduces. Fools you into thinking that there are no waves; that all is calm on the water. The Devil Wind is cruel, because it preys upon the young, the foolish, and the greedy: those who think they don't have time to wait for a friendly wind. Devil Wind tries to trick you, to make you feel that it is important to paddle away from shore. She dares you to paddle with her current. And once she has you in her embrace she tempts you to ride the current, making you think that you are strong. Until you are so far from shore that all is lost. She kisses you gently at first, convincing you that she is a warm friend. Then when you finally realize that you cannot paddle against her, Devil Wind captures you and throws you into the sea. And just before she consumes you, she makes you look back toward shore so that you will realize just how foolish you have been."

"Look out there, Hayano," the chief said, as he pointed away from the beach. "Only the God of this great sea knows how many men have been lured out into the darkness of the water, or how many are yet to die. The ways of the Indians change with the passage of the sands on the beach, but the Devil Wind is always there!"

# PART ONE

# Man Overboard

*I told that kid a thousand times,*
*not to take the lakes for granted.*
*They go from calm to a hundred knots,*
*so fast they seem enchanted.*

**Stan Rogers**

*White Squall*

# CHAPTER 1
# August 1926

[THREE HUNDRED YEARS LATER.
SATURDAY, AUGUST 21, 1926, 12:50 A.M.]

Four men were huddled in the dark, shivering on the wet floor of a tiny, fourteen-foot rowing dory. They sat in dazed silence, struggling to digest what had happened to them. Suspended in a strange new reality, they clung desperately to the gunnels of their lifeboat as it alternately ascended, then plunged down twenty-five foot breaking waves. The motion was more violent than any they had ever experienced. And these were sailors: Herman Wagerman, Bill Logan, Dick Freeman and George McMinn, of the late steamship *Howard Gerken*.

Ship's fireman Herman Wagerman was the obvious leader of the crew, even though he was outranked by first mate George McMinn. But they were no longer aboard ship and in this predicament, it was charisma and strength that spawned leadership, not rank. At thirty-five years of age, Wagerman still had the physique of the high school athlete who had been the talk of Buffalo, New York seventeen years earlier. Wagerman had played every sport, and he had played them well. He was a successful athlete because he was mentally tough and unbelievably strong, not because he was born to a privileged family that sent him to summer camps, or because he was possessed of special talent for any particular sport. At eighteen, he had broken the hearts of several college coaches by going to work on the Buffalo ore docks.

Over the years, Wagerman had added twenty pounds of muscle to his high school frame, mostly through hard physical labor. He had become legendary for his work ethic ånd strength on the Buffalo waterfront. Wagerman once won a bar bet by strapping himself to an empty railroad coal car (after several pitchers of beer) and pulling it 100 yards. At 6 feet 2 and 220 pounds he was a physically imposing man, just the right person to be with in the infamous sailor bar fights which regularly broke out in Great Lakes working class, waterfront neighborhoods. Herman didn't start as many fights as he finished, however. He was easy-going and gentle by nature.

Bill Logan was Wagerman's best friend and financial beneficiary of many of Herman's heroics. It was Logan, the ship's chief derrick operator, who staged the coal car pulling incident and held the money. Logan was the follower and Wagerman the leader, but it was usually Logan, the dreamer, whose ideas fuelled Wagerman's charisma. In fact, it was Logan's vision of shipwrecks and treasure that seemed at least partly to blame for the predicament that the four found themselves in as they tumbled helplessly in the center of Lake Erie.

As the tiny dory rose to the crest of each wave, the foursome felt the full fury of the shrieking winds. The noise from the breaking water was so deafening that they had to face each other and scream to make themselves understood. They could see the glow of city lights from Erie, Pennsylvania, tantalizingly close and to the south. Then the next cycle would begin. The tiny boat would hang perilously at the top of the wave, then suddenly drop like a stone into the black abyss between crests. The free-fall that followed the roaring and crashing of each wave top sent them into a netherworld of stark contrast: a place of absolute darkness and quiet that prevailed in the depressions between waves. The overall effect was frightening, even to seasoned sailors.

Without warning, watchman Dick Freeman began vomiting. He spewed the steak dinner that the crew had been enjoying just hours ago across the tiny dory. As he retched uncontrollably, vomit splattered on George McMinn.

"Jesus, Dick," exclaimed McMinn, "would you at least do that downwind!"

But Freeman was in no shape to take wind bearings. He was new to commercial sailing and had problems with seasickness, even under ordinary wave conditions. Freeman had pledged to all who would listen that this would be his last season aboard a ship. Right after Christmas he was going to find a job on land. But lots of seamen made that promise each winter. It was a tradition. The first of the year they would get shore jobs but soon find them so boring that when the next spring shipping season came around, they would be back aboard for just one more "last" year.

"We're gonna die out here," grumbled McMinn, "and I don't want to spend my last few hours on this earth smelling like your lousy puke, Dick."

"Nobody's going to die!" retorted Wagerman, almost yelling the words.

"So tell us what you're thinking, Herm," asked Logan. "You said you had a plan."

"Aha!" McMinn thought to himself. He had suspected that Wagerman and Logan had something in mind when they were helping all of the other crew members into the ship's two 20-foot lifeboats. As *Gerken* was sinking, it was Wagerman who rushed about the deck lighting a signal fire, organizing lifeboats and directing traffic. But when the second of the ship's two regular lifeboats was filled with crewmen, Wagerman and Logan declined to go with them. Even though he was first mate, McMinn had an intuitive confidence in Wagerman and Logan's schemes, so he decided not to put to sea with the rest of the crew. At the last minute, first mate George McMinn elected to stay aboard a sinking ship with the two crewmen who had generally made his life as *Gerken*'s deck officer completely crazy. As Wagerman and Logan pushed the last of the ship's lifeboats away, they told McMinn that they were going to follow in the captain's fourteen-foot rowing dory. Actually, their plan had been to be alone in the small dory, but McMinn's presence added a third crew member. Then, just as the three of them were launching the dory from *Gerken*'s sinking and almost-vertical stern, watchman Dick Freeman staggered on deck in a disoriented state. Freeman doubled as *Gerken*'s wireless operator along with his watchman's duties, and he had stayed below signaling SOS on the ship's wireless until the last possible moment. Too late to board the second lifeboat, Freeman became a fourth crew member by default.

"Why didn't you and Logan get into the larger lifeboats?" asked McMinn. "They're twenty feet long instead of fourteen and they have flotation chambers so they can't sink."

"Sinking isn't the biggest problem," answered Wagerman, "it's the cold water. The big lifeboats with all those people aboard will be swamped inside of an hour and the guys will likely freeze to death."

"That's what happens to most of the sailors who die on the lakes," noted Logan. "They don't drown, they die of exposure. People find them days or weeks later floating dead in their life jackets!"

"We can row this boat and bail it dry," noted Wagerman. "Once the wind dies down we'll only be two or three hours of rowing from shore," he continued. "All we have to do is stay upright and dry."

Finally, the strategy was beginning to make sense to McMinn and he reluctantly decided that he was happy to be with Wagerman and Logan. Just before *Gerken* went down, the two of them had been running around collecting tarps, buckets and extra oars. The last thing that Wagerman accomplished before pushing away from the ship was to lash bailing buckets to the gunnels of their dory so they couldn't wash away in the waves.

Even as McMinn watched, Wagerman and Logan were alternating time in the wildly gyrating boat between staying under the tarps they had stowed and bailing. They would bail in the depressions between waves and hunker down under the tarps when the tiny boat began to shoot up and over the wave crests.

"If you want to be helpful, Mr. McMinn, grab an oar and use it as a rudder," Wagerman suggested. "Try to keep the bow heading into the waves so we don't broach," he added.

"At this rate, the wind will push us backwards, all the way to Buffalo by tomorrow morning," muttered McMinn.

"Not likely," noted Logan. "By 6:00 a.m. the wind will be gone and the water will be dead calm. These summer storms don't last long."

So there they were. An unlikely bunch, fighting for their lives in the middle of Lake Erie. Just a few hours earlier the crew of eighteen had been happily eating supper in the steamship *Gerken's* dining room with company owner Howard Gerken Sr., and a guest: the cook's fourteen-year-old son Eugene. The cook's son was taking this trip as a special birthday gift from his father. Some gift!

Good meals were a tradition on Great Lakes ships, especially aboard sandsuckers like the *Gerken*. This amenity was a trade-off for the fact that sandsucker crews had more work to do than the men on the big lake freighters. Ore boat sailors were able to spend long hours off watch with little or nothing to occupy them as they rode the length of the lakes. And Saturday night's supper had been special, even by *Gerken* standards: steak, mashed potatoes, and a birthday cake for young Eugene Oaks. But as Eugene was to learn that night, things can change in a heartbeat aboard a ship at sea. One moment all was well, then in a heartbeat, twenty souls were in the water fighting for their lives.

"Jesus!" McMinn screamed. "There's a ship over there!"

"It must be a mirage," argued Wagerman. "What ship would be out here in this shit? Anybody on the east-end of the lake should be tucked in behind Long Point riding this out."

"Sit up and look, goddamn it," replied McMinn. "It's a mile or less off our starboard bow."

The news aroused Dick Freeman from his nauseous stupor on the floor. "Quick!" he said with excitement. "Let's send off a flare or do something!"

"We used them all before *Gerken* went down," replied Logan.

"Besides, they'll never see us in these seas," added McMinn. "Not a bloody chance."

"Wait a minute," countered Wagerman, "look at their course. That's not a proper course for a large ship out here on the lake. Whoever it is must be coming to help us. They probably spotted our signal fire."

On the tops of the waves, Wagerman could see the ship clearly now and he had little doubt that it was a rescue ship, since there was a light scanning the water in front of it.

"Great plan," muttered McMinn. "Us really smart guys in the small maneuverable boat have been floating away in these waves. That ship will never find us. Instead, they'll find the other two boats and we'll be screwed."

"Shut up, McMinn," countered Wagerman. "Get busy and steer toward that ship." Without another word, Wagerman and Logan shipped their oars and prepared to do the impossible: to row upwind in fifty knots of breeze and twenty-five-foot breaking waves. With Freeman in the bow bailing and McMinn perched on the stern steering, the tiny lifeboat began to turn back toward the spot where the *Gerken* went down.

"You're going to kill us all! We're going to capsize," complained McMinn as they crashed into the waves.

"Steer, goddamn it," answered Wagerman. "We're going to row to that boat."

With Freeman bailing like a madman and McMinn steering with an oar, Wagerman and Logan applied their muscle to the task of saving their own skins. Slowly, the tiny rowing dory began to make headway toward the oncoming ship. Even as they watched through the pelting rain, they could tell that the big ship was slowing.

"Probably found the other lifeboats," said Wagerman. "That's good. The boys will tell the captain we're out here. There's no way they'll leave until they find us," he added. "We're saved, guys!" he proclaimed with confidence.

"You're nuts!" muttered McMinn, who was still skeptical about their chances for rescue.

"You just keep your eyes on that ship and steer," retorted Wagerman. "Logan and I will get us there. Don't lose sight of her. She'll probably come to a stop and float right down on top of us. All we have to do is keep a bearing on her, get in her lee and row."

Despite McMinn's pessimism, Logan knew that Wagerman was right. They were well out of the shipping lanes so there was no other reasonable explanation for the appearance of this mystery ship that had somehow hooked around to the south of them in the desolate center of Lake Erie. Logan and Wagerman watched the ship's beckoning lights slowly come to a stop less than a mile away and dead upwind.

It was another thirty minutes of frantic rowing before they could make out the name of the ship that represented their salvation. It was the railroad car ferry *Maitland #1*. They interpreted that as a good omen, since car ferry crews were reputed to have exceptional close quarter maneuvering talent. Unlike the bigger bulk carriers, car ferries went in and out of difficult harbors on a daily basis. The captains and crews got plenty of practice jockeying their ships around in tight quarters.

## [SATURDAY, AUGUST 21, 1926, 1:25 A.M.]

The closer the rowers came to the rescue ship, the faster they moved through the seas. The huge car ferry was providing a calming sea in its lee and Wagerman and Logan were slowly inching the lifeboat ever closer to the *Maitland*. As they approached, they could make out the profile of a lifeboat tied to the big ship.

"It's the rest of the guys," proclaimed Logan, "and it looks like they're all saved!"

"Not quite," retorted Wagerman, gesturing to port as he rowed. Some 1,200 yards off the beam was *Gerken*'s second lifeboat and just as Wagerman had predicted it was swamped. The crew of the second boat was waving and yelling, frantically trying to signal the car ferry. "We need to get to the *Maitland* before they pull away to go after the other boat," he said sternly. "If we slip out of their lee they'll have a tough time finding us."

The four set to work again, trying to make their little dory cover the tantalizingly short distance to the *Maitland*. Suddenly, a spotlight from the car ferry found them. The light illuminated the dory as they pulled on their oars.

"We're in luck, boys," shouted Logan. "They see us now for sure!" With less than 100 yards to go Wagerman was encouraged by shouts and yells from *Maitland*'s deck. "We're going to make it after all," he thought to himself.

Five minutes later a line with a monkey's fist flew across the dory and landed in his lap. With a sigh of relief, Wagerman grabbed the line and pulled it taut, bending it to the bow cleat. And then the car ferry crew was doing the work, winching the dory and its grateful occupants toward the after section of *Maitland*'s port rail. With just a few feet to go Wagerman uncleated the line and walked toward the center of the dory, bringing its gunnels carefully toward *Maitland*'s deck. He held the dory just off *Maitland*'s rail and waited for complementary wave heights as he struggled to bring the little boat as close as possible to the deck of the car ferry. While he braced the dory, he could make out *Gerken*'s second engineer, Jesse Gerken, on the deck of the car ferry working the other end of the line. Wagerman steadied himself on the far side of the rowing dory and balanced the little boat while Logan, Freeman and McMinn positioned themselves to climb from the rail of the dory onto *Maitland*'s inviting deck.

"What do you think, Herman," asked Logan in a whimsical tone, "should we really get off or do we stay here and row back to Buffalo?"

"Get your ass out of here and stop clowning around," answered Wagerman. "Do you think it's fun holding onto this line?"

Bill Logan chuckled as he turned to step across the dory toward the rescue ship.

Logan grabbed the connecting line for support and swung himself toward the *Maitland*, but his motion was interrupted when the rope that Wagerman was holding suddenly parted with a sound as loud as a gunshot. With Wagerman bracing to hold the dory away from *Maitland* in the wildly undulating seas, the fate of the tiny boat and its occupants was instantaneously sealed. Herman Wagerman and his three friends were propelled like hapless rag dolls into the blackness of the night. And all that Herman Wagerman had to show for his superhuman effort was a rope end welded to his hands. He did a 270 degree mid-air rotation and plunged like a rock into the inky black waters of Lake Erie.

# CHAPTER 2

## [SATURDAY, AUGUST 21, 1926, 1:50 A.M.]

*It's hard to get directionally oriented underwater when a dunking comes as such a complete surprise, especially in extreme conditions. Even though he was wearing a life jacket, Wagerman did not seem to be rising to the surface. One second he had been standing in the rowing dory holding a line that tethered him to safety. Then, in an instant he was underwater struggling and confused. He was anchored to something and as he fought for the surface he had to resist his urge to breathe. Wagerman twisted against whatever was holding him under and with a massive effort he suddenly freed himself from an amorphous tangle of rigging. Realizing that he could only hold his breath for another moment he looked for lights and kicked like a man possessed toward what he thought to be the surface. But he was terribly disoriented and in that moment of struggle his own strength and determination worked against him. Wagerman was swimming in the wrong direction!*

*Eventually, increasing pressure made Wagerman realize his mistake and he turned the right way. Fighting the urge to breathe, he kicked toward the top of the water. But it was no use. Less than six feet from the churning surface, Herman Wagerman's biological instincts overwhelmed his determination and he took just one gasping breath.*

*Survivors of near drowning report that the last underwater breath is calming. Lungs fill with cool water, seem satisfied and create a sudden mood of tranquility. Panic is transformed into gentle resignation and the drowning person's mind wanders back in time. Seconds experienced in this pre-unconscious state seem to last forever, creating the illusion of revisiting one's past life. In his own personal moment of drowning, Wagerman thought about his parents in Buffalo. He recalled the precise day when he told his father that he had decided to go to work on the docks rather than play college football. He remembered tears in his father's eyes as he tried to explain that he probably wouldn't fit in with the rich kids at college anyway; that college football probably wasn't in the cards for a working class kid from a poor neighborhood.*

*As he had matured Wagerman began to understand how his father must have felt. His choice to work on the docks represented a parenting failure to his dad. While Wagerman tripped on thoughts of his father he wondered what might have happened if he had taken the other road at that moment in his life. Suddenly he was transported to a football field. He was playing college football. But by some kind of magic, he was also suspended over the field where he could see himself dressed in pads and a helmet. He was carrying the ball toward the goal line and fans in the packed stadium were cheering wildly for him. He was about to score a touchdown when a crushing tackle came out of nowhere, jarring him into a new reality.*

*The fans were screaming his name, "Herman, Herman Wagerman!" they yelled.*

*But he was lying face down on the field, unable to move. The field was soaking wet as he lay there trying to understand how he had been tackled so violently and why he had suddenly been transported back to the field and inside of his body. He was no longer watching from somewhere above himself. Sharp pains pulsated through his body. He was gasping, coughing and trying to catch his breath so that he could stand up and get back to the huddle. As he lay face down listening to the fans yelling his name, he slowly began to understand that the voices that he heard were not fans at all. It was his friend Bill Logan calling to him.*

*Wagerman reluctantly began to realize that he wasn't really on a football field. He was lying face down in the center of Lake Erie, racked with pain and coughing up water. He collected himself and looked tenuously around. Bill Logan was less than a hundred yards away calling his name and the Maitland was a half-mile to weather with searchlights slowly scanning the water. In the few moments required for Wagerman to regain his perspective he could see that he was slipping away from the rescue ship at an alarming rate. He tried to answer Logan's frantic calls, but somehow his voice didn't seem to work.*

*"Got to get back to the Maitland," he thought to himself. "I'll swim back and tell them where Logan is," he decided.*

*He put his head down in the water and began to struggle in the direction of the ship but after just a few strokes he realized that his efforts were in vain. Wagerman was completely wasted. His strength and energy had been sapped by the events of the past hours; the rowing, the failed rescue and the near drowning. His body was racked with pain from the water he had inhaled. And he was no match for the relentless motion of the waves that pushed him away from the Maitland. So he relaxed and slowly drifted toward sleep as the waves put even more distance between the rescue ship and himself. Even though he could hear Logan calling him, he couldn't respond. He closed his eyes, leaned back in his life jacket and drifted in time. In dreaming he quickly found his way to a happier moment; an afternoon near the end of the previous navigational season.*

# Dreaming

## [SATURDAY, DECEMBER 16, 1925, 6:45 P.M.]

A skeleton crew of six, including Wagerman and Logan, had delivered the steamship *Gerken* from Buffalo to her winter lay-up site in Erie. She was berthed near the Cascade Docks at the west end of the bay that formed Erie's natural harbor. *Gerken* was tied securely to a metal retaining wall and her crew was working twelve-hour days in anticipation of a ride back to Buffalo and a well-deserved Christmas vacation. As Wagerman winterized the steam engine and its ancillary equipment, he imagined the paycheck that would be awaiting him and gifts that he would buy for his family next week. Christmas was always the best holiday for the Wagerman family. It was the only time of year that Wagerman seemed to have enough cash to buy whatever he wished. Like most commercial sailors, Wagerman spent money when he had it. He was perennially flush at the end of each navigational season, then suffering, hunting for odd jobs and borrowing money to make ends meet during the weeks just before the next spring shipping season. Last year, for instance, he'd bought his dad a $30 pair of shoes for Christmas, then had to borrow $4 for food the week before he went back to work.

Next March, Wagerman would be back in *Gerken*'s engine room undoing the work that he was doing now: preparing the engines for the 1926 shipping season. *Gerken* was harder to lay-up than the typical Great Lakes steamship. It wasn't her size that made the winterizing work difficult. At 241 feet and 1,450 gross tons, she was small by postwar standards. By the 1920s, the ordinary size of a bulk carrier had reached 600 feet, dwarfing most of the older steamships and rendering them so inefficient that their only hope of economic survival was to find a niche such as sandsucking. As a sandsucker, however, *Gerken*'s machinery was far more complex than that of a traditional laker. The dredging equipment, designed to make *Gerken* competitive, created substantial maintenance headaches. In addition to her steam engine and boiler works, *Gerken* had machinery for sucking sand off the bottom of the lake, more than two hundred feet of tubing for lifting sand from the lake bottom and a deck crane for moving the dredged sand from the hold to the docks.

While Wagerman worked in the engine room, his friend Bill Logan was busy topside winterizing the crane and deck apparatus. *Gerken*'s crane was the most important part of her unloading gear and had to be carefully prepared for the impending winter. There were cables to be replaced, pulleys and sheaves to rebuild and countless fittings that had to be greased to protect against ice damage. As usual, the two friends were in cahoots on scheduling the winterizing job. While John Gerken, the owner's brother and chief engineer, walked the decks in a white shirt and tie imploring the men to work faster so that everyone could get home for the holidays, Wagerman and Logan were stretching the job. They made ten-minute tasks last an hour and turned breaks into protracted planning sessions. The "terrible twosome," as first mate McMinn had named them, were playing an age-old game with the owner's brother, who had not advanced to the position of first engineering officer entirely upon merit. They were using the *Gerken*'s expanded winterizing work as an opportunity to make extra holiday cash, a procedure that the pair had elevated to an art form over the years.

There was also a science imbedded within Wagerman's deliberateness. He understood the absolute importance of being methodical; not missing critical steps in winterizing *Gerken's* machinery. Wagerman was, in fact, doing more than a first-class job. It was a conundrum for both first mate McMinn and John Gerken, the chief engineering officer. They suspected that Wagerman was stretching the job. But they also knew that he was the absolute best at what he was doing and that they could be assured of a smooth spring startup if Wagerman was left to his own devices. Ultimately, they had confidence that Wagerman wanted to be home in Buffalo for Christmas as much as they did, and that there would be a reasonable limit to the job stretching. Plus they were being paid time and a half as well. So even though McMinn and Gerken seemed to be in charge of the winterizing crew, it was Wagerman and Logan who created the real schedule. And in the minds of the terrible twosome, tomorrow would be the last day aboard the ship this year. They would quit working tonight at 7:00 p.m., do a final easy twelve-hour shift tomorrow polishing up details, and be back home in Buffalo by midnight. Monday would be devoted to shopping, a few drinks and the beginning of the Christmas holiday.

"Come on Herman," chided Logan, "get out from under that boiler and let's get cleaned up. We can't afford to be late tonight of all nights!"

"What time is it?" asked Wagerman.

"It's after 7:00 p.m., and you are now officially donating time to the Gerken family," answered Bill Logan as he hurriedly changed out of greasy coveralls.

"Just another second," replied Wagerman, intent upon putting one last turn on a stubborn nut. "I'll be right with you. What's it like on deck?"

"Almost 50 degrees," replied Logan. "Like a spring day."

Fifteen minutes later, Wagerman and Logan were crossing the deck and heading for shore.

"Eating supper on board tonight?" asked McMinn as he watched them leave the ship.

"No, George, we're meeting someone downtown. Got some business to talk over," answered Wagerman as he crossed the gangway to the dock.

"If you find any booze, bring me some," yelled McMinn while they walked down the dock.

"Hey guys, are we still on schedule to be done tomorrow night?" added John Gerken through the pilothouse door.

"No problem, we'll be all wrapped up by tomorrow," answered Wagerman as he departed.

"Negative on the booze," added Logan. "Prohibition you know! And if we do find any we'll be drinking it ourselves," he muttered under his breath.

In the darkness, the terrible twosome climbed through a half dozen rows of parked railroad cars. From there they walked to the base of the bluffs separating Erie's "normal" citizens from its assortment of crazy waterfront characters. Silently, they picked their way up and over the steep bank using a path frequented by locals. Erie was an easy city to navigate. The streets started at the bayfront bluffs with Front (First) running parallel to the water and proceeded south in numerical order. Sixth Street was the main east–west highway. If you walked south from the water and then turned east onto Sixth Street, you could follow the road all the way to Buffalo. But Wagerman and Logan weren't going to Buffalo tonight. They turned east on Third Street and headed for Sullivan's Tavern a few blocks away. Sullivan's was Erie's sailor bar; a place where it was rumored that the occasional drink of hard liquor could be procured if you were a regular. As usual, Logan had concocted one of his get-rich schemes, and Wagerman was going along to be a partner. Tonight was to be the first meeting of three conspirators.

"Tell me again about this guy we're meeting," demanded Wagerman.

"His name is Joe Divell," answered Logan, "a veritable legend on the Great Lakes. Hard hat diver, smuggler, contractor and allegedly the meanest son-of-a-bitch on the waterfront.

You'll like him, Herm," Logan added. "We're gonna buy him dinner and he's going to tell us about the treasure."

"Sure," grumbled Wagerman, thinking that most of Logan's treasure hunts had begun and ended with buying some asshole dinner and drinks.

At 7:45 p.m. the pair walked through the front door of Sullivan's and into a cloud of cigar and pipe smoke. The contrast between the peaceful December night air and the bar atmosphere was overwhelming. Even though it was the sixth year of prohibition, the smell of spirits was strong enough inside the darkened room to make Wagerman wonder if people in Erie took the ban on alcohol seriously.

"Come on," motioned Logan, "there he is in the back booth."

They squeezed their way through the crowded barroom, and Wagerman could barely make out a wiry man of uncertain age sitting alone in the back corner. Joe Divell was, indeed, Erie's most infamous waterfront character. He was actually much younger than he looked, having earned the appearance of a man of fifty from a lifetime of outdoor work, and too much time underwater in a badly jury-rigged hard hat diving outfit. Divell was legendary for his absolute refusal to buy anything new. He had welding gear, every imaginable tool and the ability to make whatever he needed from scraps. If Divell didn't happen to have the required scraps, he would usually help himself at one of his many waterfront stops. Who would have the courage to tell him he couldn't? Telephone poles, engine parts, structural steel and more. If they were unattended on the bayfront, they often found their way into Joe's personal collection. Divell was even more legendary for linguistic creativity, having somehow managed to combine the word "fuck" with every imaginable set of regularly used nouns and verbs. He took sailor language to a new level, making no apologies to the company with whom he shared his special gift. Priests, nuns, little old ladies, school children and other innocents had all been gifted with Joe's bursts of four-letter expletives. It was just Joe Divell's way of expressing himself.

Logan introduced Wagerman to Divell and they ordered dinner.

"Think they have any booze here?" asked Logan.

"Fuck, yes," replied Divell. "I brought it to them, goddamn it, so they had better serve it to me or I'll start supplying Mosby's Tavern up the street!"

"So Herman," began Logan, "Mr. Divell is going to tell us about the treasure and how to find it and I promised that we would buy his meal."

"Bull shit," barked Divell, "you'll do a lot more than buy my dinner if I help you. You'll make me a full partner or you assholes can go screw yourselves."

Instantly, Herman Wagerman liked Joe Divell.

"Can't talk here," said Divell. "We'll eat, then go to my barge. Then I'll show you guys what I got."

Wagerman knew what was allegedly at stake. According to Logan, the dreamer, Divell could help them locate Lake Erie's legendary sunken Spanish treasure ship.

In 1717, an armada of eight Spanish ships set sail from Cuba with gold and silver, much of it smelted into coins. The treasure was needed to fuel Spain's exploration of the New World and the Spanish competition with England and France for world dominance on the seas. Mexico and the Caribbean Colonies, which had inadvertently been discovered for Spain by Columbus, were being exploited for their precious metals.

An eight-ship armada left Cuba in mid-September to return to Spain, loaded with millions of dollars worth of gold and silver. They departed a bit early that fall, betting that hurricane season was over. Soon after they had begun their transatlantic voyage, however, the season's worst hurricane hit the fleet. As the storm intensified, the armada was stretched out and separated. At least one ship sailed to safety by managing to stay on the leading edge of the storm, and making a record crossing of the Atlantic. There are a number of accounts of the plights of the remaining seven ships. Several were known to have sunk off the Florida coast where they became continuing targets for treasure hunters.

Not all the vessels were accounted for, however. For years, there were persistent rumors that one of the ships had escaped the storm by making its way along America's Atlantic coast. Legend has it that its captain decided to seize the opportunity to make himself and his crew rich. Realizing that all they had to do to escape Spanish power was continue sailing north into British held waters of the Americas, the crew of this lone Spanish treasure ship made its way north to New Amsterdam (New York). From there, it sailed up the Hudson River toward today's Albany. Near Albany, the crew disassembled the ship and hid the treasure. The following season, the captain and crew allegedly rebuilt their ship into a river barge and carried the treasure with the remaining structural parts of the Spanish galleon up New York State's river systems toward present-day Buffalo and Lake Erie.

As outrageous as the tale of the Spanish treasure ship had always seemed, its viability was fuelled by the knowledge that the French explorer Robert LaSalle had done essentially the same thing with his ship forty-eight years earlier. In 1669, LaSalle dragged the materials needed to build a proper sailing ship from the shores of Lake Ontario across the Niagara Peninsula. There he reconstructed his barque, the *Griffon*, in the Niagara River near the mouth of Lake Erie. The *Griffon*, like the fabled Spanish treasure ship, was lost somewhere on the Great Lakes in a storm. LaSalle's *Griffon*, like the Spanish ship, was also carrying a fortune. But the little barque was bearing furs, instead of gold; furs which were destined to finance the French conquest of the New World. LaSalle and other early European sailors who ventured onto the Great Lakes were caught off guard by the size and ferocity of the inland seas. Many ultimately fell victim to storms.

Thousands of commercial sailors and fishermen had been convinced by sailor bar stories that a veritable treasure trove of silver and gold coins was just waiting somewhere on the bottom of Lake Erie. The believers presumed that the Spanish Captain and his crew, with dreams of riches in the emerging New World, had reconstructed the galleon and outfitted her for a final sail to the western end of Lake Erie where they hoped to become wealthy frontier entrepreneurs. But somehow they, like the crew of the *Griffon*, were swallowed by a Lake Erie storm, never to be seen again. Both ships were consumed by the Iroquois God of the lakes who sent winds to terrorize sailors.

"Come on, let's go to my barge," grunted Joe Divell as he swallowed the last of his meal.

Wagerman paid for dinner and drinks and the three walked out the door toward the bayfront office of Erie's best known hard-hat diver. Divell's work barge was tied to a back pier along the old Canal Basin, a commercial slip created eighty years earlier. The slip was originally the entranceway for the Erie-to-Pittsburgh barge canal. Railroads ended the life of the canal after the Civil War, however, and since the late 1870s the Canal Basin had evolved into an eclectic array of waterfront entrepreneurs like Divell. An assortment of fish tugs, a coal delivery barge, and a local sand and gravel business were all jammed into Divell's waterfront neighborhood. The infamous Divell work barge was thirty-five feet long and fifteen feet wide. It was a makeshift craft, housing a variety of steam engines, a derrick with a shovel attachment, and a twelve-foot square shack on its after-end. The shack had a single door, a window and a tiny chimney which was obviously attached to some kind of coal stove since a paste of soot and seagull droppings covered the entire roof. Divell opened the door of the shack, lit an oil lamp and motioned Wagerman and Logan to sit down. As the two strained their eyes to take in the surroundings inside the tiny shack, they could hear Divell relieving himself over the side of the barge. Divell stepped into the dimly lit shack and began the conversation.

"Boys," Divell announced, "here's the deal. I'll tell you what I know, but then I become a full partner! Logan tells me that you guys have a way of sucking stuff up from the bottom in deep water without diving. I'm going to tell you exactly where to look, then I get an equal share of anything you find. One third!"

"What has Logan been telling this guy?" Wagerman wondered quietly. But he kept his thoughts to himself.

"It's a deal, Joe," added Bill Logan. "Whatever we get, we split three ways!"

As Logan blurted out his offer, Wagerman wondered just how tough this old coot really was and if Joe Divell might be hunting him and Logan down to kill them someday. An instant later, there was a chart of Lake Erie on the table in front of them with "Xs" marked all over it. Each "X" had a number next to it, and Divell systematically revealed an amazingly complex cross filing system of envelopes in drawers with corresponding numbers.

"There's hundreds of wrecks out here," he said, pointing to the center of Lake Erie. "A fucking fortune in salvage! There's steamships with jewelry and gold. Freighters carrying gold notes and bearer bonds in strong boxes. And there's the treasure ship! Millions of dollars in gold and silver. The only trouble is that the good wrecks are too goddamn deep. I can't get down on them with this equipment, and even if I could, I'm not going to be the next Johnny Green and die of the bends trying to salvage a fucking safe off the bottom. Ain't worth it! Now you boys has the way to lift the stuff up, and I know where the wrecks are," Divell added, growing much less animated and more serious. "I know where the good ones are and I can tell you which ones not to waste your time on. All you have to do is go where I tell you and do your job. I can't be sure exactly which one of them is the real treasure ship, but if you can do what Logan here says, its just a matter of time until we hit pay dirt!"

"Take wreck number 43 here on the chart," Divell growled. "Not worth a shit!" At that, Joe Divell produced envelope 43 from a drawer and opened it. "Look here," he showed them. "You line up the Presque Isle Lighthouse to the south and the first notch in the hills east of town, and you're right on top of a wreck in twenty-five feet of water. But this wreck is junk. Been on it a hundred times. In fact, it's where I temporarily dump booze that I'm smuggling if it looks like the Coast Guard is on to me. That wreck isn't worth looking at," added Divell, "but wreck number 68 could be the one. Look here! It's in sixty feet of water and it's a schooner. It's real old. Looks to be built like a military ship, not a regular working schooner. I been down to it twice but with this old equipment I have to come right back up. No time to look around," he noted. "But listen to this, boys!" Joe Divell's voice took on a new tone of seriousness. "When she hit bottom she broke into a million pieces and there's stuff laying all over the bottom. Loose stuff! If you can really do what Logan says, it'll come right up off the bottom, slicker than seagull shit."

"Jesus!" thought Wagerman. "Logan has made some kind of deal with a crazy man. I'm going to have a lunatic watching me for the rest of my life. Exactly what did Logan tell him we could do?" he wondered.

Herman Wagerman strained to listen to the conversation, but suddenly everything began to slowly transform into surreal slow motion. Words were dragging out. Sounds and textures were changing, and Joe Divell's shack began filling with water. "What's happening?" he thought. And then he was choking. Water was spurting through his nostrils and he was gasping for air. Herman Wagerman was atop a cresting wave in the middle of Lake Erie.

# CHAPTER 3

[SATURDAY, AUGUST 21, 1926, 1:50 A.M.]

*Wagerman drifted back toward consciousness. He felt like he had as a youngster on school days. He knew that he should wake up completely and get busy, but something inside of him compelled Wagerman to continue in his pre-wakeful trance state. As he dreamed, Wagerman wondered why Lake Erie had suddenly turned against him. Ever since he was a young boy and his parents had taken him to swim at Buffalo's public beaches, he had been drawn to the lake. Wagerman had gradually convinced himself that he and Lake Erie were magical friends. Even though he had been regarded as a big tough kid by most of his friends, he was an idealistic youngster who believed in the magical powers of lakes and the presence of spirits. The sandy shores and constantly changing waters were very special to a youngster growing up in a struggling working class family.*

*Wagerman was so drawn to the water as a youngster that his friends often referred to him as the dock rat. Wagerman spent every spare moment of his youth prowling the water's edge, gazing at ships and wondering what it would be like to be a real sailor.*

*When Wagerman sat in his grade school classes, most subjects seemed dull and meaningless, until a teacher mentioned the Great Lakes or Lake Erie in particular. Then he was instantly transformed to an exceptionally attentive student, even in the over-crowded catholic schoolrooms of his youth. He may not have remembered the details of lessons about sentence diagramming or verb conjugation, but the maritime history of the Great Lakes was etched indelibly into his young mind. As he floated through the water, his thoughts returned to those history lessons. Seventh grade was his very best academic year and that was quite clearly because of a special teacher. The teacher amazed young Herman Wagerman by building an entire year of history around Lake Erie and its role in the development of North American transportation. It was a context that Wagerman could finally relate to. He came to understand rather than memorize history by relating events such as the Civil War to the Great Lakes and shipping.*

*Wagerman floated along in a daze, caught between wakefulness and sleep while his memories, ironically, transported him back to the grade school class lecture where he had finally awakened as a student. Mr. Leonardi, one of Herman's rare non-religious teachers, announced that he had decided to develop a central theme for the entire academic year.*

*"Class," he stated, "I am going to base all of our school work this year around the Great Lakes in general, and Lake Erie in particular. We're going to study history, geography, civics and even math from the perspective of maritime history!"*

*The magical, idealistic part of Herman Wagerman's brain was instantly hooked as he waited to hear Mr. Leonardi's first history lesson.*

# Central Lake Erie

## [MID-NINETEENTH CENTURY]

Most North Americans are astounded to learn of the maritime history and tradition of the Great Lakes. The fact that most lake-coast towns owe their genesis to schooners, steamboats and the people who sailed them escapes even locals. When the British and French faced the daunting task of westward expansion across the immense New World, there were no railroads or highways to take them west. Movement toward the frontier was largely dependent upon ships.

The French entered the New World via the St. Lawrence River system. From there, the "voyagers" moved up river (west) to Quebec and crossed Lake Ontario with Indian guides. The French quickly claimed most of Canada, the Great Lakes region, the Allegheny River system, and the Ohio River Valley. It was clear to the French that the only way to own the New World was to control the critical waterways needed for transportation. But the French did not count upon the immensity of the Americas, or the difficulties they would ultimately face in fighting both the Indians and the English.

The British were more methodical explorers, establishing colonies and moving deliberately. They entered the Great Lakes by way of New York City. From there, they wandered up the Hudson River, portaged to the rivers of upstate New York and ultimately arrived at the eastern end of Lake Erie. Both the French and the English believed the Iroquois legend which proclaimed the existence of a connected sea so immense that it was presumed to be the Pacific

Ocean. (Decades later the immense ocean of Iroquois legend proved to be Lake Superior.) This great sea that was connected to Lake Erie was said to be reachable in less than two moons. The suspicion that there was a continuous body of Great Lakes leading to the end of the frontier and the Pacific Ocean inspired the development of sailing ships for use on the inland seas.

Lake Ontario was essentially useless for North American exploration and transportation because of the escarpment at Niagara Falls. Thus the British had an early strategic naval advantage on the Great Lakes. Their route, from the Hudson River to Buffalo at the eastern end of Lake Erie, was shorter and more practical than the French pathways that included a struggle around rapids on the St. Lawrence River just to get to Lake Ontario. Even when the French had reached the western end of Lake Ontario, they found themselves blocked by Niagara Falls.

America's inland shipping industry inevitably began on Lake Erie. It was from the vantage point of the eastern end of the lake that military sailing ships, the first commercial schooners and ultimately, Great Lakes steamships would evolve. Lake Erie was destined to become a superhighway for goods and passengers bound for North America's western frontier.

The first major sailing venture on the Great Lakes was initiated by the French explorer, Robert LaSalle in 1679. His sailing ship, the *Griffon*, was launched on the Lake Erie end of the Niagara River. From there, LaSalle sailed west to the end of Lake Erie, turned up the Detroit River and continued into Lake Huron. LaSalle's mission was to gather furs from Indians living along the Great Lakes. Unfortunately for the development of commercial sailing in the eighteenth century, the *Griffon* was lost somewhere at sea. It proved

a financial disaster and an ominous warning for future Great Lakes
sailors.

For the next hundred years, the English, who took control of
the Great Lakes basin, followed the advice of the local Iroquois who
were afraid of the Great Lakes. The Indians used the lakes only
seasonally and their usage was limited to canoe or bateau trips along
the shores. Although the Indians made regular excursions through
inland creeks and rivers, they did not make significant offshore
passages on the lakes. The Iroquois were fearful of the storms that
they had seen on the open waters of the lakes.

By the late 1700s, the military had populated the Great Lakes
with sailing ships. While lakeshore settlers were content to emulate
their Indian colleagues, using a variety of flat-bottomed cargo and
passenger boats to move cautiously along the edges of the shores,
military forces on both sides of the lake were beginning to create
offshore naval fleets. Escalating interest in military shipbuilding
motivated a number of entrepreneurs to begin construction of
commercial vessels along Lake Erie's American south shore. The first
such vessel, the *Lady Washington,* was launched near Erie in 1795.
By the beginning of the War of 1812, which featured major naval
skirmishes on the Great Lakes, more than twenty commercial
schooners were doing business on Lake Erie.

Historians credit the War of 1812, and in particular the
September 1813 Battle of Lake Erie, with launching the maritime
future of Lake Erie. While the battle itself may seem obscure in the
overall context of North American history, the peripheral activities of
the naval war alerted the population to the potential of the lakes as
shipping corridors. The naval shipyards in Erie and Buffalo attracted

shipwrights who came to the Great Lakes to practice their art, and created an interest in water travel between Great Lakes port cities like Buffalo, Erie, Cleveland, Detroit, Milwaukee and Chicago. By the postwar 1820s, there was a mad race to build grand sailing ships and to develop Great Lakes trade routes. The struggle for inland shipping supremacy was further propelled by steamships, which first appeared on the upper Great Lakes with the 1819 launch of the *Walk On The Water* in Buffalo. Steamships and commercial sailing vessels were to ply the lakes side by side for over one hundred years, while their various advocates argued the strengths and weaknesses of each type. But steamers clearly provided a technological shift that fuelled the growth of Great Lakes shipping.

What was needed to complete the transportation matrix between Europe and North America's expanding western frontier was a system of canal ways linking the Great Lakes with the oceans. And in the American spirit, canal systems were soon forthcoming. By the 1830s, the state of New York had completed a canal way linking New York City and the Hudson River to Buffalo via the Erie Canal. The first version of Canada's competing Welland Canal also opened its locks during the 1830s, connecting Lake Ontario and the St. Lawrence River with Lake Erie. The Welland arrived at eastern Lake Erie just across the lake from Buffalo and featured two alternate access channels: Port Colborne or Port Maitland. The final step in the North American waterway puzzle was a canal linkage connecting Erie, Pennsylvania—Lake Erie's central port and only protected natural harbor—to Pittsburgh. This created direct access from the Atlantic through the Great Lakes to the Ohio River and the Gulf of Mexico. The Erie-to-Pittsburgh Extension Canal opened in

1841, heralding the golden age of shipping on the Great Lakes. Lake Erie had become the virtual epicenter of North American transportation.

By the mid-nineteenth century, there was more commercial shipping on Lake Erie than in any other portion of the world, including the North Atlantic. This was, of course, the time before railroads had fully extended their east and west lines, so that most bulk shipments, package freight, passenger service and immigration were sent across the Great Lakes. Just before the Civil War 2,018 commercial ships were licensed to do business on Lake Erie including 1,625 sailing vessels and 393 steamships. The steamships in service during this period included classic side-wheelers which carried first class passengers in luxurious accommodations. These great ships featured orchestras, ballrooms and dining halls that rivaled the opulence aboard the *Titanic*. First class passengers such as Charles Dickens rode the steamers as a pastime while steerage class immigrants, below the water line, huddled in somewhat lesser comfort next to steamer trunks, waiting to be delivered to new lives on the western frontier.

Although the Civil War and the development of railroads shifted attention from Great Lakes shipping, the steamships and schooners worked on. They provided bulk transport, passenger, and package delivery through the first three decades of the 1900s. Except for the problem of an annual winter hiatus, it was difficult to beat water travel for cost efficiency. The early 1900s brought technological shifts to the ships that plied the lakes. The classic side-wheel steamers gave way to propeller-driven bulk carriers and several new types of vessels evolved. Hundreds of fish tugs went to work, harvesting the lake's bountiful freshwater fish. Luxury passenger liners, dedicated to vacation travel, and excursion ferries carried middle class North Americans to vacation spots such as Cedar Point and Mackinaw Island. In addition, two entirely new types of strictly commercial vessels emerged on the Great Lakes: railroad car ferries and sandsuckers. Railroad car ferries served as extensions of the north–south railroad lines that abruptly ended at the lakeshore. The car ferries made regular runs back and forth across the lake, carrying coal to the Canadian market. The sandsuckers were dredging ships. They mined sand and gravel from the lake bottom, feeding the growing industrial appetites of Great Lakes foundries and smelting operations and providing materials for construction. Buildings, roads and bridges in the thriving Great Lakes basin all depended upon aggregate from the lake bottom.

Shipping had changed dramatically according to Wagerman's seventh grade teacher, but it was still a big business. "There will always be a living to be made on the Great Lakes," Mr. Leonardi admonished as Wagerman and his classmates matriculated toward the eighth grade. "Think about it as a career," he added.

Wagerman could still hear those prophetic words tumbling from his teacher's lips as he dreamed about the past and remembered the events that had led him to become a Great Lakes sailor.

# PART TWO

# The Sandsucker Gerken

*Neither the people who dwell along the seaboards, nor those from the inland lakes, can understand the vastness of the Great Lakes. Here, where the high walls of water stretch in lonesome gradeur to the horizon, only seeing is believing.*

**William Ratigan**

*Great Lakes Shipwrecks & Survivals*

# CHAPTER 4

## [SATURDAY, AUGUST 21, 1926, 1:55 A.M.]

*Wagerman awoke with a start. He was fully awake now and wondering why someone seemed to be calling his name. Then he figured it out! The sound that had disturbed his dream about the history of Lake Erie was the voice of his friend, Bill Logan. Logan was yelling at him again! Wagerman turned in the water, using his hands to spin through a 360-degree circle. As he did, he spotted Logan on a wave ninety yards away.*

*Logan was shouting at him. "Herman," he yelled, "swim over here so we can stay together!"*

*Wagerman slowly came to his senses and realized the predicament that the two of them were in. He could still see the* Maitland, *but the car ferry was much further away than it had been the last time he looked. Wide awake and taking bearings, Wagerman soon realized that* Maitland *was not only further away, but that it was sliding toward the horizon at a rapid rate.*

*Logan's voice interrupted his attempts to concentrate. "Please, Herman," he yelled. "Let's stick together!"*

*"He's right," Wagerman thought to himself. "If we're together there's a better chance of someone spotting us."*

*"Bill, I'm coming," he answered. "Hold on a minute!"*

*With that, Wagerman began swimming toward his friend. He tried to stretch himself out and swim, using his arms and legs. But he had no strength. Ten minutes of swimming as hard as he could left him no closer to his friend. He decided that the problem was the life jacket; that if he were to take it off and drag it behind him, he might make better progress. So Herman Wagerman broke the cardinal rule of survival at sea. He took his life jacket off.*

*Using one of its safety lines, Wagerman tied the orange life vest to his pants. Then he took aim at Bill Logan once more and began swimming through the waves to be with his friend. After ten minutes of pounding through the disorienting crests, Wagerman stopped to get his bearings. Logan was only thirty yards away now, but he was yelling something at him. Wagerman strained to hear what Logan was saying and suddenly realized that it had to do with his life jacket. He turned to be sure that the jacket was still tied in place behind him and saw nothing. No life jacket! Only a frayed line, that had once coupled him to it.*

*"Shit!" he thought to himself. "How could I be so stupid?"*

*Logan was shouting and pointing over Wagerman's shoulder. Wagerman turned to follow his gestures and saw the bright orange life vest rise to the crest of a wave twenty feet behind him. For a split second, Wagerman was torn between chasing the life jacket and continuing to swim for his friend. But the rational part of him was quick to make a decision. Without his life jacket, Wagerman would be a dangerous burden for his friend.*

*He spun in the water like a man possessed and struck out toward the jacket, swimming with his head out of the water so he could keep an eye on the orange target. The jacket was blowing along wave tops much faster than Wagerman could swim, but it slowed in the depressions. After fifteen minutes of swimming it was clear to Wagerman that he had a chance to catch it. He put his head down and made an effort to swim even faster. After several frantic strokes, he picked his head up again and found himself severely disoriented and dizzy. The life vest was nowhere in sight. Meanwhile, he could barely hear Logan's shouts of encouragement. Moments later, in an instant of pure luck, he came crashing down the face of a wave crest and landed on top of his life jacket.*

*By the time he had strapped himself back into his life jacket, he was totally drained. The time he had spent without his jacket had left him chilled as well as exhausted. Wagerman began to realize that his life jacket was even more important for warmth than it was for flotation. Secured in the vest once more, he scanned the horizon for his friend, but they were too far apart to see or hear each other. Exhausted and disappointed at his lapse of judgement, Wagerman retreated again to sleep. In his mind, he returned to happier moments for he and Logan; a warm spring day three months earlier.*

# Springtime

## [SUNDAY, MARCH 27, 1926, 12:25 P.M.]

After a long winter, Wagerman and Logan were back aboard *Gerken* preparing the ship for a new season. They, and the rest of a skeleton crew, had been working double shifts for three days in anticipation of the regular crew's arrival the next day. Monday was scheduled to be the first day of the 1926 production season and *Gerken* was supposed to leave the dock at 6:00 a.m. to begin dredging. Wagerman was busy getting the engine and machinery ready and Logan had been preparing *Gerken*'s dredging equipment, vacuum lines and deck derrick. Both men were doubly motivated this year since they had spent the winter devising an almost-practical plan for dredging up treasure using Joe Divell's designated locations. Logan modified the dredge so that it would accommodate medium sized items, hopefully silver or gold coins and other valuables. Wagerman had completed adjustments to *Gerken*'s below deck filtering screens and developed a plan for diverting interesting bottom artifacts into a special bin between bulkheads where he and Logan could sort through them.

Sandsuckers were always bringing up miscellaneous items from the lake bottom. Ordinarily such jetsam was considered a nuisance and motivated the deck sweeper to move the underwater dredge to a new location. This year, however, things were to be different. Wagerman and Logan would be hunting for bottom material rather than avoiding it. Providentially, the senior Gerken and his two engineer brothers, John and Jesse, had spent the winter devising a new in-hold separating system for dredged aggregate. They had met with Wagerman in March and given him a set of engineering drawings for reconfiguring *Gerken*'s hold compartments. Senior Gerken hoped to develop a business advantage by presorting dredged materials aboard the ship. In that way, the unloading and sorting process would be streamlined. The crew would spend more time dredging and less unloading. Senior Gerken had charged Wagerman with rebuilding *Gerken*'s under-deck hold structure to contain his new system and Wagerman was using the construction project as an opportunity to create his own "special" compartments for treasure.

The work of prepping the ship was almost completed and Wagerman and Logan had decided to celebrate by walking along the bayfront to the Public Dock for lunch. Fortified with smoked whitefish from Dailey's Restaurant at the foot of the dock, the two reviewed plans to search for Joe Divell's buried treasure. As they sat in a corner table, Logan unfolded a chart of the lake, a copy of the one the first mate used to direct the ship's sand dredging navigational efforts. Over the winter, Logan and Divell had worked together to transpose the sites of the "most promising" potential treasure ship wrecks onto copies of *Gerken*'s charts.

"Divell says that one of these five wrecks is most likely to be the Spanish ship," Logan noted with an air of assuredness.

"Well, that's just great," replied Wagerman. "They're all in places where we're not supposed to dredge. How do you plan to handle that?"

"Easy," replied Logan. "We took on a new partner—the guy who drives the boat!" Grinning like a Cheshire cat, Logan continued with his plot. "He will take us wherever we need to go to dredge. Once we're there, pumping sand into the hold, who knows or cares where we actually are? It all looks like water to the brass as well as the crew!"

"You mean McMinn?" asked Wagerman. "He's the first mate! He'll never do it! He hates us!"

"I already took care of him," replied Logan. "And he doesn't really hate us, Herm. He's just generally pissed because we're so good at what we do and because we have too much fun. Besides, for all his rank, McMinn doesn't make that much more money than us. He has a big family to support. He's an Irish Catholic, you know!"

"What did you have to promise him?" asked Wagerman.

"Just the Spanish treasure," replied Logan. "The poor guy's already planning what he's going to do with the money."

"But what if Captain Gamble or one of the Gerkens catch on?" Wagerman objected. "If they do, McMinn is going to rat on us."

"Not likely," answered Logan. "I introduced him to Joe Divell over the winter and mentioned that if anything like that happens Divell will probably kill him! Would you want to have Joe Divell looking for you?" he added with a chuckle. "So we start tomorrow," Logan continued. "We use Divell's instructions, put the ship over top of the wrecks, one at a time, then suck up everything we can: sand, boat parts, treasure and whatever else we find on the bottom. Divell says there's lots of really good stuff down there just waiting for the picking. Old silver plates, candlesticks and the like. Even if we never find the actual Spanish treasure, we can still make thousands. When we start to get a bunch of stuff we'll filter the material to your special bin and check it for valuables later. You're the one who keeps up the sand screens in the hold, so who would know what we're up to? If we don't find anything at one location, we move on to the next."

"Divell will always keep ahead of us by a few wrecks. He can go down thirty or forty feet in that old rig of his and check to see what each wreck looks like. If it's a bulk carrier full of coal or lumber, we leave it alone. But if it has the look of a treasure ship we'll go after it and hope that the hull broke up when it went down. Divell says that some of the wrecks have loose stuff lying all around them on the floor of the lake. It's as if someone just scattered treasure in the wind and let it float to the bottom. This time next year, Herm, we'll both be men of leisure."

"Come on, we'd better get back from lunch or by this time next week we'll be unemployed," retorted Wagerman.

They paid their bill and headed back to the *Gerken*. Skeptical as he usually was about Logan's get-rich schemes, Herman Wagerman found this one compelling. At the very least he was impressed by the time and energy Logan had invested in planning. Trips to Erie in the off season, meetings with Joe Divell and more. But mostly it was Divell's faith in the plan to vacuum treasure off the bottom which had convinced him.

The terrible twosome walked south to the bayfront railroad tracks, then turned west to trudge the last mile to *Gerken*'s dock. As they walked the tracks, silently alternating steps between wooden ties, they thought about sunken treasure and about what it might be like to have enough money.

"Maybe we'll be doing that this time next year," remarked Logan as they passed the Erie Yacht Club.

Wagerman followed Logan's glance and saw two young men preparing to launch a sailing yacht. The glistening white boat was hanging in straps, suspended just above the water.

"Ah yes, yachting," said Logan. "We'll buy a sailboat just like that one, join the Buffalo Yacht Club and wear clean white clothes like those guys! Any boating that we do next year will be with the richies from the club on varnished wooden sailboats! No more greasy sandsuckers for us, Herm."

But Wagerman wasn't listening. His gaze had riveted itself upon one of the two women who were helping to launch the boat. She was strikingly beautiful. Jet black hair and large, soft brown eyes. Eyes that were piercingly visible even from the distance that separated them. What attracted Wagerman to this woman was not so much her beauty as her strength and agility. As he watched, she climbed onto the boat's stern, pulling herself up and over the gunnels with a quick athletic motion. Once aboard, she tightened the turnbuckles that held the rigging in place, tuning the mast with assured confidence, all to the apparent amazement of the second woman. The other woman was a fragile looking blond who stood watching the assorted launching action from a safe distance.

Wagerman altered course from the railroad tracks and headed directly toward the foursome and their sailboat. Freshly painted gold letters on the stern included the name of the wooden yawl, *Pterodactyl*, and the letters EYC, indicating that the pretty little boat sailed out of the Erie Yacht Club. She was a classic yawl, perhaps ten or fifteen years old, with a glistening new coat of white paint and brightwork that shined like a mirror. Wagerman approached, with Logan in tow, while the two yachtsmen were lowering *Pterodactyl* into the water with a giant dockside winch. The dark-haired woman was gliding athletically across the deck, placing bumpers against the hull to protect it from the adjoining concrete and metal dock.

Wagerman looked directly at the girl and said, "Beautiful! The boat, I mean!"

"God, is he smooth," thought Logan as he laughed at Wagerman's clumsy approach.

"Thanks," answered the closer of the two men. "We're taking advantage of this weather to get her in the water and let the hull swell shut. *Pterodactyl* is always first in the water at the club," he added with pride. "Hate to waste any good spring sailing days!"

"Need any help?" asked Wagerman. "We're from the crew of the *Gerken* right over on the next dock," he added, pointing in the general direction of his ship.

"Sure," replied the young man, "we'll always take a hand with launching!"

Quickly, the men introduced themselves.

"I'm George Stickle and this is my friend Ben Cooley," offered the first man. "*Pterodactyl* belongs to Ben," he added.

"If you guys would help hold *Pterodactyl* off the docks while we lower her into the water, we would appreciate it," chimed in Cooley. "Hate to screw up her new paint the first day, you know!"

In an instant, Wagerman, who wasn't all that interested in the men's names, was at the little yawl's beam, just inches from the dark-haired woman. Wagerman carefully held *Pterodactyl* away from the pier as the boat was lowered and even more carefully made sure that his fingers brushed against the young woman's hands when she pushed a fender over the side.

"Thanks a lot for the help," offered the young woman. She smiled brightly as she tied bowlines in lines on Wagerman's side of the boat. "My name is Suzanne Franzesi and my friend over there is Nancy Giles."

"Looks like you've been around boats before," remarked Wagerman.

"Grew up right here on the water," answered Suzanne, brown eyes flashing in the midday light. "My dad is Italian, but my mom is Portuguese and her whole family is in the commercial fishing business. We live just on top of the bluffs, on Fourth Street."

*Pterodactyl's* hull softly caressed the water, and Wagerman took a line from Suzanne. He quickly tied the boat up before it rubbed against the metal pier.

"Looks like you've done that before, too," noted Suzanne.

"I'm a sailor, it's my job," replied Wagerman. Reading her expression, he noted that Suzanne seemed more impressed than put off by the fact that he was a sailor. When he had first blurted out the word sailor, Wagerman wondered if the opposite might happen. It seemed to him that yacht club women might feel that commercial sailors were part of the underclass. Suzanne's apparent comfort with Wagerman sparked his interest and made him wonder what she was doing with guys in prissy white outfits. Somehow she didn't seem to fit with them.

Logan spoiled the moment. "Speaking of being commercial sailors, Herman, we had better go. We're late from lunch and the first officer will have our heads if we don't get back soon."

"Nice meeting you," offered Wagerman as the two left, but when he said it his gaze did not include Stickle, Cooley or the second woman.

"Forget it, Herman," chided Logan on their way back to the ship, "those people are way out of our league. The guy on my side of the boat, George Stickle, said that he and Cooley are architects at Erie's biggest building design firm. He also mentioned that the girl you were staring at has been going with the owner of the boat for more than three years. Any woman with them would be disgusted by the thought of a rag-assed sailor like you, Herman," he added.

"I'm not so sure," thought Wagerman. Somehow Suzanne Franzesi didn't seem to be like any woman that he had ever met and she didn't seem to fit well with her yachting friends.

"We're privileged that you two could return from lunch," barked first mate McMinn as they climbed aboard ship almost two hours after leaving for lunch. "What do I tell the old man if the *Gerken* isn't ready to go in the morning?" he added impatiently.

"Don't worry, Mr. McMinn," offered Wagerman, "we're way ahead of schedule. She'll be ready in plenty of time for tomorrow."

Wagerman returned to the engine room to finish turning bolts on *Gerken's* steam boiler, but he couldn't stop thinking about Suzanne. She was surely beautiful, but that alone wasn't what had caught his attention. It was her spirit; the twinkle in her soft brown eyes, her strength, her agility and her directness that had engaged him. He had a strange premonition that they would meet again.

As he tugged on a particularly stubborn bolt, a jet of water suddenly shot from the steam boiler and hit him square in the face. He jerked his head away to avoid the jet of steaming water, but the stream wasn't boiling hot as he would have expected. It was cold.

"Something is very wrong here," he thought when the water didn't scald him. While he mused, the cold wet shower continued until it jolted him back to his reality. When his mind cleared, he wasn't in *Gerken's* engine room. He was floating in the middle of Lake Erie, heading northeast in relentless waves and current. Wagerman had been dreaming again.

Except for the misty light of the moon, the evening sky merged with the blackness of the water in a 360-degree panorama, creating a continuous dome of deep gray seascape. *Maitland*'s reassuring lights were out of sight, and Herman Wagerman was alone. Completely alone.

# CHAPTER 5

[SATURDAY, AUGUST 21, 1926, 2:00 A.M.]

*The screeching of a tattered gray seagull completely revived Wagerman from slumber and instantaneously reminded him of his predicament. He was lashed to a life jacket, bobbing up and down on ugly white-bearded waves in the middle of a hostile lake. When he looked south, breaking crests glistened like cruel phosphorescent monsters in the blackness. The din created by breaking water on the rabidly frothing wave tops was louder than any freight train Wagerman had ever heard.*

*The moon was high on the southern horizon, and it was slowly beginning to provide some illumination in an otherwise mass of dark confusion. The lake was a conveyor belt of relentless whitecaps and Wagerman was its prisoner. He floated helplessly, suspended in the cold and hoping that dawn would come to warm him. The seagull made a second pass and Wagerman wondered if it was awaiting an opportunity to become a water buzzard and feast on the remains of a dead sailor.*

*In an angry gesture Wagerman waved and yelled, "Beat it, I'm not ready for you yet!" Wagerman thought briefly about setting off for the south shore, which was clearly visible from wave tops. But he quickly reasoned that using his limited energy for swimming against the waves would be foolhardy.*

*"Thank God it's mid-August and the water is relatively warm," he thought to himself. In this warm August water he had a chance of staying alive until dawn. With daylight, he might be spotted by a rescue vessel. Wagerman knew that commercial sailors and*

*fishermen always pitched in to assist in a search when one of their brothers was lost at sea. So he took comfort in the hope that he would be found if he could stay awake and on top of the water until morning. His chances would be vastly improved if the wind eased, as Logan had predicted. Flat water made finding someone at sea a lot easier.*

*Bill Logan, who had been only a few yards away before Wagerman drifted to sleep the last time, was gone. He scanned the water in all directions, finding no trace of his friend. As Wagerman's thoughts turned to Logan, he recalled the details of the plot that had propelled him and his friend on their ill-fated treasure hunt.*

# Dredging

## [MONDAY, MARCH 28, 1926, 7:00 A.M.]

"Look here, Herman, we have to talk about something," growled first mate McMinn as he interrupted Wagerman's work. George McMinn had cornered Wagerman in the engine room shortly after *Gerken* left port on her first dredging run of the 1926 season.

"Something wrong in the wheelhouse?" Wagerman asked.

"I didn't come down here to talk about the wheelhouse," answered McMinn. "It's this treasure hunting thing that we need to get straight!"

"Sure," replied Wagerman, "but Logan said he already talked to you about it."

"He did," replied McMinn, "but I want to talk with you before we get too far into this deal, Herman. When Logan first told me about his hare-brained scheme, I told him he was absolutely nuts. I said that if I caught the two of you doing anything that looked even remotely like you were trying to dredge up treasure, your asses would both be fired."

"What changed your mind?" asked Wagerman.

"In two words: Joe Divell," answered McMinn. "Logan took me to meet him last January and frankly the old coot made sense. I've been in this business for twenty years and I don't have a pot to piss in," said McMinn. " If what Divell says is even close to being true, we can each make a few thousand bucks. Then I could send my kids to school so they won't have to live a shit-life like mine. But let me tell you something, Wagerman. I need this job! So you guys have to be careful. If old man Gerken or Captain Gamble get wind of what we're doing they'll have our heads."

"How could we possibly get caught?" asked Wagerman. "We'll be careful, and watch for your cue. If things aren't right on the bridge, just give us the high sign and it will be back to regular dredging." Wagerman was trying to be reassuring, but McMinn didn't seem comforted.

"I hear you, Herman," he responded, "but I came down here to tell you exactly how we're going to work this deal," added McMinn. "First, we'll do some regular dredging, fill the ship to seventy percent capacity. Then we'll 'somehow' run dry on the bottom and shift to a new location. That's when we'll go to the spots that Divell will be giving us. Treasure hunting will take place when I say, and only after the hold is already almost filled. That way we're not screwing the company out of too much time."

"Sounds fine to me," replied Wagerman.

"I always thought Logan was half crazy," offered McMinn as he stepped toward the engine room door to leave. "All of his money-making ideas added together over the years have amounted to jack shit. The only reason that I even went to meet Joe Divell was because you're involved. So don't let me down, Herman! I'm counting on you to hold it together. And just because we're in this together doesn't mean that you two can ignore ship's rules. You can't do things like you did yesterday when you took two hours for lunch. Otherwise somebody is going to figure it all out!"

The door of the engine room closed and Wagerman once again wondered what he was getting himself into. He was growing increasingly uncomfortable with the treasure scheme, or at the very least distracted from it. Most of his thoughts lately had been occupied by the woman from the Erie Yacht Club. He just couldn't stop thinking about Suzanne Franzesi. A bell rang, signaling the fact that *Gerken* had reached the dredging grounds. Wagerman left his warm corner of the engine room for the hold where he would soon be activating the machinery that ran the dredge. There was a lot of sand to be pumped up and delivered before there would be any treasure hunting. *Gerken* had contracts to deliver sand to Erie as well as Buffalo that year. They would be working double shifts for the first weeks of the spring season.

Wagerman reached for the valve that would allow him to direct the incoming dredged sand toward the main hold, but somehow his hand got wet. He stared at his fingers with confusion, watching as frothing water passed through his hand rather than sand. Then he slowly came to his senses. Fully awake once more, Wagerman found himself back in his life jacket, floating in Lake Erie.

# CHAPTER 6

[SATURDAY, AUGUST 21, 1926, 2:10 A.M.]

*Wagerman's mind was racing; speeding back and forth without control between memories. It was as if he realized that his time was limited and his subconscious wanted to cover as much thought-distance as possible. As he dreamed, he couldn't help wondering about the improbable decisions that had led to his career as a sandsucker crew member. He had been working on the Buffalo ore docks one day and having serious reservations about how physically difficult the job was. Shoveling coal twelve hours a day is not a pleasant way to make a living! It seemed a more plausible career for a twenty year old than for a mature man. Wagerman realized that he would some day have to find a different job.*

*Wagerman was haunted, at the time, by occasional meetings with his old high school chums. Many had graduated from college and seemed to be enjoying white-collar careers and promotions while Wagerman was still shoveling.*

*Sometimes while he worked, he looked enviously at the sailors who brought the big coal ships in and out of the harbor. Their life seemed easy and glamorous by contrast, and Wagerman had always loved the big boats. But jobs aboard ship were scarce and Wagerman's attempts to apply for them had met with little success.*

*Then he met Jesse Gerken. Jesse was a regular at the waterfront bar where Wagerman ate lunch and the two became fast friends almost immediately. Gerken was a big bear of a man who worked for his brother Howard at Gerken Sand & Gravel. And when Howard Gerken acquired a dredging ship (a sandsucker), he had charged*

*Jesse with the responsibility of recruiting a crew. Jesse Gerken arranged for Herman to interview with his brother for a job, but his description of Wagerman had all but convinced Senior Gerken to hire him. Unbeknownst to Herman Wagerman, the interview itself was just a formality.*

*As Wagerman floated along, trapped by an uncontrollable avalanche of random memories, he recalled his first meeting with Senior Gerken. Howard Gerken was professorial, and the interview seemed to take on the tone of a history lesson. Senior Gerken didn't seem interested in asking Wagerman anything about himself. Jesse had already impressed his brother with details of Herman's work ethic. Instead, Senior Gerken regaled Wagerman with the evolution of the sand dredging industry and the development of his sand and gravel business. Howard Gerken's colorful descriptions of the industry began at the very beginning.*

*"Herman," he said, "sand has always been big business on the Great Lakes. Unfortunately, most of the people who work in the business don't understand the history of the industry or the importance of what they are doing. In my company," he added, "I expect everyone to have a complete knowledge of the business! So let's start with some history."*

# The Wisconsin Glacier

## [12,500 B.C.]

Long before North America's Indians ventured into the Great Lakes Basin or Europeans showed up to race across the Americas fighting over ownership of the New World, there was the glacier. The Wisconsin Glacier! This unimaginably huge mass of moving ice slowly and relentlessly plowed its way south, advancing at a geological rate of several hundred feet per year. It grew from the North Pole and the arctic ice caps to a point just south of Lake Erie. While the glacier's one-mile thick, plow-shaped leading edge pushed along, it systematically ground the rocks and soil in front of it into glacial grist. Sand. Then suddenly and unexplainably, long term seasonal climate trends mysteriously reversed themselves.

For unknown cosmological reasons the atmosphere began to warm up and just as relentlessly as it had advanced, the great glacier started to retreat to the north. Its southern extremities slowly began rotting in place, releasing melted water where there had once been a mile high slab of ice.

The glacier completely changed the behavior of the Great Lakes. As it retreated, it ultimately created the pattern of water flow that continues to this day. First, it connected the three northern Great Lakes with the Lake Erie–Lake Ontario system. Then it sealed off the Georgian Bay outlet that had previously allowed the three upper-most lakes to flow north into the French River. This resulted in four Great Lakes—Superior, Michigan, Huron and Erie—sending gravity-driven water rushing from one lake to the next.

Lake Erie became the last in a series of four upper lakes. Its waters rush along the lake's longitudinal axis, flowing from southwest to northeast and driven by the pressures of the three lakes to its north. All of this water ultimately cascades over Niagara Falls and the Niagara Escarpment. From there it passes into Lake Ontario, the St. Lawrence River and finally the Atlantic Ocean.

The Iroquois had a word for Lake Erie which loosely translated meant river-sea. To the Indians, Lake Erie was as big as a sea but it behaved as though it were a river. Its river-like characteristics were caused by the relentless gravity-driven currents pushing water from Superior, Michigan and Huron down the middle of the lake.

The glacier did more than influence the shapes and flow patterns of Lake Erie. As it withdrew, it dropped millions of tons of sand in strips along the lake bottom, making Lake Erie a huge repository of pure, glacially-deposited sand. The Iroquois discovered the sand when they traveled to the lake's two great sand-nourished peninsulas: Presque Isle at Erie, and Long Point directly north on the Canadian shore. When the Indians returned to their villages after fishing expeditions, they took sand with them. It had dozens of uses in Iroquois culture; drying meat, serving as a base for cook-ovens, and pottery making. However, it was the white man whose interest in sand was to create an entire new industry on the Great Lakes, sand mining.

By the mid-1800s, the Industrial Revolution was well underway. Great Lakes cities were producing goods as fast as entrepreneurs could build factories and hire people. Sand was an essential ingredient in many early industrial processes, including foundries, smelting operations and glass making. In addition to the demand created by industry, sand was needed for the construction business.

It was an essential ingredient in the concrete used for bridges, buildings, harbor jetties and road systems.

White men followed the Indians to the lakeshore where they mined sand directly from the beaches. Sand and gravel companies in towns such as Buffalo and Erie would typically shovel the beautiful white native material directly onto barges that had been towed to local beaches. Once filled, the barges were taken to downtown docks where their contents were piled in a huge mound and offered for sale to industrial and construction interests. It wasn't long before these sand-shoveling operations had incurred the wrath of local citizens, especially the ardent nature lovers. By the late 1800s, sand and gravel companies had moved their mining operations away from the beaches and adopted the process of dredging sand directly from the lake bottom. Dredging was carried out far enough offshore that the ire of the citizenry was, at least for a brief time, placated.

Dredging technology was rudimentary. A dredging ship, or sandsucker, was taken to a place where there was known to be a sand deposit on the floor of the lake. Once there, a dredge, or sweeping device, was sent overboard and dropped onto the lake bottom. The dredge, itself, was like a giant vacuum sweeper, powered by a shipboard engine that created suction. The dredge, or sweeper end, was held on the floor of the lake while bottom material, along with water, was sucked up a long flexible hose and into the hold of the ship. Once the sand and water mixture was suctioned aboard, pumps were used to send the water back overboard. Once loaded, the sandsucker would return to shore, tie up at a dock and empty its load of material. Early sandsuckers often used deck-mounted steam shovels to scoop the sand out of their holds and place it in dockside piles. Thus the traditional mountains of sand at waterfront docks.

By the early 1900s government agencies had become alarmed by unregulated dredging. They soon chased the sandsuckers out into the water with guidelines, rules and regulations for offshore dredging. The intention of the regulating agencies was to prevent over-mining and to prohibit dredging in close-to-shore areas where the removal of bottom material could cause beach erosion. Dredging companies were assigned specific offshore areas within which they were allowed to dredge materials. The regulatory agencies had no practical way to enforce these designated area regulations, however, and some companies would dredge in unauthorized areas because they were closer, shallower, or contained a specific type of material.

Sand and gravel companies were generally reputed for their ability to save money on steamships. They often purchased undersized old-timers that were about to be phased out of the bulk delivery business because they were too small or too slow. Once acquired, the undersized steamers would be retrofitted with gear specific to sand dredging and unloading, including on-deck steam shovels. In the world of Great Lakes commercial sailing, the officers and crew of the large bulk delivery freighters regarded sandsuckers and their sailors with some disdain. The romance of long voyages to Great Lakes ports or oceans seemed far more exciting than the numerous milk-runs required to suck up sand and deposit it on local piers. But within the sailing community, the same credentials and skills applied to both venues. Engineers and firemen were needed to work on the engines, and first officers and watchmen were required to navigate and drive, regardless of a ship's size or the type of work she was doing. And there was something to be said for life aboard a sandsucker. Because of the multitude of short runs, sailors from the dredges were likely to keep regular schedules and to see their families during the shipping season. Finally, there was the important issue of safety. While the sandsuckers were not as new or powerful as the larger modern ships, they were also far less likely to be at sea in storms. When the weather was foul, sandsuckers stayed in port. It was nearly impossible to keep a long dredging tube on the lake bottom in high winds and waves.

## [EARLY JANUARY, 1920]

In 1920, the Gerken Sand & Gravel Company acquired its own sandsucker and named her the *Howard Gerken Jr.* The *Gerken* was a prototypical sandsucker. At 1,320 gross tons and 241 feet long she was far too small for use as a modern bulk carrier. She was also a bit broad for her length, with a beam of 41 feet. *Gerken* drew only 16 feet when loaded, giving her the advantage of being able to work near docks which did not have deep water access. But this shallow draft made her less stable than deep-draft vessels of similar size. She was also relatively new for a sandsucker, having originally been launched as the *Rosamund Billete* in 1910.

The *Billete* was designed as a bulk freighter for use in Manitoba's Red River. Her first owners went out of business, however, and she was sold, then renamed *City of Winnipeg* in 1914. She continued in the Red River until 1917, when her second owners sold her to a company in Quebec who dismantled her and shipped the vessel to the St. Lawrence River. There she was rebuilt and placed into service in 1918 as a small bulk steamer named *T. P. Philbin.* By the late teens, however, modern 600 foot bulk carriers carried more than five times the cargo of a tiny ship like the *Philbin.* So she was offered for sale.

Howard Gerken purchased the *Philbin* and converted it to a sandsucker in support of his Buffalo-based company, Gerken Sand & Gravel. The *Gerken* was outfitted with a large high-capacity deck-mounted steam shovel, which allowed for efficient off-loading at the dock. The shovel, coupled with her on-deck machinery, made *Gerken* appear top-heavy and caused many sailors who observed her profile to snicker. They made sarcastic comments about *Gerken* being a converted river barge and a capsize waiting to happen. On balance, however, *Gerken*'s crew regarded her top-heavy deck structure and rounded hull as an acceptable trade-off for the regular schedule that they enjoyed. Besides, they reasoned, she was unlikely to encounter any of Lake Erie's really dirty weather since she only steamed between Buffalo and Erie and she was almost always within sight of shore.

Howard Gerken's pride in his accomplishments with his new flagship was matched only by his enthusiasm for the history of the sand-mining business. In many ways, Gerken's animated lessons on the glaciers, Indians and sandsucking reminded Wagerman of his finest grade school history days and the teacher who had excited him about the Great Lakes and history. Mr. Gerken's pitch had been so compelling that Herman Wagerman would have gladly taken a pay cut to work on his ship. So he stood to shake hands with his new boss and agree to an engineering position as Gerken's fireman. But as he tried to stand he fell forward, pitching violently toward the floor.

# PART THREE

## The Other Ships

*These grand freshwater seas.*
*Erie and the rest,*
*possess an ocean-like expansiveness.*
*And they have drown many a midnight ship,*
*with all its shrieking crew.*

**Herman Melville**

# CHAPTER 7

[SATURDAY, AUGUST 21, 1926, 2:20 A.M.]

*Wagerman's history lessons were abruptly interrupted by reality
when his face was immersed in water. He bolted upright in his life
jacket and found himself floating in cold water rather than sitting in
Howard Gerken's stuffed leather office chair. Alone again, the inky
black center of Lake Erie was becoming a terribly desolate place for
Wagerman and he longed to talk with someone. Anyone! As he grew
depressed about his isolation he began taking mental stock of his life
and chastising himself for things that he had not accomplished. By
his age Wagerman's parents were married and had children and he
knew that his mother shook her head in disbelief every time another
year passed and Herman failed to show the inclination to settle
down. With little to do but self-examination,
he resolved not to waste any more of his years.*

*"If I'm lucky enough to get out of this scrape," he thought to
himself, "I am going to change things. Get a steady job on shore,
save money and settle down."*

*Strangely, his psychological resolve seemed to bring him new
strength. Even though the water hissed and boiled around him,
he felt a sense of inner calm.*

*To distract himself, he struggled to think of useful things to do
while he waited for dawn. He made some adjustments to his clothing
and equipment, hoping to make himself feel warmer. Working
diligently, he untied his life preserver. Then he managed to slide it
down lower on his body so that he would ride higher in the waves
with less skin exposed to the cold water. Next, he found a length of*

*braided line in his pocket. Unraveling it, he made it into three individual pieces. He used the first two lengths to tie his pant cuffs closed so that water would not flow in and out of them. It was a trick he had learned from an old navy man. By closing off the flow, the body has time to heat the water trapped between the legs and the pants, creating an insulating layer. Wagerman used the last piece of line to lock his life preserver into its new lowered position.*

*When he had finished his work he was exhausted from the effort. So he closed his eyes and allowed himself to return to his dreams. Given his newly aroused interest in changing his approach to life, Wagerman began to think about Suzanne Franzesi. Herman knew that if she were his girlfriend, he would treat her quite differently from the way Ben Cooley, her current boyfriend, had. He had come to know that because of a chance meeting. Slowly, his mind wandered to the glorious moments that he had enjoyed with Suzanne just a few days earlier.*

# Yachting Days

[THURSDAY, AUGUST 19, 1926, 2:00 P.M.]

*Gerken* was tied to the Cascade Docks after a morning of dredging. As usual, there was no Spanish treasure to be had that day. But there were bits of old wood and a sizable collection of miscellaneous ship's hardware. The hardware had become a target for Wagerman and Logan as they were beginning to realize that this apparent junk had antique value. They had begun their treasure hunting adventures by collecting baskets of it on their "stealth" dredging trips. Their first reaction was to presume that it was a disappointing bunch of junk. They sorted through it begrudgingly, complaining that they didn't seem to be finding any real treasure. But as the hunt continued, Divell's creativity in the junk brokerage business helped them to understand how potentially valuable the bits of ship parts and hardware could be. So now, Wagerman was cataloging it and tucking it away behind his workbench.

Logan and his deck crew were busy emptying the ship's hold onto a growing sand mound on shore and Wagerman was officially off duty for another three hours. Then he would be firing up the boilers for their next run. Another day of dumping sand on this pile and *Gerken* would begin taking its loads to Buffalo. They would not be tied up at the Erie docks again until the ship was ready for its annual winter lay-up. Wagerman was standing on deck, wondering what to do with his last hours in Erie when Logan whistled at him from his seat on the derrick.

"Herman," he yelled, "check this out!"

Logan's finger directed Wagerman's attention down the bayfront toward the Erie Yacht Club. A dark-haired woman, dressed in jeans and a cotton blouse, was walking the tracks with a wicker basket. It was Suzanne Franzesi and the sight of her walking toward him seemed more dreamlike than real, since he had been thinking about her just moments earlier. He had seen her on the waterfront several times since their encounter at *Pterodactyl*'s launching and they had regularly exchanged greetings when their paths crossed, but they had not yet had an extended conversation.

Suzanne walked toward the *Gerken*, stepping along the tracks that Wagerman and Logan had traversed so many times that season. But her head was pointed toward the ground, her pace had lost its bounce and the electric fire was clearly gone from her brown eyes. Wagerman wondered why she seemed so upset as she passed the ship and in an instant of impetuousness, he was off the *Gerken* trotting toward her. Any hope of his being subtle was instantly dashed by the howling and hooting of the crew from *Gerken*'s deck.

"Hello, Suzanne," he called as she turned to see what the commotion onboard the *Gerken* was all about. "Is something wrong?"

"As a matter of fact, yes, Herman," she answered, "I've been stood-up again and I'm really upset! I have a picnic lunch and no one to share it with. Would you be interested?"

"Of course," he responded. "It's lunch time and I'm starving."

"Then let's go and have a picnic," Suzanne replied, with brightness returning to her eyes.

"Come on. We'll get away from here," Wagerman suggested, as cat calls and whistles continued from the deck. "I apologize for my friends," he added.

"It's okay, Herman, I have brothers who are worse." She turned and waved one last good-bye to the crew, then she and Wagerman crossed the tracks and headed for the bluffs. "Follow me," she said. Silently, she led Wagerman up the steep bank and through a stand of brush. The terrain abruptly changed to a path that traversed the face of the bluffs. "I'll show you my secret place," she said with a laugh. "It's a special spot that I have been coming to since I was a little girl." Suzanne broke into a trot and Wagerman had to struggle to keep up with her. They rounded a culvert in the bluffs and came to a limestone formation that jutted out from the brush, offering a spectacular view of the waterfront.

"Here it is," she proudly announced. "We always called it white rock house when we were little. Isn't it wonderful? My friends and I used to come here to play dolls," she added.

The place was surrealistically beautiful to Wagerman. He stood in silence while Suzanne began to unload the picnic basket. It was hard to believe such a spot could have been hidden on the bluffs. Wagerman wasn't sure if the rocky promenade was the source of his enchantment or if it was the woman who had just divulged her secret place with him. Being there with her seemed like an incredible intimacy. Wagerman could barely believe that she was sharing it with him.

"They're such jerks!" she said, with venom. Her tone jostled him back to reality.

"Who, and what did they do?" asked Wagerman. He was confused by this meeting with the woman who had occupied his thoughts lately. He couldn't imagine why he was so fortunate to be sitting there so close to her, eating sandwiches, cookies and fruit from a wicker basket. Wagerman sensed that this chance encounter represented some kind of fated opportunity, but he was puzzled by it. He suspected that Suzanne was upset with Cooley and his friends from the Yacht Club, and that he was the surprise benefactor of this picnic because of her feelings. But he wasn't sure if he should continue probing. He had assumed that she was Cooley's steady girlfriend but deep within Wagerman's spirit of optimism, he sensed a connection with her and wondered if her relationship with Ben Cooley might be troubled.

Her voice shattered his musings once more. "Herman," she said, "I have been going with that guy off and on for almost five years. Our relationship is basically on when the boat is laid up for the winter and he's not seeing his yacht club friends. Immediately after I help paint *Pterodactyl*'s bottom and get her into the water, then it's off. Sometimes I love that boat, but most of the time I absolutely hate it," she continued. "This year was going to be different. We were going to do lots of sailing together. Ben was supposed to take me on a romantic trip today. We were going to sail across the lake to Long Point for a weekend. We had planned and planned, and today was supposed to be our day."

"What happened?" asked Wagerman.

"At the last minute he decided to take George Stickle instead of me. He told me that they're going to a place called Gravely Bay with another sailboat and that it's going to be a men-only weekend. This happens every year, and I'm really sick of it," she added. "Actually, I think he's ashamed of me. I grew up in a fishing family and I don't fit very well with the bottle-blond Yacht Club girls he sees during the summer," she added.

As Wagerman ate, he was acutely aware of the fact that this was his cue to say something. But the words didn't seem to come out.

Something about Suzanne had paralyzed his brain and made the usually charismatic and talkative Herman Wagerman a shy stumbling boob; a personality which was so different from his shipboard character that he wasn't sure what to do. He desperately wanted to explain that he was really not like this; that if she was patient he would soon have the courage to speak clearly and let her know that he was not really a moronic sailor. But somehow all he could do was watch the horizon as clouds began to stack up over the bay. The summer clouds turned deep gray and began to rumble, warning of an impending August storm.

"Looks like we could get rained on," he said, glancing at the sky.

"Wouldn't be the first time," she responded as giant droplets began to fall on their picnic. "We'll just think of it as a free shower," she added, laughing.

Herman Wagerman could barely believe his fortune. Here he was, sitting with the most beautiful woman he had ever met, on a castle made of limestone watching a refreshing summer rainstorm roll across the water. While he sat, mesmerized, a hard rain began to fall, soaking the food, the tablecloth that was spread on the rocks and Suzanne's shirt. The increasingly moist fabric revealed a woman whose shape had previously been hidden by the modesty of a loose fitting cotton shirt. As her shirt grew wetter, the contours of her breasts became visible and her nipples were clearly outlined under the fabric. It struck Wagerman that he was in the company of an angel.

"I have something for you, Herman," she said, jolting him back to reality.

He was embarrassed at having been caught staring at her chest, and quickly reestablished eye contact. She handed him a small package wrapped in brown paper and string.

"Go ahead and open it," she said. "Perhaps you can use it aboard the *Gerken*," she continued.

So there in the pouring summer rain, Wagerman unwrapped a gift that had probably been purchased for Ben Cooley. But he didn't mind. As he fumbled to untie the string, Herman hoped that this might be the beginning of a long series of attentions that would now be directed toward him instead of the architect who clearly didn't appreciate his good fortune. The last piece of wet brown paper fell away, revealing a beautiful pearl handled utility knife.

"Just the right size for a sailor," she remarked. "And it even has a fid on the after-end," she noted.

"It's beautiful," he blurted out, half-amazed that Suzanne knew what a fid was. "I don't know what to say," he responded. "I would never have bought myself such a nice knife, and I've always wanted one!"

As he looked at her, the rain seemed to melt Suzanne Franzesi away leaving only gray waves where there had once been a beautiful woman in a clinging wet blouse. Wagerman had been having another dream. But now he was back in the middle of the cold lake rather than enjoying a pleasant summer picnic. Wagerman reached in his pocket and was relieved to feel the knife that Suzanne had given him just days earlier. At least a part of her would be with him on the lake that night. Comforted by her knife, Wagerman fell back into a deep sleep.

# CHAPTER 8

[SATURDAY, AUGUST 21, 1926, 2:30 A.M.]

*Even though Wagerman had slowly returned to consciousness in the middle of Lake Erie, he still was thinking about Suzanne Franzesi. Her image in the wet blouse haunted him. She was so incredibly beautiful that his imaginings of her were far preferable to the cold reality of Lake Erie. Reluctantly, however, he returned to the responsibilities of wakefulness and his watchman's vigil. Every time he rose to the top of a wave crest, he scanned the horizon for signs of help. He was getting colder and he desperately wished that the incessant rain would stop.*

*Wagerman's mind was wandering more spontaneously now, making it impossible to concentrate on the horizon for more than a few moments at a time. As he floated along, he was sliding uncontrollably between fantasy thoughts of the beautiful woman who was appearing in his dreams and the reality of the rescue ship that was searching the lake for him and his friends. Wagerman realized that the car ferry was his best and perhaps only hope for salvation.*

*The southerly wind was driving the current relentlessly offshore, and Wagerman could see that the lights from the American shoreline were fast fading from sight. He wondered how long the Maitland would stay out on these seas looking for him and if the captain of the railroad car ferry would realize how rapidly he was drifting north. Wagerman had faith in the Maitland and its captain, however. The car ferry sailors would never abandon a brother sailor who was adrift at sea.*

*Car ferries and their sailors were not without their own share of adventures on the Great Lakes, either. Just seventeen years earlier, the car ferry* Marquette & Bessemer #2 *had gone down in a similar storm, possibly right out here where Wagerman was floating. But the* M&B *went down with all hands. A lifeboat with nine sailors, frozen to death in their seats, was found off Erie, just about where the* Gerken *had sunk. Wagerman struggled not to think about pictures of the* Marquette & Bessemer's *lifeboat that he had seen as a high school senior. Front-page photographs featured the bodies of the frozen sailors as they were lifted out of the lifeboat, one by one, and delivered to a funeral home in Erie. He fought this image while he struggled to remain alert, but he ultimately slipped back into his dreams.*

*His unfocused mind was recalling another seventh grade history lesson from Mr. Leonardi that had brought the business of railroad car ferries to life for him. As usual, Mr. Leonardi's lessons integrated history, business and technology. According to his teacher, it all had begun with the Civil War!*

# Maitland #1

## [JUST AFTER THE CIVIL WAR]

The Civil War dramatically changed shipping on the Great Lakes.
At the onset of the war, every reasonably seaworthy Great Lakes ship
was commandeered for the Union war effort. Steamships, barges and
schooners were taken out of their customary service and converted
to war material delivery vessels. Many, if not most, of these vessels
were moved to the Atlantic Ocean, never to return to the Great
Lakes. More importantly, the war demonstrated the efficiency of
railroads for moving goods and people over great distances.
Railroads could be built between any set of towns, even if they were
not located near bodies of water. And with railroad transportation,
unlike water conveyance, there was no winter navigational hiatus.
So while bulk carriers continued working their specialized inland
waterway delivery niches, the railroads were destined to have a huge
impact upon Great Lakes shipping.

In a bit of business irony, it was often the owners of steamship
companies who pioneered the development of Great Lakes regional
railroads. Their vision and business sense warned of impending
railroad competition. And their loyalties were far more directed
toward profits and investments than to the romance of steamships.
Charles Reed of Erie, who was known throughout North America as
the "Steamboat King," was typical of these entrepreneurs. Reed
quietly sold his shares of stock in the Erie-to-Pittsburgh Extension
Canal and purchased two railroad companies after the Civil War.
It was Reed and his fellow steamship owners who had the necessary
capital to make the new railroads work.

The first efforts of the nation's railroad companies were directed toward connecting the major cities of the east. The next step was to link the east coast with the western frontier. By 1868, this link was completed and railroad owners began to think about north–south spur lines. There was special interest among railroad companies in connecting the coalfields of Pennsylvania, West Virginia and Ohio with the growing Canadian market. Residents of the "great white north" were desperately in need of efficient heating fuel and it seemed that there was an endless supply of coal to be mined just south of Lake Erie. In a stroke of entrepreneurial genius, several major railroads simultaneously developed the concept of the railroad car ferry, a specially designed ship whose decks were equipped with railroad tracks. Car ferries allowed the companies to avoid the arduous task of building tracks all the way around Lake Erie to reach the Canadian market. Ontario had its own east–west tracks linking Toronto with Windsor and the Canadian frontier. The American companies just had to devise a way of reaching them. So they would place railroad cars filled with coal onto car ferries on the American shore, then haul the precious loads of heating fuel across the lake to the Canadian market.

Railroad car ferries usually had three or four sets of tracks running from bow to stern so that several coal cars could ride across the lake at a time. Coal cars were hauled north from the United States to Canada and unloaded. Then the ferries would bring empty cars back to the south (American) shore.

When Wagerman began working on the *Gerken*, he was able to integrate his seventh grade lessons with his new profession. He watched the car ferries trundling back and forth on the lake and paid special attention to accounts of their comings and goings. The two busiest American ports were Ashtabula and Conneaut, Ohio; both of which were within forty-five miles of Erie. The Marquette & Bessemer Railroad operated the car ferry service out of Conneaut, sending cargoes to Port Stanley, Ontario. The New York Central Railroad ran its car ferries out of Ashtabula sending them diagonally across the course of the *Marquette & Bessemer* to Port Maitland, Ontario on the eastern end of the lake. Car ferries were traditionally named after either the company that owned them or their destination port followed by a number designating the order in which the ship was launched. Thus *Maitland #1* was so named because it serviced the port of Maitland and it was the New York Central Railroad's first, and oldest, car ferry.

Car ferries ran such steady and predictable routes that passengers regularly utilized them for trips across the lake. Businessmen and travelers with a need to commute between car ferry ports would regularly pay a ticket fee to cross Lake Erie. Accommodations were Spartan, but prices were cheap and the old ships could be counted upon to leave and arrive on time. The port cities serviced by the car ferries grew used to the comings and goings of these ships. The 9:00 p.m. hour in Port Stanley, for example, was invariably punctuated by *Marquette & Bessemer #2*'s whistle as she powered into the harbor. Old timers on the docks would consult their watches when they heard the evening whistle and proclaim conditions on the lake. An early whistle meant that the water was as smooth as glass. A late whistle, on the other hand, indicated rough seas. The later the whistle, the rougher the water. Each of Lake Erie's four major car ferry towns, Ashtabula, Conneaut, Port Maitland and Port Stanley had similar traditions. The only variable was the accustomed hour of the whistle.

The greatest tragedy in the history of Lake Erie car ferries occurred on December 7, 1909, when residents of Port Stanley heard *Marquette & Bessemer #2*'s steam whistle for the last time. It was blowing mournfully and it was more than an hour late. Observers watched as the old ship sat in place outside the Port Stanley harbor. The channel entrance had become a maelstrom of breaking waves in the seventy-mile-per-hour winds that piped up after the car ferry left Conneaut. Following several moments of apparent indecision, the captain decided that the harbor entrance was too rough to risk an entry. *Marquette & Bessemer #2* slowly turned her bow west and began steaming upwind toward the Detroit River end of the lake. Observers assumed that the captain had decided to ride out the storm, taking the waves on his bow. This was the traditional conservative strategy. Even if storm winds continued to blow, a ship could ultimately find shelter in the lee of Rondeau Point to the west.

No one ever saw the *Marquette & Bessemer #2* again after she steamed away from Port Stanley that night. People in cities along both shores of Lake Erie (United States and Canada) reported hearing her steam whistle at various times during the night. But the car ferry itself was never seen again. The ship went down somewhere in Lake Erie that night, taking a crew of thirty-three with it, as well as an Erie businessman who was riding to Port Stanley with $50,000 in cash. Mystery surrounding the *Marquette & Bessemer #2*, which has never been found. Grizzly accounts of the nine frozen survivors discovered off Erie in the ship's lifeboat kept people talking about the ship for years. In fact, there were three people who had good reason to be thinking about her the evening of August 20, 1926. They included Herman Wagerman, who kept seeing visions of the frozen sailors in their lifeboat, as well as the captain and first mate of the car ferry *Maitland #1* who were about to go for the ride of their careers.

*Maitland #1* served a route similar to that of the old *Marquette & Bessemer*. She left Ashtabula, Ohio, each day with a load of railroad cars bound for Port Maitland, Ontario. Port Maitland lies approximately three miles up the Grand River, which flows into the eastern end of Lake Erie, halfway between Long Point and the Niagara River. Acting Captain Thomas Heyman and First Mate Bill Burke knew that it was blowing hard out on the lake. They had completed the crossing from Ashtabula just hours earlier. But the Ashtabula to Maitland run had been relatively easy since the wind was on the stern and the ship was fully loaded. As *Maitland #1* pulled away from her railroad docks Friday evening, the two men in the wheelhouse realized that their return trip would, at the very least, be unpleasant. Cottonwood trees along the sheltered banks of the Grand River were bent almost double in the wind. To make matters worse, *Maitland #1* would be traveling light on the ride home with a load of empty cars. This would raise her freeboard and expose more of the hull to the waves.

As the car ferry neared the entrance to the open lake, Burke peered through the bridge windows and proclaimed his opinion of the weather: "Shit! Tomorrow is my day off, and we're not going to be getting home on time tonight."

## [FRIDAY, AUGUST 20, 1926, 9:00 P.M.]

Without responding to Burke's complaint, Heyman powered *Maitland* out of the sheltered river and into the evening seas, carefully noting time and position in his log. Heyman was an acting captain and he knew that he was on a probationary trial with the company. The owners would be pleased if he brought the ship home through this summer storm. But he realized all too well that conditions on the lake that night held the potential for disaster. Heyman's first concern was not the waves. It was August, and summer storms generally didn't last long. It was the duration of the wind along with the fetch of the lake that caused problems, not just wind velocity. In addition to the fact that Heyman discounted the winds as part of a short summer storm, the waves were running from the south/southeast and wouldn't have a chance to build like waves from the southwest. Heyman judged the winds to be in the neighborhood of forty miles per hour, not yet a major problem. His more immediate concern was keeping track of his position in the waves so that he would not hit Tecumseh Reef, Lake Erie's major eastern navigational hazard. Tecumseh was sheer sharp rock, and it would make quick work of *Maitland #1*'s steel hull if she were to hit it in waves like these.

The door to the bridge opened suddenly, letting in a great gust of wind as Pete Brinley stepped inside. Pete was in his thirty-fifth year as a watchman on the Great Lakes and had sailed aboard car ferries since his first grandchild was born ten years earlier. Brinley said he wanted to live to see him graduate from high school, so he gave up his career aboard the big ore carriers. Although Pete had never advanced to become an officer, he was regarded as the most knowledgeable and experienced crew member. He had also been a mentor when an ambitious young Tom Heyman was first moving up the ranks aboard the car ferry.

"Can I have a word, Captain?" asked Brinley.

"Sure, Pete, what is it?" responded Heyman.

"I had two good friends on the old *Marquette & Bessemer*, you know! Weather looks a lot like it did that night, Captain!"

"This is a summer storm," answered Heyman. "It's bound to let up soon."

"Take a look at the way the wind is shifting," responded Brinley. "It's going southeast on us. A Devil Wind for sure! And it won't let up soon. In fact, it's probably going to pipe up," added Brinley. "I talked to the crew," Brinley continued, "and they don't mind turning back. We could spend the night in Port Maitland. The old-timers always said that you should never tempt a Devil Wind," he added.

"I'm going to try running into it for a while, Pete," said Heyman, "but thanks for the advice. Maybe I'll ask you to come back up here in an hour and take another look."

"Sure, Cap," replied Brinley, " I'll be below if you need me."

"*Marquette & Bessemer #2! Tempt a Devil Wind!*" muttered First Mate Burke. "Jesus, what a nice thought! I think he's overreacting."

"I'm not so sure," responded Heyman. "We'll get around Tecumseh Reef and take another look at it."

He pushed the old car ferry toward Tecumseh, but Heyman could see that Brinley was right about the wind. It was building and shifting southeast. The wind and waves were right on the nose and the ship's motion was not pleasant! But if pressed to decide between pleasing the crew or making the owners of the company happy, a young acting captain almost always chose in favor of his career. So Heyman settled into his chair on the bridge and began doing the navigational geometry required to predict when *Maitland #1* would arrive at the Tecumseh Reef Buoy. By 10:00 p.m., *Maitland* had still not reached the buoy at Tecumseh Reef, ordinarily a thirty-minute ride from the entrance of the Grand River. Choosing discretion over the possibility that he would be making his inexperience and insecurity seem obvious, he sent Burke to bring Brinley to the bridge. When the door opened and Brinley walked in, the blast of air was even stronger than it had been before.

"What's up, Cap?" asked Pete Brinley.

"I'm a little worried about not spotting the Tecumseh Reef Buoy," answered Heyman. "Don't you think we should be able to see it by now?"

"Look at the wind," responded Brinley. "It's moved ten points to the southeast since I was up here an hour ago. That means you're probably heading directly for the reef. You need to steer to port to correct for the drift!"

"Think so?" asked Heyman. "I've been careful to stay on course."

"In winds like this, the waves give an empty car ferry a terrible leeway," responded Brinley. "You need to correct."

"By how much?" asked Heyman.

"Two degrees to port for every degree the wind shifts when it's blowin' fifty or more. And it's blowin' at least that," noted Brinley.

"Correct by 20 degrees?" asked Heyman.

"Yup, and do it now," Brinley added. "You can't afford to take a chance with Tecumseh. In a Devil Wind like this she'll tear the livin' shit out of the bottom!"

Heyman knew that Brinley was probably right. In fact, he probably had been right earlier when he had suggested returning to Maitland. So Acting Captain Thomas Heyman took Watchman

Brinley's advice and turned *Maitland*'s wheel until the big ship came down 20 degrees to port. As he continued thinking about his career, Heyman was developing a plan of action. Once he passed Tecumseh Reef, he decided to himself that he would steam directly for the American shore. In a southeast wind, the bluffs along the New York and Pennsylvania shorelines would eventually shelter him. Once he reached the lee of the American shore, he would bring *Maitland #1* to the southwest and take her home to Ashtabula. Satisfied with his mental plan, he went back to searching the horizon for the Tecumseh Reef Buoy. Thomas Heyman was concerned that he had over-corrected with the wheel and taken the ship too far east, adding to time and fuel consumption en route to Ashtabula. But he resolved to stay the new course for a while and search for the buoy.

"Jesus, look at that!" exclaimed First Officer Burke.

"What?" asked Heyman.

"It's the Tecumseh Reef Buoy, dead ahead and not a mile away," answered Burke.

"Christ!" muttered Heyman as he wheeled *Maitland* another 10 degrees to port. "That was way too close. Go below and get Brinley up here again."

The close call, along with Brinley's prophetic advice had momentarily shaken Heyman. He had assumed that the buoy would appear on the ship's starboard beam. Convinced that he had overreacted with the wheel, he was even worried that he might be so far east of the reef that he wouldn't even see it. Having the buoy appear dead ahead had not helped bolster his confidence.

It was almost 10:30 p.m. when Brinley arrived on the bridge for a third time that night to counsel his young acting captain and protégé. This time, Heyman was prepared to take any advice that

Brinley might give. Brinley stepped through the door, accompanied by a gale forced blast of wind that propelled him into the wheelhouse.

"At least seventy miles an hour, Cap," he offered. Spying the Tecumseh buoy just to starboard, he made another observation. "Felt the boat come to port a few minutes ago, Cap. Did the buoy surprise you?"

"I'm a little concerned, Pete," offered Thomas Heyman. "It took us ninety minutes to make a half hour run and I almost hit the reef. I'm wondering what to do next. Do you still think I should go back to Maitland, Pete?"

"What were you planning to do?" asked Brinley.

Tenuously, Heyman shared his idea to run due southeast. "I was thinking that we could make directly for the American shore and get some shelter behind the cliffs. What would you do?"

It was at this point that Watchman Pete Brinley made a fated suggestion that was to prove lifesaving for *Gerken*'s crew.

"Cap, if you go southeast," Brinley reasoned aloud, "you won't find much shelter. The waves near the south shore will be crazy in a blow like this, and sooner or later the wind will shift back to the southwest. Then she'll be on our nose again. The only thing to do is to get past Tecumseh, come to starboard, and then do what the old ship captains have always done in a Devil Wind."

"What's that?" asked Heyman.

"Tuck in behind Long Point and wait it out," replied Brinley. "The winds will be blocked by the point and there's 100 feet of water behind the north beaches. We'll just hunker down and wait. By morning, the wind should let up and we can steam directly to Ashtabula."

Without thinking twice about Brinley's advice, Thomas Heyman rounded Tecumseh Reef and brought the car ferry 90 degrees to starboard. The steering maneuver eased the ship's motion considerably and Heyman headed his ship for the lee of Long Point, twenty-five miles due west. Heyman was rapidly forgetting about saving money for the company at the risk of the ship and crew. Shelter in the lee of Long Point suddenly seemed like a perfect interim destination.

# CHAPTER 9

[SATURDAY, AUGUST 21, 1926, 2:40 A.M.]

*Wagerman made a concerted effort to dream about more positive things as he drifted between reality and sleep. While he pondered the likelihood of rescue, his thoughts turned from the* Maitland *to the* Erie Coast Guard. *He knew the* Maitland *would have a wireless, and he presumed that by this time they would have contacted the Coast Guard Station. So even if the "Coasties" hadn't seen* Gerken's *distress signals, they would almost certainly be out searching by now. Wagerman knew some of the crew at Erie's station and he imagined them putting out to sea so that they could join the search. So as he scanned the horizon for signs of rescue he watched for more than one ship.*

*He let his mind drift back to grade school again and to his seventh grade teacher. Mr. Leonardi was young and enthusiastic. He didn't seem to be going through the motions of teaching like so many of the other teachers and he was obviously more excited about helping the students learn than disciplining them or forcing them to follow the many catholic school "rules." One day in November, when there had been a Coast Guard rescue near Buffalo, Mr. Leonardi excitedly rushed into class and read the entire newspaper account to the class. Fifty children in bolted-down desks sat in rapt silence, hanging on every word. And when Mr. Leonardi had finished the article he announced that he was going to abandon the day's lesson plan and use the opportunity to tell the history of the United States Coast Guard. Ironically, his lessons had included the Coast Guard*

*Station at Erie, Pennsylvania, a classic case of the evolution from lifesaving stations to the modern Coast Guard.*

*Wagerman thought about Mr. Leonardi's lessons from that day and about the Coast Guard. He reasoned that he was fortunate in a way. There was a rescue station ashore on the channel at Erie. They had two vessels capable of a mid-lake rescue and Wagerman knew that they would not hesitate to join Maitland in the search. Hope tripled!*

# The Lifesaving Service

## [SPRING, 1876]

Commercial shipping eventually led to the development of lifesaving services in both the United States and Canada. During the late nineteenth century, American businessmen put pressure on Congress to redirect the monies previously earmarked for Civil War military activities toward the safety and security of the Great Lakes commercial shipping fleet. Shipping volume grew exponentially after the Civil War, and entrepreneurs on both sides of the lakes were convinced that a lifesaving service would provide economic benefits for ships and their passengers.

Erie's Lifesaving Service was organized in the early 1870s and construction of its first beach station was completed in time for the 1876 shipping season. The station house was located on the beach at Presque Isle Peninsula. It was positioned so that personnel had a bird's-eye view of the northern-most section of open beach. The thinking was that this location would provide an optimum view of the lake, offering watchmen an unlimited panorama of the open water. The station structure looked like a nineteenth century firehouse, with huge double doors facing the beach and a seagoing, high freeboard lifeboat mounted on tracks. The rails extended from inside the lifesaving station to the beach, theoretically enabling the crew to launch a lifeboat in seconds by pushing it directly down the tracks and into the water. In addition to lifeboats, the lifesaving crew had mobile cannons used to shoot rescue lines to vessels which foundered close to shore and a breeches buoy system which could be deployed for evacuating people from ships.

Lifesaving was a highly romanticized activity on the Great Lakes. The lifesaving station crew regularly practiced activities such as rowing, swimming and underwater diving, training on the beach during the July and August idyllic northern weather. Townspeople from Great Lakes cities would often make summer excursions to lifesaving stations to watch the heroic crew members practice running on the beach, swimming for distance and performing feats of strength and agility. Young boys who lived near lifesaving stations dreamed about becoming lifesavers and rescuing damsels in distress.

The grim reality of lifesaving stations generally set in about mid-October. The weather became cold and unpleasant and the water took on a life-threatening chill. In addition, October marked the beginning of high wind season on the Great Lakes. Late fall and early spring months on Lake Erie are traditionally punctuated by severe storms. Winds often reach hurricane proportions and last for days on end. For ships at sea, this meant that the non-summer months were the most likely times for shipping emergencies. It was no easy task launching a twenty-five-foot rowing vessel in sub-freezing weather with high winds and brutally cold water. To make matters worse, fall and spring storms soon evidenced another grim reality for the early lifesaving stations. Their locations, while handy to the beach and providing excellent visibility, were impractical for several reasons. First, the stations were subject to shifting beach sands. Once a particular location had been selected, storms would either erode the sand, placing the station structure at peril, or deposit hundreds of yards of sand between the end of the lifeboat tracks and the water. But the primary dilemma presented itself when there was a pressing need to deploy a lifeboat during a storm and the crews found that the beach surf made a launch impossible.

By the 1880s, Erie's beachfront Lifesaving Station had proven to be as much of a functional failure as it was a romantic delight. Yet the politicians who provided the funding were reluctant to abandon its basic idea. Alternatively, they decided to move the building to a more sheltered location. Thus the Erie Station was reconstructed on the north side of the commercial channel connecting the open waters of the lake to the city's protected natural harbor. The major strength of the new location was the fact that it was sheltered from the lake's winds and waves. On the down side, however, the new station was over a mile from the beaches, thus making it difficult to keep a physical watch over the lake's open waters.

And so it was that the tradition of the beach patrol emerged. The crew of the lifesaving station would make regular walks along the beach near the location of the original beach station, scanning the offshore waters and noting any vessels observed during stormy weather. If a ship was spotted during a storm, the frequency of the beach patrol was increased so that the station crew could keep a vigil and monitor its progress. A dead-reckoning position was noted and recorded every hour until the ship departed the Erie Lifesaving Station's jurisdiction. Beach patrols were routinely increased during storms; often the case during fall and spring seasons when there was a shipping rush, with owners and captains anxious to squeeze in an extra season's run. These were, therefore, the months when the likelihood of disaster was the highest and when members of the beach patrol paid the greatest attention to the details of their duties.

From five feet above the water's surface the horizon is approximately seven miles away. Thus members of the beach patrol, walking on the hard-packed sweep of surf sand along the beaches at Presque Isle, commanded a half pie-shaped field of vision with a radius of seven miles. This distance seems small in consideration of the fifty-mile width of Central Lake Erie. But with the tip of Long Point (immediately north of Presque Isle Peninsula) only twenty-seven miles away, visual observations of shipping were actually quite likely, especially since ship superstructures would often extend the range of sight well beyond seven miles.

Any ship transiting Lake Erie had to pass through the narrow corridor between Presque Isle and Long Point (which had its own lifesaving station). Thus there was a good chance that in clear weather, beach patrols from either the U.S. or Canadian shore would see any but a ship driving right down the center of the lake. And since distressed ships had a tendency to make for one of the two shores, there was a good chance that a shore patrol might actually spot a ship that was in trouble.

When there was a rescue, the media would be filled with accolades for the Lifesaving Service. The reputation of the local Revenue Service, however, was quite another matter. The Revenue Service, which was related to the Lifesaving Service by virtue of a common funding source (the federal government), maintained a fleet of ships along the Great Lakes, ostensibly for purposes of defending the United States against Canada and enforcing customs regulations. While this seemed a somewhat logical notion during the early nineteenth century (just after the War of 1812), the practicality of a fleet of warships for protection against Canada seemed far less sensible by midcentury. As the Revenue Service fell from favor, it began a progressively negative spiral in which the ships in service grew more outdated and ill-equipped because of funding shortfalls. This would, in turn, be followed by glaring examples of interdiction failure. The Revenue Service argued that they needed more funds to update their fleet, but public opinion made politicians reluctant to provide money to a service that rarely seemed able to accomplish much of anything when called upon.

In 1915, the federal government made an amazingly reasonable decision, which calmed public tensions regarding the Revenue Service. It merged the Revenue Service with the Lifesaving Service, creating the United States Coast Guard. This decision provided a fleet of ships for the Lifesaving Service so that they would no longer be relegated to rescues within sight of shore. The shift allowed the newly-formed Coast Guard to design ships specifically for search and rescue (rather than using the old Revenue Service's antiquated warship "cutter" designs) and inspired the tradition of Coast Guard cutters.

The birth of the Coast Guard took place at an exciting time of technological change. Wireless ship-to-shore radio and other navigational technologies were emerging. Eventually it seemed that all commercial ships would have the capacity to speak with each other and keep in touch with on-shore interests such as the Coast Guard. With its ability to bring up-to-the-minute weather reports, wireless promised a new era of safety. But not every commercial ship was equipped with a radio transmitter. Coast Guard stations throughout the Great Lakes were inadvertently trapped between old and new technologies for the first years of the twentieth century. Paradoxically, it was the older, at-risk ships that were usually not so well-equipped. And these were precisely the vessels that were most likely to have problems.

Wagerman dreamed about the Erie Coast Guard Station and its beach patrol. He knew that the Erie Station had carried on the tradition of beach patrols that had been originated by the first lifesaving stations. And as he dozed, he imagined that they must have spotted his signal fire and run to the station to sound an alarm.

# PART FOUR

# Lake Erie's Wrath

"John Maynard," cried the captain, "can you hold on five minutes longer?" "I'll try, Sir," he said. And he did. The flames came nearer and smoke almost suffocated him. Crouching, he held the wheel firmly, driving the great steamer for shore where its passengers, women and children first, could be saved. He held with his left, until flesh shriveled and muscle crackled in the flames. Then he held for a time longer than his right. All but he were saved. Now he to whom they owe everything, sleeps in peace in the green of Lake Erie.

**Charles Dickens**

*The Brave Helmsman
of Lake Erie*

97

# Chapter 10

## [Saturday, August 21, 1926, 2:45 a.m.]

*Wagerman awoke with a start. Something had aroused him from his dreams and as his mind cleared he realized that it was his own shivering. He was so cold that he knew he would soon be in serious trouble if he couldn't think of ways to warm himself. Searching for signs of hope, he turned slowly through 360 degrees, scanning the horizon. Nothing!*

*The effort required to propel his body through the simple turning maneuver was alarming. Yet he noticed, as he kicked his legs and moved his arms, that the easy physical motions were restorative. He could feel heat pulsate through his extremities as he moved them. Raising his arms above the water he began to rotate them holding them straight out and away from his body. He counted as he rotated. One, two, three, four. Sixteen rotations, and he could actually feel heat passing back through his swollen hands. His fingers came alive once more and he found that he could manipulate them. Systematically, Wagerman exercised each part of his body; his neck, his legs, even his ankles. The result was the same with each body part. The simple exercises warmed him. As he continued his program of water calisthenics he remembered physical education at his catholic grade school in Buffalo. There were more than fifty children in Wagerman's first grade class. They sat in tiny desks, bolted to the floor. There they learned reading, the multiplication tables and how to pray. Midway through each morning and afternoon, ten times per week, they also had physical education. The children stood in place at their desks and did the precise exercise routine that Herman was doing now in the center of Lake Erie. And sometimes, especially during Lent, they combined praying with exercise.*

*"I wonder if they were preparing me to be a shipwrecked sailor?" he thought to himself.*

*Wagerman's biggest problem in grade school had been daydreaming. It seemed that there was always something far more interesting going on inside his mind than in the class. And it seemed quite the same way in the lake. So with nothing else to do, Wagerman allowed himself to succumb to daydreaming during his water exercises. In the warm haven of his mind he returned to the* Gerken *and treasure hunting. This time, however, his dreams were more practical and focused. He was imagining what might have happened if he had been able to earn enough extra money to ask Suzanne for a real date. To save up enough cash to do a proper job of courting, he knew that the* Gerken *treasure scheme would have to be a success.*

# August Run

[THURSDAY, AUGUST 19, 1926, 3:00 A.M.]

There were two mission control centers aboard *Gerken* during the summer of 1926. One was in the traditional location on the ship's bridge. There, Captain Gamble, First Mate McMinn and engineering officers John and Jesse Gerken plotted courses and developed navigational plans for their regular sandsucking runs. The second and unofficial control center, at least for the summer of 1926, was in the hold just behind the main bulkhead. There, Wagerman, Logan, and sometimes McMinn would pour over Joe Divell's charts and muse about how many more wrecks they might have to sweep before they "struck it rich." On the last run they thought they had found the mother lode. They were at Divell's Wreck #83. It was a wooden schooner in forty-four feet of water, nine miles due north of the Presque Isle Lighthouse. This wreck was difficult to find because it was in relatively deep water and so far offshore that it was hard to line up with features from land. Divell's instructions had been to power due north from the Presque Isle light for exactly nine miles. Joe accomplished this feat in his old tug by driving at half throttle for an hour. But it took Logan, Wagerman and McMinn four tries to locate the wreck, since it was hard to calibrate *Gerken*'s speed with that of Divell's tug. When they finally did find it, their first sweep proved extremely productive. In little more than an hour of dredging, a number of interesting artifacts came tumbling through the strainer and into the hold. There was nothing of major value, but the load of junk assured them that they were onto something.

Divell had been insistent that this particular wreck had the most potential so far. He had grown more and more enthusiastic over the past weeks as Wagerman and Logan moved systematically from one wreck to the next. Even the relatively unproductive wrecks had produced lots of artifacts. Amazingly, the things that Wagerman would have regarded as absolute junk: nails, chunks of waterlogged wood and the like, were fetching remarkable prices. Divell found several second-hand dealers who were brokering their assorted shipwreck "junk" to collectors. Apparently there were lots of individuals across North America who would purchase assorted pieces of shipwreck debris and convert them to treasured keepsakes. Old pieces of wooden ribbing were saturated with varnish and affixed to placards as wall hangings. Rusted nails were sandblasted and made into framed decorations. Collectors were literally crazy for shipwreck artifacts.

Logan suspected that Joe Divell had been "salting" the treasure trove of actual marine artifacts with his personal collection of waterfront junk but Wagerman found that hard to believe. Divell was a curmudgeon, but he also had the reputation of being honest to a fault.

When the dredging operation had uncovered a recognizable artifact, a spoon or candlestick for example, Divell was able to get a handsome price for it. To date, the partners had sold almost $2,000 worth of stuff, and Wagerman had three more packing crates filled with newly mined pieces to take to Divell. He guessed that the new shipment was worth at least three times what they had already collected. Wagerman and Logan were excited to return to Wreck #83 since they had done so well there the last time they were out. In less than an hour they had picked up some of the very best and most valuable articles yet including cups, plates, flatware and hardware. This was just the kind of stuff that was sure to fetch a great price from Divell's collectors. Even if they never found the Spanish treasure, the revenue from this site could easily make the entire summer operation worthwhile. McMinn was the most excited of all. When they had approached him with his first share, almost $500, he nearly cried with joy. George's family was going through tough financial times and the extra cash was a godsend.

The biggest problem with Wreck #83 was that is was well outside of the approved dredging area. It was several miles northwest of the grounds where *Gerken* was authorized to dredge and just barely within clear-weather site of the Coast Guard's beach patrol. There wasn't much of a risk of being caught, however, since the beach patrol would not be paying careful attention to shipping unless there was a storm. There was a far greater chance that the operation would be discovered by the rest of the crew and in particular by John Gerken, the chief engineer. It was he who seemed to take personal responsibility for doing the proper and legal things with respect to *Gerken*'s dredging patterns. As the official family representative on the bridge, he apparently felt that it was his duty to be sure that Coast Guard sand dredging regulations were not violated.

This run was likely to present some other special difficulties for Wagerman, Logan and McMinn, as well. They were tied to the Buffalo dock that morning waiting for company owner Howard Gerken who was due to board for the trip. Senior, as the men called him, didn't go along too often, but when he did the captain and crew pulled out all of the hospitality stops. There was a party atmosphere aboard ship that day since the crew knew they would be eating well for the duration of the trip. In fact, Leland Oakes, the ship's cook, had asked for help the night before, loading a case of T-bone steaks into the galley for Saturday's dinner. As he hauled provisions onto the *Gerken*, Oakes introduced his son Eugene who was to celebrate his 14th birthday aboard on Saturday.

Both young Oakes and Senior Gerken were there for the same reason. This was to be an August run. Great Lakes weather has always been macroscopically predictable. The shipping season begins and ends with the stormiest months, March and December. The transitional months of April, May, October, and November can also be volatile, spawning sudden storms of frightening proportions. But midsummer months are generally docile, a time when air and water temperatures are approximately the same. There is an absence of fog, temperatures are balmy and the winds almost always blow gently from the prevailing southwest direction. This was traditionally the time when owners joined their crews, bringing friends or business associates to enjoy the tropical midsummer delights of Great Lakes travel.

Sometime after the middle of August there is inevitably a late summer storm which heralds the end of tropical times. But most years, these pattern-changing storms occur between early and mid-September. Thursday, August nineteenth was a beautiful summer day. As the crew waited for Senior to come aboard during the predawn hours, they lounged about the deck in short-sleeved shirts enjoying rare moments of leisure. They smoked, drank coffee and talked to each other about off-season plans as they waited, unaware of what the weather gods were cooking up for them in the upper atmosphere.

"Where the hell are you guys?" barked McMinn as he dropped down the ladder and into the hold.

"Over here, George," called Wagerman from behind his
bulkhead station.

"Look at what we dredged up at Wreck #83 on our last run,"
added Logan, pulling out a packing crate filled with artifacts. "Divell
will probably get another $2,000 just for this one crate."

"We have to get *Gerken* back over that wreck," added
Wagerman. "A few more hours of dredging and we can make another
$5,000 at this rate."

"I know," responded McMinn, "but we have to be careful.
Senior is going to be aboard and everyone will be minding the boat
and all of her details. So here is what we're going to do." McMinn was
now even more anxious to continue the unofficial dredging than the
terrible twosome, so Wagerman and Logan listened carefully as he
outlined his plan. "We won't go anywhere near the wreck on our first
run," noted McMinn. "We're going to go from Buffalo directly to the
Erie dredging grounds. We'll fill the ship, then take her to Erie and
tie up. Senior is planning to join some business associates for dinner
in Erie tonight, so we'll unload and wait for him. Friday when we
leave to dredge the load for Buffalo, we'll go back out to Wreck #83.
Senior will be hung over and tired and he won't be paying attention
to ship's operations. Everybody else on board, including Captain
Gamble and the two Gerken boys, will be paying attention to Senior.
We'll pick up a three-quarter load at the regular dredging site, then
head out to Wreck #83. If we plan things right we'll get to the wreck
at suppertime and I will volunteer to drive. Then I can put you boys
right on top of the wreck. While everyone is busy eating steak
dinners and having a good time, we can work on our treasure."

Wagerman was delighted. With McMinn's cooperation, he knew
that he and Logan would have at least a few hours to mine the

bottom. Wagerman had long given up hope of finding Spanish gold. He had always regarded the legend of gold and silver coins as a pipe dream. Instead, he was thinking about the five hundred extra dollars that he had already made selling the assortment of junk that had been pumped up off the bottom. A few more loads like that, and he knew exactly what he would do with his share. A thousand dollars in a bank account would be more than enough to make some winter trips to Erie. Who knows, perhaps he would buy a diamond ring. Wagerman had aspirations of serious courting. As he contemplated his fortunes, he could see himself taking Suzanne Franzese to a fine restaurant. In his mind, he was wearing a suit and tie, clothing befitting yacht club types. She would be wearing a black dress with a plunging neckline and they would be seated at a formal restaurant with white linen tablecloths. He wouldn't be taking her to the kind of places where he and Logan ate, but to a fancy establishment. A hotel with a ballroom.

Wagerman gazed across the table at Suzanne. Her soft brown eyes sparkled in the candlelight as he looked at her. Barely believing his good fortune for being with her, he reached into his pocket to produce the diamond ring. Wagerman wondered how she would react to his directness. They had known each other for such a short time! His fingers fumbled furiously inside his pocket, clumsily groping for the ring. For some reason his hands were swollen and stiff, and they failed to respond to his intentions. Finally, he found something. But it wasn't the ring that he had planned to give to Suzanne Franzesi. It was a jack knife! As he gripped it, Herman Wagerman was instantly transported back into his cold, wet life jacket.

# CHAPTER 11

[SATURDAY, AUGUST 21, 1926, 2:55 A.M.]

*Wagerman pulled the shiny new jackknife from his pocket and examined it carefully. As he held it, he was more intent upon the image of the woman who had given it to him than the knife itself.*

*"Ironic," he thought to himself. "All these years as a sailor without a proper knife. Then when I finally get one I'm dumped into the water to die. I'll probably never really be able to use it!"*

*For the first time since he had been thrown into the lake, Wagerman stumbled mentally over the possibility that he might die. Perhaps it was his first grade exercise program that had propelled him toward such thoughts. After all it was in his early catechism classes that he had first encountered the notion of death. Prior to that time in his life, he had enjoyed the invincibility, immortality and innocence of childhood. He could still remember his teachers admonishing the children to be vigilant, since death could come at any time.*

*"Sister, is Death a real person?" he had asked once in first grade.*

*"No one knows, Herman," was Sister's answer. "But many believe that there is an Angel of Death," she added, "a creature who comes when it is your time and helps in the transition to the other side."*

*"Will the Angel of Death be a man or a woman?" asked Herman Wagerman, with eyes and mind wide open to the impending answer.*

But there was no response! Such esoteric questions of theology were not the mainstay of first grade.

With a jolt of energy Herman Wagerman suddenly sat bolt upright in the water and decided to stop feeling sorry for himself. Indeed there was something to celebrate. The knife! It was the gift of the woman of his dreams and he had it with him. His happiness warmed him temporarily and as he sat suspended in his life jacket, Wagerman gripped his new knife as tightly as a child who had just received the best Christmas present of all time. Wagerman's mind drifted back to his second meeting with Suzanne, a wonderful evening that had included dinner and a kiss.

# *Devil Wind*

## [THURSDAY, AUGUST 19, 1926, 11:00 A.M.]

*Gerken* was poised over a productive sandsucking spot on the bottom of Lake Erie, just a few miles northwest of Erie's harbor. The dredge was down and Wagerman was watching the last of a load pour into the hold. At 11:05 a.m. Wagerman rang the bell signaling that the ship's hold was filled. Within minutes, *Gerken* was headed for Erie's commercial docks to deposit its load. Wagerman climbed to the deck where he could see Senior Gerken smiling and chatting on the bridge. The weather was perfect. The wind had been dead calm and the water was like a millpond, but a new southerly breeze was filling in, cooling the deck and breaking the humidity. *Gerken* moved easily across the flat surface, leaving a wake that was visible for miles behind her stern. She was fully loaded and her decks were almost awash from the combination of sand and water in her hull. As she powered along at eleven knots, her pumps were discharging a muddy stream of excess water from the load of sand. She certainly did not give the appearance of a romantically beautiful steamer, as she plowed along with her waterline five feet below the surface. But then the *Gerken* was supposed to be profitable, not pretty. And judging from the mood on the bridge, this had been one of Senior Gerken's best business years.

An hour later, they were tied to a pier unloading. The engineering crew, including Wagerman, was off duty as Logan piled sand on the dock. Senior Gerken was ashore with his Erie cronies, apparently negotiating a delivery deal for next season. Unloading sand in Erie was unusual at this time of year. There were rumors that this particular August delivery signaled the beginning of a new, lucrative deal between Senior Gerken and several interests in Erie. By 5:00 p.m., the unloading was completed and Wagerman had returned to the ship after enjoying his picnic lunch with Suzanne. With the load of sand piled neatly on the dock, the crew was patiently waiting to learn the ship's schedule for their next run. Herman Wagerman had returned to the engine room to do some regular maintenance and as he worked, McMinn and Logan entered the room for a conference.

"Looks like we'll be pulling out late tomorrow morning," said McMinn. "The old man told us he would be staying ashore tonight and to expect him back at the ship around 9:00 a.m. That means that the crew has the night off starting now, except for us. We're going to stay on board for a few minutes and do some high level planning."

"What's up?" asked Wagerman. "Is something happening that we didn't count on?"

"No," replied McMinn. "I just want to make absolutely sure that there are no slip-ups."

"We're going to leave for the dredging grounds late tomorrow morning, right?" asked Logan.

"Yes," answered McMinn, "and when we get to the dredging area we'll go slow and stall for time so that it's late afternoon before we pull the dredge and head out to Wreck #83. Hopefully by that time the steak dinner will be underway and everyone will be distracted. I will take the wheel while everyone goes to the galley. Then I'll put us right over the wreck, and you guys can go to town. With any luck it will be late afternoon, but well before dark. If we're not running any lights the Coast Guard won't be able to see that we're dredging in the wrong place. I should be able to give you guys at least a couple of hours out there!"

With that, Logan hauled out the crates of artifacts from behind Wagerman's tool crib and showed their latest haul to McMinn. "Since we'll be in port tonight, I think that Herman and I should make a delivery to Joe Divell. The sooner he gets this stuff, the sooner we all get our money."

"Okay," said McMinn, "but be back aboard by midnight, just in case Senior returns early and wants to get started."

McMinn left the terrible twosome and headed for the bridge.

Wagerman quickly finished working on the engine, changed into fresh clothing and helped Logan carry the crates of artifacts off the ship. They waited until no one was on deck so they wouldn't be questioned about what they were doing. Alternating hands on the crate's metal handles, Logan and Wagerman lugged their booty along the railroad tracks to the West Slip, then carried it to Joe Divell's barge. There was a light in the shack and they could see Divell inside the tiny office hut. After they dragged the crate to the door of the shack, Wagerman excused himself.

"Look, Logan," he said, "you take the stuff in and talk with Divell, I have an important phone call to make. See you back at the ship."

Before Logan could respond, Wagerman was gone, trotting toward Dailey's Restaurant on the Public Dock and the telephone booth inside the entrance. Fumbling for a coin, he dialed the Franzesi's number, hoping that Suzanne would answer. His heart sank when a strange female voice responded. Haltingly, he asked for Suzanne. The woman at the other end introduced herself as Suzanne's grandmother.

"You must be the young man Suzanne had lunch with this afternoon," she responded.

"Yes, ma'am, my name is Herman Wagerman," he answered.

"Suzanne is working tonight until 7:00 p.m. at Beckman's Grocery & Ship Supply Store down the street," she offered. "I'm sure that she would love to have you visit her, Herman. Do you know how to find it?" Suzanne's grandmother asked.

"Yes, I do. We get our ship supplies there," he answered. "I think I'll take your advice and stop in." With that, Wagerman took off at top walking speed, heading west for Beckman's store.

## [THURSDAY, AUGUST 19, 1926, 6:00 P.M.]

Wagerman walked, and he worried. The closer he got to the store, the more he mused over what he was doing. "How would Suzanne respond to me just popping in on her like this and would I be getting her in trouble at work?" he wondered. He was still struggling with his internal voices when he found himself stepping into Beckman's. A sign on the front door noted that weekday store hours were from 7:00 a.m. to 7:00 p.m. Wagerman moved uncomfortably toward the candy counter and divided his attention between hunting for a piece of candy and looking for Suzanne.

"Herman! What are you doing here?" a voice asked from behind him.

He was so startled that he almost sent the candy display tumbling onto the floor.

"Hi," he answered sheepishly. "I was hungry for some candy," Herman replied haltingly. "Well, not really," he continued. "Your grandmother told me I might find you here and I wanted to see you again. Is it okay that I stopped?" he asked.

"Of course, Herman," she responded. "There are hardly any customers tonight and I could use the company."

For the next hour, Suzanne and Herman sat at the counter of Beckman's, talking about everything from families to holidays, jobs and childhood experiences. Herman had never felt so comfortable talking to anyone before.

The chiming of the store clock interrupted their conversation. It was 7:00 p.m. and time to close up. Suzanne turned off the lights and exited the store as Herman held the door for her.

"Can I walk you home?" he asked.

"I have a better idea," she responded. "Are you hungry?"

"I'm always hungry," he answered.

"Want to get a bite to eat?" she asked.

"Yes, let's go!" responded Wagerman with enthusiasm.

She led him to a small restaurant a few blocks from the store. It was a friendly little place just steps from St. Andrew's Church.

"I often eat here, Herman," she chirped as they entered. "The food is inexpensive and good, plus it's a handy place to hide if I skip Mass."

They could have been eating dirt for all Herman Wagerman noticed. He was so caught up with Suzanne that the evening took on a magical quality. He had never met such a woman. She was incredibly beautiful, and at the same time warm, direct and friendly. Wagerman was rapidly growing comfortable with her, behaving less like the shy fumbling person that he had been earlier in the day. As Wagerman began to feel at ease, he sensed that she really liked him, too.

After a two-hour dinner, Suzanne and Herman left the restaurant and walked toward the Franzesi house. Herman took her hand in his, half expecting that she would reject it, but she didn't. She gently squeezed it and continued walking. Herman hated to see the walk end, so he slowed his steps. Suzanne followed his lead, stopping at various places in the neighborhood to point out icons of her youth: the tree where she stumbled and got a black eye in fifth grade and the field where she learned to play softball.

Reaching her house, Herman pulled Suzanne to him and kissed her. As their lips touched, he felt a wave of anxiety. He wondered if would she be repelled by his clumsy efforts. Herman's romantic skill and experience were inversely proportionate to his strength and work ethic and he, of all people, was well aware of these limitations. He was often the brunt of shipboard jokes when it came to matters of romance. But Suzanne did not reject his advance. Instead of pulling away, she softened and melted into his embrace. The kiss lasted for several minutes and ended with both Suzanne and Herman gasping for air.

"I'm sorry," said Herman nervously. "Was it too soon?"

Before he could finish the words, Suzanne was kissing him again, and it was a passionate kiss.

"It wasn't too soon, Herman," she responded softly after their lips parted. "It was right on time!" She hugged him tightly then pulled away. "It's getting late, Herman, and I should go in now. My family will be worried. But please call again soon," she said. With that she stepped onto the front porch of her house and disappeared.

Wagerman's heart pounded as he returned to the ship. At that moment, he was the happiest man on earth. He didn't care how

much Joe Divell was about to fetch for the caseload of junk that he
and Logan had dragged to his barge.

Boarding the *Gerken*, Wagerman noticed that the wind had
begun to pipe up. It had been dead calm all day but since the
afternoon rainstorm, the humidity had increased and the water had
taken on an ominous gray tone. Wagerman was standing on deck
next to the gangway, gazing mindlessly at the evening sky and
thinking about Suzanne when Logan unexpectedly appeared.

"Looks like a summer thermal, Herman," Logan reported.

"I don't think so," answered Wagerman. "Looks more like a
south wind," he added.

"I hope not," answered Logan. "The last thing we need is a big
wind for tomorrow's dredging."

Wagerman was awakened in his berth the next morning by
wind whistling in *Gerken*'s rigging and a strange new ship's motion.
He dressed quickly and climbed onto the deck to check the weather.
It was indeed a new wind, blowing at least twenty-five knots and
almost from the dead south. Cottonwood trees along the bluffs were
bent under the burden of the wind with their leaves blowing against
their normal grain. The leaves revealed a silver underside color that
enhanced the deep-gray sky. As Wagerman studied the weather,
McMinn came by the rail to chat.

"Maybe we should skip a day, Mr. McMinn," he offered. "Could
be pretty rough out there in this stuff."

"Won't happen," replied McMinn. "The old man wants to get
back to Buffalo with a load of sand and we may never get back here
again this season. And besides," continued McMinn, "it's a south
wind so we'll be under the lee of the shore all the way home to
Buffalo. As soon as Senior gets back, we'll leave."

With that, First Mate George McMinn left Herman Wagerman and walked to the bridge.

## [FRIDAY, AUGUST 20, 1926, 9:45 A.M.]

A long black Packard pulled up to the ship. The door opened and Senior Gerken stepped out of the back seat. Waving to his companions from the previous evening, he hurried to the bridge and struck up a conversation with his engineer brothers and Captain Gamble.

Moments later, McMinn gathered the crew for an announcement. "The weather is a bit rough out on the lake, but it's blowing from the south so the waves aren't that big. We're going to wait until noon to shove off since we expect the wind to calm down by then. That will still get us home to Buffalo this evening, but we may be a bit later than we planned."

With more than an hour of slack time before he had to fire up the engines, Wagerman trotted down the companionway and headed for the closest phone booth. He had time to call Suzanne one last time. Logan watched him jogging down the tracks toward the downtown docks and shook his head.

"Poor guy," he thought to himself. "He's really lost it!"

Herman dialed the Franzesi's phone number for the second time in twenty-four hours and waited with anticipation. This time Suzanne answered the phone herself.

"Hi," he responded. "I hope that you don't mind my calling so early!"

"Not at all," she answered, "it's wonderful to hear your voice, Herman, but I thought you were leaving early this morning."

"We're going to sit out this wind and wait until noon to ship out," he answered, "so I had time to call you one more time.

I had the best time last night," he added. "Could we please do it again soon?" Wagerman asked.

"Of course, Herman," she answered. "When will you be back in Erie?"

"Officially, not until we winterize the ship in November," Herman answered, "but I can't wait until then to see you. As soon as we're back in Buffalo and I see the ship's fall schedule, I'll call you. I will arrange to get to Erie somehow and then I'll take you to dinner. Maybe we can go to a really fancy place downtown."

"That would be wonderful," answered Suzanne. "I'll be waiting to hear from you."

Just before he hung up, Wagerman blurted out one final sentence, and he couldn't believe the words as they spilled out. "Suzanne," he said with a fumbling voice, "I'm in love with you!"

As soon as he put the phone down, he began to wonder if he had just done something stupid. He should have waited to tell her in person.

"Sometimes I'm so dumb," he muttered to himself.

Dejected, he decided that the phone call had probably been a bad idea. He returned to the ship, all the while noting that the wind velocity seemed to be increasing rather than settling down. Back aboard ship, Wagerman kept a vigil at the deck hoping against hope that Suzanne had taken his call well. He secretly wished that she would come by the ship before it left. As departure time approached, Wagerman found himself questioning his spontaneity again.

"How could I have been such a moron? I should never have called her this morning," he thought to himself.

*Gerken* pulled away from the pier at precisely 1:00 p.m., turned east and headed down the bay toward the channel. Her engines were purring. Wagerman, at least, had the satisfaction of being a competent assistant engineer. The ship had run flawlessly since its spring commissioning. At 1:20 p.m., the captain cut the throttle back to quarter speed, indicating that *Gerken* was entering the channel to the open lake. Moments later, Bill Logan stuck his head down into the hold and yelled at Herman Wagerman.

"Hey Herm," he said, "better get up here on the double!"

Wagerman climbed quickly to the deck, concerned that there was a mechanical problem. Logan grinned and pointed to the channel wall ahead. There, not one-hundred feet away, was a beat up black Ford truck parked along the channel entrance. And sitting on the front fender waving, with her hair blowing in the stiff breeze, was Suzanne Franzesi. Wagerman was stunned. He couldn't believe that she had driven all the way across town to wave good-bye to him. He waved back, walking from mid-ships to the stern as he did so. When he had walked as far aft as he could, he stopped at the aft rail. There, he gazed at a vision of astounding if not contradictory beauty: an angel standing in a Devil Wind.

By 3:00 p.m., Wagerman wasn't thinking of Suzanne Franzesi anymore. He was in *Gerken*'s hold grabbing onto whatever he could use to steady himself as he monitored the flow of sand into the bowels of the ship. The wind was howling and Herman was having serious reservations about McMinn's plan to move farther offshore to Wreck #83. The site where they were dredging was less than three miles from shore and the waves, even that close to the protection of shore, were running six to ten feet. Herman knew that if *Gerken* were to venture farther offshore in a building southeasterly, the waves would double in height. He wondered if the ship could take such seas with her hold three-quarters full.

With the violence of the motion, Wagerman began to feel seasick, a rarity for him. Suddenly and without warning, he was vomiting; retching uncontrollably. Wagerman struggled to wipe the bile off of himself and was shocked to see that he was wearing a life vest. And then, he realized that he wasn't really in *Gerken*'s hold. He was back in his cruel reality, floating in his life jacket. He was cold, sleepy, despondent and now sick. How could he die out here in a puke-stained life vest just hours after the woman of his dreams had indicated that she was actually interested in him?

Despondent, Wagerman began to turn his mind back toward school days again, but this time he didn't get as far back as grade school.

# CHAPTER 12

## [SATURDAY, AUGUST 21, 1926, 3:00 A.M.]

*Wagerman was in ninth grade. He had just begun high school in a Buffalo catholic boys' school which offered a revolutionary new structural development: class changes. Instead of sitting in undersized bolted-down desks for hours at a time, Wagerman could now get up and move to a new location once an hour. But the best part of this new arrangement was the variety of teachers. Instead of having just one teacher for the entire day, there were now seven class periods. Seven different teachers. As his cold, almost lifeless body floated northeast, his mind drifted back to his first year of high school and to the one teacher who compared to the quality of Mr. Leonardi in seventh grade. Ninth grade was the year that Wagerman discovered General Science and met a second truly inspirational teacher. His instructor, Fr. John Mitchell, had been a geologist by trade before becoming a Jesuit, and Wagerman immediately struck up a relationship with him because of their common interest in Lake Erie. Wagerman was fascinated by weather and forecasting, and he looked forward to his 1:00 p.m. General Science class. He enjoyed the lectures but he eagerly anticipated the times when Fr. Mitchell would expound on questions. Although the young Wagerman didn't realize it at the time, Fr. Mitchell looked forward to Herman's questions as much as his student enjoyed the answers.*

*Wagerman's mind returned to a cold and windy day in November, 1905 when he had asked Fr. Mitchell why Lake Erie was reputed to be the stormiest of the Great Lakes. The answer that he received was destined to haunt Herman Wagerman's dreams for many years.*

*Herman had asked his question at the very beginning of class that day, inspired by the sheets of sleet that pounded the windows of his classroom. Fr. Mitchell thought for several minutes, then he discarded his lesson plan and spent an entire period developing an answer.*

# Lake Erie Storms

## [NOVEMBER 1905, GENERAL SCIENCE CLASS]

The Great Lakes system and Lake Erie in particular, act as weather-making barriers to the eastward flow of the upper atmosphere. They sit directly in the path of global weather systems that trundle west to east across the continent. They also create a geographic margin that separates southerly Gulf of Mexico systems from the Arctic patterns that develop in the north. When atmospheric high- and (especially) low-pressure systems hit the freshwater seas, the temperature differentials created by the water, in combination with the humidity that constantly boils off the lakes, have the capacity to produce local weather chaos. The dynamism of the region's atmospheric conditions can lead to astounding shifts in weather in extremely short time periods.

Lake Erie has been particularly problematic over the years. The shallow Western Basin waters quickly spawn steep, breaking waves as westerly storm winds build. Lake Erie's longitudinal axis lies along the prevailing wind direction. Thus its waves have an opportunity to grow and develop as they travel the length of the lake, and wave heights are ultimately driven by fetch (the distance that waves are free to travel across open water before reaching land). Lake Erie's prevailing waves mature gradually as they move east. But when they arrive at the Long Point/Presque Isle corridor, the relatively deep water of the Central Basin adds a new and potentially frightening dimension to the growing seas. The deeper waters hold heat in the winter and cold in the summer. A thermocline (layer of insulating water) forms between the dynamic top water and the more stable bottom water. Thus the insulated bottom waters continue at the same general temperature, 40 to50 degrees Fahrenheit, year round. This creates a heating effect in the winter when lake waters act as a radiator, warming and humidifying the air. In the summer, an opposite cooling effect occurs, causing the lake to radiate cool air upward into the atmosphere.

The lake bottom drop-off that the waves encounter as they move east, along with temperature changes radiating up from the deeper waters, combine to create a remarkable aquatic metamorphosis. Waves grow in height, turn an ominous deep-green color and take on the infamous Lake Erie square shape: a wave whose height is approximately the same as its period (space between crests).

From the perspective of the upper air wind currents, Lake Erie's Central Basin is a traffic director. It slows, speeds, or deflects the flow of air that would otherwise pass longitudinally along the lake. Atmospheric currents are generally redirected south during winter months and north during the summer. This has the effect, in the winter, of allowing strong Arctic low-pressure systems that would otherwise pass harmlessly north of Lake Erie to flow over the center of the lake. These arctic disturbances are accelerated by the sudden shift in upper air direction. An eddy is created in the atmosphere immediately over the top of the lake; encouraging low pressure cells to intensify and winds to increase. Summer storms work the opposite way. Upper-air flow is suddenly redirected north, allowing Gulf of Mexico low-pressure disturbances to roar up the Ohio Valley into the Lake Erie basin. But for pure terror, there is the continuous potential for an arctic low pressure to collide with a Gulf system. While this is a rare statistical occurrence, the potential for a monster storm to emerge by adding the strength of two contrary low-pressure systems is a continuous threat on Lake Erie.

The fact that two of North America's most significant escarpments border Lake Erie's Central and Eastern Basins, further exacerbates the dynamism of the lake's weather patterns. The Niagara Escarpment punctuates the eastern end of the Lake Erie region and causes a dramatically different weather system to dominate the Niagara Peninsula just east of the lake. To the south, the Appalachian Escarpment, a nearly 1,000 foot high table separating the Gulf of Mexico and Lake Erie drainage regions, comes within ten miles of Lake Erie's Central Basin. The Appalachian Escarpment is high enough to be visible to sailors as they travel down the center of Lake Erie. And its geological effects are easily seen within the region. The escarpment creates a microclimate along the southern coast of the lake, a place that is so warm in the winter that it is ideal for grape growing.

The two escarpments, which lie at a right angle to each other, create an upper-atmosphere fence; a weather-gate which slows the progress of low pressure cells transiting the lake. The gating effect also has a way of stalling low-pressure systems right over Central Lake Erie causing 180-degree wind shifts over relatively brief time periods. These sudden, dramatic wind shifts are responsible for fanning wave heights, creating wave disturbances and spawning the infamous Lake Erie seiche effect.

A seiche can occur when high winds push the lake's top-water to one end of the lake, where it stacks up on itself. A strong south-westerly, for example, ordinarily causes the water level to drop by two or three feet at the western end of the lake and rise by a similar amount on the eastern end. A seiche occurs when the persistent, long-term wind is suddenly followed by a strong wind from the opposite direction. This causes all of the water stacked at one end of the lake to rush back in the opposite direction.

During the 1880s, an eastward flowing seiche caused a torrent of tidal wave proportions to hit Buffalo, New York. Two young boys who had taken shelter from the rain a block away from the downtown docks were carried away by the waters and drowned.

Central Lake Erie's boiling weather cauldron has spawned hundreds of major storms in the years since sailing began on the lakes. Sailors have grown accustomed to sudden shifts in weather, and storms have become a regular part of Lake Erie's maritime commerce. What Great Lakes sailors worry about, however, is not the average storm. It is the hundred-year monster; the one-in-a-thousand spring or fall storm whose violence defies description.

### [THE UPPER-ATMOSPHERE OVER LAKE ERIE: AUGUST 20, 1926]

For as much as he had learned about Lake Erie's storms Wagerman still was not prepared for the winds and waves that he was facing. The 1926 August Gale began as another of Lake Erie's surprise storms. This time, however, the upper atmospheric currents ruptured from the south instead of the north. An extreme northerly bulge in the jet stream brought a vicious low-pressure center roaring up the Ohio Valley, then accelerated its intensity as it sped toward the Great Lakes. Somewhere over Lake Huron, the Gulf Stream low-pressure cell collided with an Arctic low-pressure system, creating the formula for atmospheric chaos. The compounded low-pressure cell took a hard easterly turn and headed across southern Ontario, running parallel to Lake Erie. As it moved east, pressure from the high Arctic cell caused the entire system to sag south toward the lake. The system stalled over the water and sat spinning for almost a day as it tried to push its way beyond Central Lake Erie's escarpments.

Upper-atmospheric lumps caused by the Niagara and Appalachian Escarpments acted like fences, containing the August 1926 low-pressure cell as it sat over the lake, growing in intensity. The storm cell paused, spinning over the lake's warm open waters, and the barometric pressure dropped alarmingly. Wind velocities accelerated at an astounding rate.

While the 1926 August Gale lacked the chilling cold and numbing snow squalls of many of her late fall predecessors, the surprise arrival of this summer storm, coupled with its extreme wind velocities made it just as dangerous!

# PART FIVE

# Shipwrecked

*No charts, lighthouses or navigational aids
can ever prevent the loss of ships in the sudden,
unpredictable storms of Lake Erie. One storm alone,
in November 1838, is said to have accounted
for twenty-five vessels lost.*

**Harry Barrett**
*Lore & Legend of Long Point*

# CHAPTER 13

[SATURDAY, AUGUST 21, 1926, 3:10 A.M.]

*The night wore on and Wagerman grew obsessed with the impending arrival of dawn. He wondered just what kind of a day Saturday would be and if the sun would shine on him. While he floated, he tried to imagine the sun rising on the eastern horizon and beams of light bringing him the warmth that he so desperately needed. As a small boy, Wagerman had been both attracted to and terribly afraid of the dark. It was a strange psychological confusion that had followed him into his adult life as a sailor. He hated the finality of sunset and looked forward each morning to light cresting across the eastern horizon.*

*If life on the water offered one special benefit to Wagerman, it was the sunrise. For him, there was nothing quite like the beauty and hope offered by each morning's arrival of the sun. Friends with shore jobs were oblivious to sunrise. They knew sunsets and often commented upon their beauty, but most had never even seen a sunrise. This seemed backwards to Wagerman who sometimes found sunsets depressing. As much as he enjoyed the evening sky of summer and its stars, he was always overjoyed to experience the glow of new light the next morning. The warm red sun peaking over the eastern horizon never failed to mystify him. He always found an excuse to climb out of Gerken's hold with a cup of coffee and watch the waxing of the morning light.*

*Wagerman knew that this could be his last sunrise and he hoped that he would be able to last long enough to see it. As he* contemplated the warmth of the sun he wondered if Suzanne's boyfriend, Ben Cooley, had ever seen a sunrise.

"What kind of guy could he be?" Wagerman wondered, thinking about how and why Cooley had decided not to take Suzanne sailing with him.

Wagerman began to suspect that belonging to a fancy yacht club and sailing a pretty varnished yacht might erode common sense.

"How could anyone who knew Suzanne not want to spend every available moment with her?" he thought to himself.

Herman Wagerman decided that if he survived this ordeal, he would show her a sunrise.

# Pterodactyl's Final Cruise

## [THURSDAY, AUGUST 19, 1926, 12:00 NOON]

George Stickle and Ben Cooley were anxious to clear the dock and begin their anticipated sailing trip. Especially since the long weekend which the pair had planned suddenly had to be abbreviated by a last minute business entanglement at their architectural firm. Instead of returning Sunday, as originally planned, they had just learned that they were obliged to be back Saturday for an evening dinner with a client. They had both left their jobs before lunch and driven to the Erie Yacht Club where they planned to meet the crew of the sloop *Eagle* for the sail across Lake Erie to Long Point. Sickle was removing covers from both the main and mizzen sails as Cooley packed a weekend's supply of food and drinks into *Pterodactyl*'s small below-deck icebox. They prepared the yawl to leave the EYC docks and listened to *Eagle*'s crew, a few slips away, similarly readying their sailboat. *Eagle* was almost eight feet longer than *Pterodactyl* and she was faster, so they were anxious to get a head start. It was reassuring to have company on a lake crossing and Cooley knew that if they could get away thirty minutes ahead of *Eagle* they would still be within sight of her when they reached the Canadian side of the lake and rounded Long Point.

"Nice fresh breeze," commented Sickle. "Looks as though it's a bit south of the prevailing direction."

"Yup," answered Cooley, "and that's good for us. We can keep up with *Eagle* if it's a run and the wind blows hard."

And the wind was suddenly beginning to blow after a dead calm morning. It was gusting to almost twenty knots, a fresh breeze to be sure but one which they could easily handle in the old sailboat, especially if they were not beating into it.

"We're almost ready to go," noted Cooley as he poked his head up from below. "Just one last problem to deal with!"

"What's that?" asked Stickle.

"Somebody has to tell Suzanne that she's not coming along," answered Cooley. "She still thinks that this is a date weekend."

"Christ!" responded Stickle. "How are you going to tell her now?"

"I'll just be honest and explain that it's a guy's weekend on Long Point," answered Cooley. "She wouldn't have any fun out there with the Anderson boys, anyway," he added.

Even as he spoke, Suzanne Franzesi walked through the gates of the yacht club carrying a basket of food.

"I wouldn't want to be you," commented Stickle. "She's really going to be pissed off."

"Don't worry, I can handle her," replied Cooley as he stepped off the boat and walked across the docks to meet Suzanne. Stickle watched, half expecting that Suzanne would hit Ben Cooley over the head with the picnic basket, and he wondered just how many more times Cooley would get away with treating her so badly before she dumped him. After a few brief and obviously uncomfortable words, Suzanne turned on her heels and walked away, keeping the picnic basket.

"How did she take it?" Stickle asked.

"No problem," commented Cooley. "She loves me!"

Somehow Stickle doubted Cooley's analysis but he untied *Pterodactyl*'s lines and the little wooden yawl slipped out into the bay. In moments, *Pterodactyl*'s main sail, mizzen, and small jib were all up, and the yawl was racing west through the channel. Just before they entered the open lake, Cooley looked over his shoulder to see *Eagle* pulling into the middle of the bay and raising her main.

"Good," he commented to his friend George Stickle, "they won't catch up to us until we're at least half way across the lake." *Eagle* was newer and faster than *Pterodactyl* and sloop rigged, a modern trend among club racers. Her large main and jib required a larger crew, however, and Cooley was content to own the smaller, more easily managed yawl rig with its balanced sail plan. Cooley took the cover off of the cockpit compass and brought the yawl to port until she was on a heading of 12 degrees, the rhumb line course to the tip of Long Point. As he pulled away from the beaches at Presque Isle, the peninsula which guards Erie's natural harbor, the wind seemed to strengthen and shift even more to the south.

"A perfect breeze," commented Stickle.

"For today," added Cooley with somewhat less optimism. "Let's hope that it goes back to the southwest by the time we come home. I would hate to have to beat back against a southerly."

"No problem," remarked Stickle, "how often does a south wind last for more than a day?"

And Thursday was, indeed, a remarkable sailing day. The sky was crystal clear, the waves were relatively flat and a freshening wind drove both *Pterodactyl* and *Eagle* effortlessly toward the tip of Long Point, Ontario, twenty-seven miles north of Erie. Cooley and Stickle alternated at the helm, and from time to time, they glanced astern at the reassuring spectacle of *Eagle*'s overlapping jib bearing down on them. They judged that they were sailing at about six knots, and that *Eagle* was making almost seven. At this rate both boats would be around the tip of Long Point and anchored in Gravely Bay by 6:00 p.m. Their plan was to rendezvous with Canadian friends who had cottages near the tip of Long Point among the infamous Anderson Properties. Gravely Bay and the Anderson Properties were on the north beach, only a few miles from the tip of Long Point. There would be perfect shelter from today's southerly breeze in the bay behind the north beach. In fact, the only time that Gravely Bay was an inhospitable anchorage was when the winds piped up from the northeast. When and if that happened, boats anchored inside Gravely Bay would traditionally run west with the wind toward Port Dover or Port Rowan where there was shelter regardless of the wind direction.

The Anderson cottages, near the tip of Long Point, represented the only civilization on the barren twenty-mile sand spit. Their existence on Long Point's north (Outer Bay) shore was created by a remarkable surveying error at the time that the Long Point Company purchased the entire sand spit peninsula from the Canadian government in 1868. In the early 1800s, Long Point developed a reputation as a mysterious and dangerous spit of land. The dangers of Long Point came first and foremost from the fact that the low-lying sand spit extended almost twenty miles into Lake Erie, presenting a danger to navigation. Long Point's shoal waters became legendary for their proclivity to attract, then capture sailing ships as they tacked their way up or down Lake Erie's axis. But the most infamous dangers during the 1840s and 1850s came from land-based pirates or wreckers, as they were called by locals. The wreckers would use a variety of techniques to lure unsuspecting ships close to Long

Point's shoal waters in hopes that the vessels would run aground. Once aground and held prisoner by Long Point's sandbars, the wreckers would pounce upon the ships, quickly emptying the cargo for personal use or resale. Since Long Point was so remote, almost 100 miles from either London or Toronto, there was little chance for authorities to react to the activities of Long Point's wreckers.

By the mid-1850s, the United States Congress was under pressure from American shipping interests who had been losing cargo to Long Point's wreckers. There was serious talk of the U.S. military occupying and claiming the peninsula for the sake of controlling it. Cooler business heads prevailed, however, and a cartel of U.S. and Canadian industrialists was organized. They developed a plan to buy Long Point, lock stock and barrel, from the newly-formed Canadian government. This group of twenty (ten Americans and ten Canadians) calling themselves the Long Point Company, incorporated in 1866 and formalized the purchase of the lands known as Long Point by sending a check to the Canadian federal government in 1868. One of their promises to Canadian and U.S. authorities was to end the pirating which had been growing in seriousness along the southern beaches of Long Point.

The mid-1800s were high water level years on Lake Erie and a navigable channel had spontaneously broken through the sand near the base of the point. This channel allowed ships to avoid the long trek around the tip of the point by ducking behind the sand peninsula and traveling along the lake's relatively sheltered north shore. The British government placed a lighthouse at the base of the peninsula to mark the channel to the sheltered Inner Bay. A favorite trick of Long Point's wreckers was to attack the lighthouse, extinguish the light and build a false beacon light a few miles up the beach. Ships would be lured toward shore where they would run aground thinking that they were, in fact, heading for the channel to the Inner Bay.

Long Point's wreckers were clearly locals seeking clever entrepreneurial ways to increase their wealth. Many of the residents of Port Rowan and Port Dover knew who they were, but there was no way to gather proof and prosecute them. In 1870, the Long Point company hired the world famous Pinkerton Security Company which sent an undercover agent. His job was to seek the confidence of the locals and gather evidence against the wreckers. The agent, whose name was Allen, was never heard from again. The next year, colleagues found his headless body in a shallow grave near the sand ridges at the tip of the point.

Seeing the folly of their approach, the Long Point Company tried a fundamentally different tactic the next year. Realizing who the wreckers were, they hit upon the idea of hiring the meanest and toughest of the suspected locals to work for the company and clean up the point. Thus began the long tradition of the Long Point Company's keepers. By 1872, the company was well on its way to cleaning up Long Point, posting it as a no trespassing area and operating it as a wildlife refuge. Company members established a duck-hunting club near the center of the point for the exclusive use of members and their guests, a club that continues to the present day. Unfortunately, the Long Point Company's original surveyor made a significant error in his calculations. Working under great pressure and fearful for his life, he understated the length of the sand spit. This mistake resulted in the company not acquiring the last few miles of land on the tip of the point. Seizing upon this surveying error, one of the locals (Anderson) who was not selected as a keeper, exercised his creativity by purchasing the unsurveyed tip of the peninsula. To deflect political pressure from himself, he divided his newly acquired land into beachfront lots and offered them to townspeople in protest of the Long Point Company's acquisition.

The Anderson properties were contested, first by the Long Point Company, and then by the federal and provincial governments. But the original members of the Anderson properties near Gravely Bay prevailed, keeping the legal right to build and maintain cottages on the tip of the point and to pass them along to direct family members. Slowly, the twenty-cottage compound near the tip of the point became a local hangout for men. In the tradition of boathouses which were springing up all along the Great Lakes, the cottages gradually evolved into summer havens for groups of men who used them for fishing, playing cards, drinking and other general male mayhem.

*Pterodactyl* and *Eagle* were bound for a weekend of carousing with the Anderson boys. Cross-lake friendships had developed over the years between Erie's yachting community and the Anderson gang and it was common for members of the Erie Yacht Club to visit the cottages. When they did, they brought boatloads of steaks and other food stuffs in exchange for the alcoholic beverages that were available in Canada. Prohibition in the United States made liquor difficult to find, but in Canada it was perfectly legal to manufacture and sell alcoholic beverages. There was almost always a weekend party at Long Point's Anderson Cottages and both sailboat crews planned to overnight at Gravely Bay on Thursday and Friday. *Pterodactyl* had to return to Erie on Saturday so that Stickle and Cooley could attend their evening party. But the crew of *Eagle* was going to sail into the Inner Bay and spend a few more days visiting Port Rowan.

At 3:00 p.m., *Eagle* caught up with *Pterodactyl* in mid-lake. The crews bantered about their boat speeds and the poker party at Gravely Bay while they watched a dramatic change in the weather. The sky turned slate gray and without warning the wind velocity increased as its direction shifted southeasterly. Cooley and Stickle donned raincoats and reduced sail just before the skies opened up and spilled a heavy load of summer rain on the two sailboats. By 5:00 p.m., the rain slowed and the lighthouse at the tip of the point was in clear view. *Pterodactyl* followed *Eagle* around the tip of the point, taking care not to trip on the sandbar that stretched east from the tip. Hardening sails, both boats turned to port and reached along the north beaches of Long Point, arriving at Gravely Bay on schedule. *Pterodactyl* anchored a few hundred yards offshore and even as they were securing the sails and running gear, a rowboat was pulling toward them with a happy boatload of Canadian friends laughing and shouting about the poker game which was about to begin.

By 8:00 p.m. Thursday evening, the game was in full operation. Twelve players, including the crews of *Pterodactyl* and *Eagle*, were drinking Canadian ale, placing penny-ante bets and swapping tall tales about Long Point. As the games progressed, the weather worsened. Southerly winds were howling across the point and rain pelted the roof of the cozy brown cottage where the friends gathered. At 11:00 p.m. the crews of the American sailboats excused themselves and rowed back to their anchored vessels. It's hard to relax with a sailboat riding at anchor in a blow. Canadian Hubie Barrett rowed the Americans to their sailboats and warned them to be wary of a wind shift.

"Looks like a storm could be building tonight," he said. "If the wind swings east we'll be digging these sailboats off the beach tomorrow. Keep an eye out," he admonished, as he left them and rowed back to his cottage.

Cooley and Stickle arranged an overnight watch system with *Eagle*'s crew so that there would be someone on deck from one of the sailboats all night watching for a wind shift.

"If it turns east, we're heading for Port Rowan," exclaimed the captain of the *Eagle*.

"Not us," answered Cooley. "We have to be in Erie Saturday. If the wind shifts, were going to head back!"

Cooley and Stickle took the first two sixty-minute watches, sitting on the deck of *Pterodactyl* from 11:30 p.m. until 1:30 a.m., when they were relieved by a crew member from *Eagle*. By 2:00 a.m. Friday morning, both sailors were sleeping soundly in the berths below decks.

Cooley woke up first. It was 7:00 a.m. and he had a headache from drinking. The wind had eased, but the skies were grayer than ever and the wind direction had shifted even more toward the southeast. As he sat in the cockpit wondering about the security of their anchorage, *Eagle*'s crew raised anchor and put up a sail.

"Good-bye, guys," the captain called. "We're heading for Port Rowan before the wind switches east."

Stickle heard the conversation and climbed through the companionway to watch *Eagle* pull away. "Wish we could go with them," he muttered.

"Let's fix breakfast and wait a while," suggested Coole., "There's no sense leaving just yet. If the wind goes east on us we can wait until this afternoon and have a nice sail home."

"Great idea," answered Stickle diving off the stern with a bar of soap. While the two cleaned up and brushed their teeth, Hubie

Barrett rowed out to *Pterodactyl* and offered breakfast at his cottage. After they ate, Stickle and Cooley walked south across the tip of Long Point to check conditions on the open lake. The sight that greeted them on the beach was not pleasant. A deep gray sky, roaring winds and a confused sea with leftover waves from the previous evening's winds did not offer a promising sail home.

"We'll wait until this afternoon," suggested Ben Cooley, "maybe the waves will die down. Let's not forget to mention to Suzanne that this would have been a lousy trip. She probably would have been seasick if she had to cross with us!"

Looking at the ugly conditions on the lake, Stickle offered a different suggestion. "Maybe we should wait and go back Saturday morning," he muttered.

"I don't think so," answered Cooley. "We'd better leave before the wind goes east. Besides, if we get back Friday evening, I'll take Suzanne to lunch Saturday to make up for leaving her behind."

# CHAPTER 14

[SATURDAY, AUGUST 21, 1926, 3:20 A.M.]

*The wind was growing noticeably calmer and the waves, while still monstrous, were beginning to flatten out. Now that the huge breaking crests were subsiding, Wagerman could see that he was drifting rapidly north and east and he began to wonder if the confusion of the seas would make it impossible for the Maitland to find him. He knew that it was difficult to sense shifts in wind direction and velocity from the bridge of a large ship and puzzled over whether or not anyone could predict the drift-course of a man in a life jacket.*

*Wagerman began to have another hopeful thought about the potential for rescue. As soon as the winds calmed, he knew that commercial traffic would pick up on the central lake. Ships that had been waiting for the weather to clear before leaving port, as well as vessels sitting out the storm behind Long Point, would be anxious to make up for lost time. Realizing that his only hope for survival was to be spotted by a ship, Wagerman began to do some mental navigation. He assembled an imaginary chart of Lake Erie and visualized a mark designating Gerken's final location just before sinking. Then he mentally transposed the track of the rowing dory before he and his friends had been intercepted by the Maitland.*

*Wagerman knew that breaking seas, such as the waves that were carrying him, were said to generate a current roughly equivalent to ten percent of wind velocity. Estimating average wind speed over the past hours at forty to fifty miles per hour, he concluded that he had probably drifted four or five miles north. He was drifting rapidly toward Long Point, but the wind was shifting and he realized that there was no hope of him reaching it. He would be washed east of Long Point long before his drift pattern took him that far north.*

*But there were the shipping lanes! Eastbound commercial ships passed through the center of the lake, along an east–west line approximately five miles south of Long Point. With luck, Wagerman knew that he might drift into that general location by dawn. On his mental chart of Lake Erie, he estimated that he was already fifteen miles north of Erie. Another two hours at this drift rate and he would be in the shipping lanes! So as he waited for sunrise, Wagerman contented himself with the possibility that he might be spotted by commercial traffic. Buoyed with new hope, he allowed his imagination to take him back to the fateful evening just hours before the* Gerken *went down.*

# Gerken's Last Treasure Hunt

## [FRIDAY, AUGUST 20, 1926, 7:00 P.M.]

"Okay, Herman, are you ready?" asked First Mate McMinn. "I told the captain we were almost full but that we ran dry at the last spot. He thinks that we're going to pull the sweeper and move a few miles."

"I don't know, chief," replied Wagerman. "I'm worried about going further offshore in this blow. Do you think she can handle it?"

"No problem," answered McMinn. "Now that we're almost full, the ship is going to ride low and steady in the water. She'll be much more stable. All we need is an hour or two on Wreck #83, and we might bring up some really great stuff. Besides, everybody is just about to go to the dining room for steak dinner. Nobody will know what we're doing out there. This is the perfect opportunity," McMinn continued. "It'll be almost dark, the old man is going to be distracted and we can have a couple of good hours to search the bottom. One big load and we're on easy street for the winter, Herman, so concentrate on what you're doing."

"Okay," Wagerman replied reluctantly. "I guess we should try."

At 7:15 p.m. *Gerken* raised her dredge and headed north for her August date with destiny. The dinner bell rang at 7:30 and the crew, including Senior Gerken and his two brothers John and Jesse, filed into the dining hall for the evening's much anticipated dinner. Even though the waves and winds were howling, *Gerken* was making slow steady progress, running dead downwind for her appointed spot over Wreck #83. En route, McMinn extinguished the ship's running lights so that no one from shore would realize where they were headed.

Wreck #83 was well outside the approved dredging grounds, so Wagerman, Logan and McMinn had to be cautious about working the area. First they had to distract the ship's officers from the planned treasure mining activities. Then they had to be careful not to be spotted by the U.S. Coast Guard or other sandsuckers whose crews might report them for being in an improper location. McMinn had become adept at putting the ship over the top of Divell's wreck site and the dredge was finding its way right onto the old wreck which sat almost upright on the lake bottom. So as the *Gerken*'s crew and top brass began their meal of T-bone steaks, fresh corn on the cob and birthday cake, McMinn headed the ship toward the site of the mystery schooner! *Gerken* plodded northward with her almost-filled hold keeping her low and steady in the water. The sandsucker developed a slow but steady wallowing motion, even though a procession of waves passed under her hull.

Logan swung into the hold to see how Wagerman was doing. He was excited about the possibilities of today's dredge, but also miffed that he was missing a fine meal.

"Shit!" exclaimed Wagerman. "I'm too sick to eat all that food anyway. Three hours of rolling back and forth down here and you'd be puking your guts out too, Logan."

"Come on, Herm," Logan kidded, "one more run and we could hit pay dirt."

"Sure," said Wagerman, "if we don't roll over in these waves and sink."

"Don't worry, Herm," replied Logan, "with a load of sand in the hold, the old girl will sit steady in the water. And besides, the wind has to let up pretty soon. It's been blowing like hell all day!"

A change in the pitch of *Gerken*'s engines indicated that McMinn was slowing the ship down.

"We must be getting close, Herm," said Logan as he bounded up the ladder toward the deck to lower the dredge.

*Gerken*'s engines slowed to idle speed and the ship strained to come about into the waves. It was then that Wagerman realized just how big the seas had gotten. McMinn swung the ship through 180 degrees and tried to head into the breaking waves, but Wagerman could tell from his position in the hold that it was not going to be easy to steady the ship. McMinn spent more than ten minutes after bringing *Gerken* around and into the waves, steering the ship from starboard to port and back. He was trying to get the sandsucker into a steady groove. The engine's pitch changed several times as McMinn attempted to use the propeller to hold the ship in place.

From the confines of the hold it seemed obvious to Wagerman that dredging in waves like this would be next to impossible. Muttering to himself about the stupidity of coming this far offshore, he swung away from his workbench and headed for the deck. He was convinced as he began climbing the steps that McMinn would soon give up and head *Gerken* back toward the shelter of shore. Suddenly three huge breakers in a row caught the ship on her port side and rolled her more than 20 degrees to starboard. Wagerman lurched forward and fell against the bulkhead next to the stairs with a resounding thud. *Gerken* took several additional big waves before McMinn was able to bring her bow back into the seas. Even when he did manage to bring the ship head-to-wind, the motion of the waves was terribly harsh. Wagerman assumed that Logan would not even be thinking of putting the dredge down. In seas like this, there was no way to keep the sweeper on the bottom, much less aim it at a shipwreck. Instead of stopping head to seas, however, *Gerken* was being blown in a continuous circle. Her starboard side was now taking the huge breaking waves at a 60-degree angle.

Wagerman picked himself up and climbed to the deck to see what was happening. Topsides, a quick glance convinced him that they were in trouble. Logan had deployed the deck-mounted dredge as McMinn brought the ship into the wind, but the sweeper end and its hose were rocking wildly against the side of the ship. Logan was working like a madman trying to get the apparatus back on board. Meanwhile, the evening meal had ended abruptly. The ship's motion had caused dishes, silverware and serving bowls to spill in a calamitous crash onto the laps of the assembled crew. Even the birthday cake meant for the cook's son had landed upside down on the floor. Captain Gamble, Chief Engineer John Gerken and his brother Jesse were all climbing the bridge to ask McMinn what had happened and the deck crew was rushing to help Logan retrieve the dredge.

"Bad idea," Wagerman muttered to himself, as he strode across the deck of the pitching ship to help Logan. As he made his way along the rail, twenty-five foot breaking waves were crashing over *Gerken*'s bow, soaking the deck and equipment. Green water rushed across the deck, and the deck-mounted steam shovel was gyrating back and forth across the darkening sky like a ghostly pendulum. The undulating shovel punctuated *Gerken*'s wild motion.

"Jesus, Logan, let's get that dredge back aboard so we can get the hell out of here!" shouted Wagerman.

But the motion of the ship was working against the crew as they struggled to retrieve the dredge. On the bridge, Captain Gamble stumbled through the cabin door and grabbed the wheel from McMinn.

"What the hell are you doing?" he demanded. "We can't dredge in waves like this!"

"I know," replied McMinn. "We're going to bring the dredge up and head for Buffalo."

"How far out are we?" asked Gamble. "These waves are unbelievable."

"Just a mile or so from our original dredge site," replied McMinn. "I'm not sure how the waves built up like this."

Grumbling about general incompetence, Gamble powered the old ship up and began moving south through the waves. The ship's engines calmed the motion momentarily. As soon as Gamble brought the engines to three-quarter speed he swung the wheel to bring *Gerken* east and head for Buffalo. Even as John Gamble turned the wheel to port, Jesse Gerken burst through the door of the bridge yelling for him to stop the maneuver.

"The dredge is still down!" he screamed.

But it was far too late. *Gerken* slowly tried to round up to port, but it was anchored in place by the dredging apparatus. Then as it sat in place churning against itself, a rogue wave broke against the starboard side, pitching the ship more than 30 degrees to port. The men at the port rail, who had been on the verge of retrieving the dredge, abandoned their efforts and grabbed for their lives before they were swept overboard. Gamble increased the power, trying to move the ship through the waves, but *Gerken* began to cavitate against the force of the dredging apparatus. The harder Captain

Gamble pushed the ship, the more she rolled to port. Gamble ordered a hard starboard rudder and increased the throttle to its maximum. For a brief time it seemed that *Gerken* would right itself and pull the dredge and hose along as she struggled to starboard. But there was a sudden resounding crash on the deck. The deck-mounted steam shovel broke loose and began a slide across the deck to port, following the dredging hose toward the rail. The ship, which had seemed almost on the verge of recovering, stopped in mid-motion and hesitated, apparently trying to decide if it would straighten out or continue its roll to port. Captain Gamble acted decisively during the momentary delay. He ordered an anchor set from the starboard side of the bow and the ship's pumps turned on. After sending deck crew off on their missions, he ordered watchman Dick Freeman to send off a distress signal using *Gerken*'s wireless.

"What should I say about our location?" asked Freemen as he headed for the radio room.

"According to McMinn, we're about four miles east of Erie and a few miles offshore," answered Captain Gamble.

McMinn swallowed when he heard the location report, but said nothing to contradict Gamble's instruction.

*Gerken* continued to balance motionlessly on her port side for several moments that seemed to last an eternity. The entire crew was frozen in place, watching in shock. Then there was a grinding sound from below indicating that the load of sand in the hold was shifting toward the low side of the boat. The grinding finally gave way to terrible crashing sounds as bulkheads collapsed and the rush of below-deck materials accelerated. With each groan and pop from below, *Gerken* seemed to give up and roll a little further onto her side. Then in moments the ship was clearly lost; sitting like a tired old warrior on her port side with her deck apparatus dangling overboard from the side of the ship and anchoring her to the bottom.

Wagerman watched in horror as bits of gear slipped from the starboard or high side of the ship, tumbled across the deck and dropped over the port side. It was a surreal vision. *Gerken* was wallowing on her side, dead in the water. Her fires had gone out as the cargo shifted toward the low side of the hold. Her engines were silent but the magneto lights were still on, leaving her dead in the water but bright. The wild ship's motion had stopped and as Wagerman surveyed the situation it appeared that the Gerken might lie on her side almost indefinitely. At least it seemed so until Wagerman began to notice that the ship was making a gurgling sound and that water was running into the hold at an alarming rate. A deep brown swath of sandy effluent, streaming leeward from *Gerken*'s compromised hull clearly indicated that they were going down, and fast. The waves were pushing *Gerken* north and she was literally tripping on her dredging gear as she drifted. The sound that *Gerken* made as it tripped on itself was clearly the ship's death rattle!

## [FRIDAY, AUGUST 20, 1926, 11:00 P.M.]

"What do we do, Herm?" asked Logan, who had pulled his way across the deck to join Wagerman at his position next to the disabled steam shovel.

"We're going down," replied Wagerman. "That means we'll need the lifeboats. You fetch the one on the low side of the wheelhouse and get it in the water. I'll get the one on the high side and lower it."

"What about the officers on the bridge?" asked Logan.

"Look at them," Wagerman replied. "They're running around like chickens with their heads cut off. If the ship goes down with the lifeboats tied in place we're all going to go with it!"

In an instant, Wagerman and Logan sprung into action. Wagerman climbed to the starboard side of the wheelhouse, now some twenty-five feet above the water, and freed one lifeboat from its davits with the axe that hung on the wall next to it. Slowly but surely he worked the twenty-foot rowing dory along the elevated side of the wheelhouse with a winch until it was close to dropping along the deck. From his vantage point above the now nearly vertical deck he tied the boat's painter to *Gerken*'s wheelhouse and lowered it with the winch until the lifeboat rested on *Gerken*'s port deck rail. Climbing down the wheelhouse wall to the low side of the ship, Wagerman watched out of the corner of his eye as the bridge officers set flares off. Meanwhile, Logan dropped the second lifeboat onto the deck with its winch.

"Think anyone will see those flares?" asked Logan as he joined Wagerman on the port rail.

"Not a chance," replied Wagerman. "They don't realize that we're almost ten miles offshore. They're wasting their time."

Working together, Wagerman and Logan slid both lifeboats over the port side and tied them securely to the rail.

"What's next?" asked Logan.

"Come with me," answered Wagerman. "I found something which is going to help us." Without asking questions, Logan dutifully followed Wagerman who climbed up, then around to the rear of the wheelhouse.

"Here is our ticket to shore," noted Wagerman, pulling himself up onto *Gerken*'s wheelhouse roof. "The captain's personal rowing dory! Fourteen feet long, hard chines and a proper shape for rowing. When the big ship goes down, we'll get into this baby and pull for shore. Come on, we're going to take it forward and tie it to the rail so only we know where it is." As Wagerman and Logan muscled the captain's rowing dory forward and tied it to the rail in an innocuous location, the bridge crew was busy lighting the last of *Gerken*'s flares.

"Let's get to the bridge and see what's going on," said Wagerman after they had secured the dory. Slowly, the terrible twosome worked their way along the port rail toward the wheelhouse.

"How long do you figure we have before she goes all the way over?" asked Logan.

"Twenty minutes, maybe thirty," answered Wagerman. "She's going to turn turtle, look at how the rail is dropping into the water."

"Christ!" said Logan. "What should we do?"

"Get our life jackets on," replied Wagerman, "and be ready to abandon ship."

When Wagerman and Logan climbed through the wheelhouse door into the now sideways bridge, they were greeted with chaos. People were yelling at each other, the cook's young son was sobbing and Senior Gerken was cursing up a storm because the Coast Guard had apparently not responded to their display of flares. They could just barely see the flashing light at the Presque Isle Lighthouse and Senior Gerken was just now beginning to get a sense that they might be too far offshore to be seen by Erie's Coast Guard Station. But the severe angle of the ship was making them so disoriented that the bridge officers were still not aware of the fact that they were almost directly north of the Erie lighthouse rather than east as Senior Gerken, his brothers and Captain John Gamble had been led to believe. McMinn sat sullenly in a corner of the bridge without volunteering any information about *Gerken*'s actual position.

"What now?" McMinn growled. He aimed his rhetorical question at Wagerman and Logan as they pushed their way into the wheelhouse.

"I have an idea," replied Wagerman. "Look north. You can see the Long Point Light! We can't be more than fifteen miles from the tip of the point. In weather like this there's bound to be ships either hunkered down in the shelter behind the point or heading that way. We need a signal that can be seen from Long Point. If nothing else, maybe the lighthouse keeper will see it and radio for help. Come on, let's make a real signal fire!"

Carefully, Wagerman led Logan and McMinn out of the wheelhouse and downstairs into the officers' quarters. While they descended the stairs toward the rooms Wagerman grabbed an axe. He stopped at the first wooden door that they encountered and swung the blade directly into the middle of it, shattering it into dozens of shards of wood.

"Let's get these strips of wood up on deck and start a fire," Wagerman shouted as he chopped.

Working like men possessed, Wagerman chopped wood, splintering anything that he could find: furniture, chairs, bed posts and joinery, while Logan and McMinn dragged the pieces to the highest level spot on Gerken's wheelhouse. Slowly the pile of wood began to grow. When the bridge crew began to comprehend what Wagerman and his mates were up to they pitched in, dragging flammable materials onto the deck as rapidly as Wagerman could liberate them. When the pile had reached a precarious balance point atop the starboard side of the now sideways wheelhouse, Jesse Gerken poured lamp oil onto it and set it aflame. Just as the flames seemed to reach a maximum height Wagerman appeared with the Captain's mohair mattress, which he deftly tossed into the middle of the flames. When the mattress ignited, a wall of flames shot forty feet into the night sky, illuminating the bedraggled and desperate crew. Almost all of the men gazed past the fire toward Erie, hoping that somehow their signal fire would be spotted. But Wagerman looked the opposite way. In the distance, toward Long Point, he thought that he saw navigational lights.

### [FRIDAY, AUGUST 20, 1926, 11:30 P.M.]

The crackling of the dying signal fire was suddenly drowned out by gurgling water rushing into *Gerken*'s hull. As Wagerman and Logan watched the fire settle and die, *Gerken* made a terrible moaning sound and began to roll even further to port. It was *Gerken*'s death roll and would obviously result in the old ship turning upside down. But the ship seemed to be holding her own for the time and no one was anxious to put to sea in twenty-five foot waves. So the crew milled about near the lifeboats trying to decide how long the ship would stay afloat. Just before midnight the ship made another loud groan and lurched ten more degrees to port. She was now lying at almost a 90-degree angle and the gurgling sound was accelerating. Several more lurches to port convinced everyone that it would be safer on the lifeboats and the crew silently began to board. In an instant everyone was in one of the two lifeboats.

"Let's go," urged Jesse Gerken, "before the ship goes over and takes the lifeboats with it!" Wagerman and Logan released the painters so that the lifeboats would be clear if *Gerken* were to sink.

Just as they were releasing the two boats, McMinn, who had been the last to climb aboard, looked at Wagerman and Logan and asked, "What about you two? Are you coming?"

"Not yet, chief," Logan answered. "We have something else to do!"

With that, McMinn returned to the deck and helped push the lifeboats away. "What's up?" he asked, looking Wagerman in the eye.

"We're going to take the other lifeboat," answered Herman Wagerman. "It's a bit small but it will hold the three of us," he added. Just as he uttered the words, Dick Freeman came staggering across the deck, looking dazed and confused.

"Shit!" muttered McMinn. "We almost forgot Dick. He was below, radioing for help."

"Come on!" yelled Wagerman to Freeman. "We have to get out of here right now!"

With McMinn and Freeman in tow, Wagerman and Logan raced to *Gerken*'s bow, climbed aboard the Captain's rowing dory and pushed themselves from the ship. The dory drifted away quickly in the waves and within a few minutes the big ship rolled all the way over and sat bottom up in the waves. As they watched in shock, *Gerken* made a last mournful groaning sound and slipped below the surface. The magneto was still running and ship's lights continued to glow while *Gerken* paused, resting just below the water's surface. But the crew of the captain's dory didn't have time to ponder the strange specter of the underwater lights. The small rowing dory, which had been riding in *Gerken*'s lee, was now fully exposed to howling southeasterly winds and the full fury of the waves. Wagerman and his colleagues were suddenly fighting with monster waves.

Wagerman stopped to take his bearings and decide what he should do next. He reached for an oar and noticed that his hands were bloated and white. Puzzled, he tried to manipulate his fingers, but they wouldn't move. He reached forward to look more closely at his hands and rolled into the water, coming up coughing and sputtering. Wagerman was awake again and he was floating in a life jacket, not riding in the captain's rowing dory.

# CHAPTER 15

## [SATURDAY, AUGUST 21, 1926, 3:30 A.M.]

*The wanderings of Wagerman's mind were beginning to distract him from his feelings of cold and loneliness. He was tired from fighting the water. So tired. But he took solace in his recollections, even though he found himself increasingly unable to direct them. His memories were far more pleasant than the thoughts that plagued Wagerman when he was fully awake and thinking about his predicament. So he continued his random reflections, welcoming them as old friends.*

*He was drifting backwards in time from the present moment to so many former time periods that he was growing confused by his mind's association processes. For some strange reason he seemed to continually regress to his school years.*

*In seventh grade, his mother had reluctantly agreed to take him to a lecture on Great Lakes shipwrecks. A young Herman Wagerman, like most of his friends, was absolutely fascinated by stories of shipwrecked sailors. And his teacher, Mr. Leonardi, had announced the lecture to his class and encouraged all to attend. Most of Wagerman's classmates were far more repelled by the thought of a weekend lecture than drawn by the topic. But not Herman! He harassed his mother for days until she finally agreed to take him.*

*On the day of the lecture, he convinced his mother to arrive almost an hour early to ensure they would get good seats. When the lecture began, Herman Wagerman and his mother were planted in the front row. Herman was anxiously waiting, while his mother was wondering what had gotten into her son to make him so excited about such a strange and gruesome topic.*

*Retired Great Lakes ship captain Robert Wall slowly walked onto the stage. He was a large man with a full head of white hair. Wall introduced himself as the son of an Irish immigrant and one of the lucky sailors who had somehow escaped tragedy and mishap on the lakes.*

*As Wagerman recalled the tales that he had heard at that lecture, he wondered if his childhood interests had been a premonition. A warning! He could still see Captain Wall with his shock of brilliant white hair, standing at the podium more than twenty years earlier.*

# Lake Erie's Shipwrecks

## [December 1903, Buffalo: A Lecture on Lake Erie Shipwrecks]

Captain Wall introduced himself to the audience, then began his discussion of the Great Lakes and shipwrecks.

"I spent the bulk of my career right out there," he said, motioning in the general direction of Lake Erie. "In the most dangerous of all the Great Lakes! For that matter," he continued, "the most dangerous body of water in the world! I'm here tonight," Wall added, "to explain why Lake Erie has had so many shipwrecks, and to tell you the stories of two of the most interesting ones."

Captain Wall gathered himself for a moment and then began his lecture as Herman Wagerman sat spellbound.

The central portion of Lake Erie is the world's most dangerous section of navigable water. Statistically, its waters have taken more of a shipping toll per square mile than any other area in the world. The most important reason for all these shipwrecks is a simple one: the sheer volume of Lake Erie shipping traffic. In the nineteenth century, when westward expansion was at its peak, there was a traffic jam of ships out there, in the smallest of the Great Lakes. Lake Erie was worse than a big city street at rush hour! This incredible traffic pressure in Central Lake Erie was, in itself, primarily responsible for the danger. Insurance records indicate that there was more shipping volume in Central Lake Erie by the middle of the nineteenth century than in any other portion of the world, including the Atlantic Ocean.

Adding to the dangers of this traffic volume was the dismal state of the art with respect to navigation and shipping safety. When shipping was at its mid-1800s peak, there were no uniform requirements for navigational lights aboard ships. And there were few aids to navigation. Lighthouses were just beginning to appear on the lakes, and modern nuances such as ship-to-shore radio, weather forecasting and charts of the lake bottom were the vague dreams of visionaries. So all of this traffic, essentially uncontrolled by navigational systems, ultimately found its way into Central Lake Erie. There were crude schooners tacking back and forth across the lake on cargo runs between small town ports, and steamships driving straight up and down the lake's axis. The grand old steamships had holds bursting with hundreds of immigrants and package freight, while their top-decks carried first and second class passengers. Most of the wealthy people rode the lake for the sheer thrill of the voyage, enjoying opulent cabins, ballrooms with orchestras and fine restaurants. It is little wonder, given the volume and state of shipping, that there were not even more collisions.

The central portion of the lake was also the midpoint of most voyages; the place where trouble was logically most likely to occur. Mechanical failures or bad weather at a trip's start, for example, would usually result in an immediate return to the departure port. If a ship were to find itself in real distress, where else would the problems be more likely to occur, than in the middle of the trip?

But it wasn't just traffic that caused the dangers in Central Lake Erie. In fact, Lake Erie winds and waves are world-renowned for their cantankerous character! When Lake Erie's winds blow in the prevailing direction (southwesterly and down the axis of the lake) they build monstrous waves in short order because the wind velocity is added to the lake's complementary current. Unlike the Atlantic Ocean or even the other big lakes (Michigan, Huron and Superior), Erie's waves grow quickly because of the relatively shallow nature of the western basin. The western end of the lake is only twenty to thirty feet deep, so waves trip on the bottom and develop steep, breaking faces. And fresh water, which is less dense than the salt water of the oceans, allows the waves to grow much faster and become steeper. A few hours of breeze on Lake Erie, and you're looking at nasty ten to fifteen footers!

But for pure excitement (or terror, Captain Wall muttered under his breath) you must experience Lake Erie during a nor'easter. On Lake Erie, that's a wind that blows opposite to (against) the prevailing current. Ocean sailors call it Lake Erie's "Gulf Stream Effect." A stiff nor'easter quickly spawns unbelievable waves with crests that are steeper and closer to each other than the worst conditions facing ocean sailors.

No matter which direction the waves come from, they become even more dangerous when they reach the central basin because the waterway suddenly narrows. Central Lake Erie's two great peninsulas, Long Point to the north and Presque Isle on the south side, cause the lake and its relentless eastern currents to narrow. It's just like a narrowing creek or river but on a much larger scale. The compressed waves speed up, grow taller and break up into directional eddies, changing the normal current behavior. Right at this central point between the two peninsulas, the lake's width changes from almost fifty miles to twenty-seven.

When the waveforms collide with the narrowing lake between the two peninsulas and the shoal waters surrounding them, the crests swing toward shore raising the dangers of being driven aground. And the closer a ship gets to either of these two peninsulas, the higher and steeper the waves! Old time sailors have reported waves near both Long Point and Presque Isle that utterly defy description; breaking crests in which it is impossible to control a ship of any size.

Long Point has traditionally been the biggest problem, since the regular shipping lanes pass within a few miles of its tip. Hundreds of ships were driven onto its beaches by storm waves over the years. And even if a shipwrecked sailor were able to get off a sinking ship and row or swim to shore at Long Point, he would find himself afoot on one of the largest stretches of wilderness beach in North America.

Captain Wall paused once more and seemed to collect himself in front of the audience. "This brings me to the first of my tales," he added, "the story of the *Jersey City!*"

It was the terrible misfortune of the crew from the steamer *Jersey City* to be driven ashore at Long Point on November 25, 1860. Caught in a fierce storm, the 182-foot ship carrying a hold filled with processed meat and a deck load of cattle was struggling west along the south beaches of Long Point. While the crew had the apparent security of being within sight of land, they were subjecting their ship to a terrible pounding as they crashed through Long Point's infamous waves. The captain later reported that seas along the point were running steady at twenty-five to thirty feet, with five-foot breaking crests. By 11:00 p.m., it was clear to the captain that the ship was in serious trouble. They were making no progress against beach landmarks and the *Jersey City* was slowly being washed leeward, toward the beach.

When the cattle on deck began to fall and bellow in terror, the captain decided to come about and run downwind. He hoped to round the tip of the point and make for shelter behind the north beaches. But just as he put the ship's wheel to port and the *Jersey City* swung broadside to the waves, a rogue forty footer broke over the starboard side, rolling the ship severely to port. The load of live cattle fell and slid along the deck, propelling the *Jersey City* even further to port. Most of the cattle were washed overboard where they began to moan in horrendous frantic tones.

By the time the five-year-old ship had turned so that it was 90 degrees to weather, she was pitched over at more than 45 degrees and the fires in her boiler went out. The ship was, for all intents and purposes, doomed. She was floating east along Long Point's south beaches, absolutely dead in the water, with the hull leaking faster than the pumps could evacuate the water.

An hour later, the *Jersey City* ground to a halt on a sandbar 400 yards from the beach. Recognizing this as their best opportunity to make for shore, the captain, crew and passengers launched two lifeboats and headed for the beach. The captain, eighteen crew members, and two passengers successfully made the trek to the icy-cold beaches through the winds, waves and a raging November snowstorm. One crew member was lost at sea as the lifeboat crews pulled for shore.

After almost an hour of arduous rowing, a frozen, exhausted and wet crew finally dragged their two lifeboats ashore, then walked to the relative shelter of the trees just off the beach. The captain assembled his crew and passengers and developed a plan. A blizzard was raging and the southwesterly gale literally stung the skin as everyone listened to the captain's plan.

"If we walk west," he reasoned, "we'll be heading into the wind. We'll never make it to Port Rowan. It's much too far away," he told them. "Our only hope is to walk with the wind at our backs, toward the lighthouse at the tip of the point. It's closer and we can get there in a few hours," he added.

But the crew rebelled against the captain's orders to walk east toward the tip of the point and the lighthouse. The disenfranchised crew members and one passenger decided that it would be safer to walk west toward civilization. Their confidence in the captain had been badly shaken by the shipwreck and the death of the watchman who fell overboard during the row to shore. They just couldn't understand the logic of walking away from the closest city. Thus sixteen souls set off on foot across snow-covered beaches for the base of Long Point.

The captain took a party of five in the opposite direction, hiking for the lighthouse. Half-frozen, they arrived at the lighthouse near midnight where they were offered shelter and food.

Early the next morning, the lighthouse keeper and the captain left the lighthouse and walked back toward the site of the *Jersey City*. Trudging through a foot of new snow, they searched the south beaches hoping to find the missing crewmembers. And they did. But the men that they found were all frozen to death. It was apparent that the dissident crew had subsequently disagreed with each other. Some, who must have backtracked, were found frozen to death on the beach near the *Jersey City*. Others were found inland. Those desperate crew members must have been making for the apparent shelter of the north beaches.

Frozen bodies were found on Long Point throughout that entire winter with the last one appearing at spring thaw in March. It was the body of a sailor, sitting upright next to a quaking aspen tree. The sailor seemed to be lazily looking out over the Outer Bay.

Captain Wall's second tale was the story of the steamer *Atlantic*,
another victim of Central Lake Erie. She was a state-of-the-art, 267-
foot, luxury sidewheel steamer heading west on the calm summer
night of August 9, 1852. The *Atlantic* carried a crew of more than
twenty and a passenger manifest numbering between 500 and 550
depending upon estimated family sizes of the immigrants who were
heading west in the big ship's steerage compartment. As the *Atlantic*
steamed past the tip of Long Point under clear evening skies, she
collided with the steamer *Ogdensburg*, eastbound for the Welland
Canal. For some unexplainable reason, neither wheelman saw the
other ship.

*Ogdensburg*'s impact holed the *Atlantic* on the port side just
forward of her sidewheel. Hardly believing what had happened, the
captain of the *Atlantic* regained his composure on the bridge, steered
away from the *Ogdensburg* and resumed his westward course for
Detroit. The *Ogdensberg*'s captain watched in amazement as *Atlantic*
steamed away, hardly missing an engine beat. Within a few moments,
however, the *Atlantic*'s engineer rushed to the bridge to report that
the ship was severely holed and that the engines would soon be
flooded. Captain J.B. Petty decided that his best hope was to run for
shallow water near the beaches of Long Point. His plan was to run
the *Atlantic* aground rather than let it sink in the deep water just
south of the point. At 2:30 a.m., the *Atlantic* turned for Long Point
and headed at full steam for the south beaches. At 2:50 a.m.,
however, the fires went out in the boiler and *Atlantic* began to settle,
bow first, into 175 feet of water.

Even though the *Atlantic* went down quite slowly (witnesses
claimed that the stern was still afloat at mid-morning the following
day), there was absolute panic aboard the ship.

As *Ogdensburg* returned to provide assistance, chaos broke out among the steerage-class passengers. Immigrants, who barely spoke English, ran for the rails and literally threw themselves overboard, thinking that there was a fire aboard. Most did not know how to swim, and many drowned immediately when they hit the water. Others were caught in the ship's massive sidewheels where they were crushed by the blades, trapped and dragged underwater as the ship settled. In all, 250 to 300 persons died that tragic evening. When the steamer *Ogdensburg* reached Erie with the survivors and crew, the captain blamed the accident on traffic volume. "With all the ships out there at night," he said to the media, "it's little wonder that there aren't even more collisions!"

Herman Wagerman didn't sleep for days after hearing Captain Wall's stories about the *Jersey City* and the *Atlantic*. Instead, he lay awake in his bed thinking about what it must have been like to be a shipwrecked sailor. All the way home from the lecture, his mother had chastised him for convincing her to take him to such a frightening talk.

"What kind of crazy person would even think about becoming a Great Lakes sailor?" she had asked him.

# PART SIX

## Rescuers

*The waves resembled rows of snow-capped
mountains marching in unison.
The mountains were not particularly terrifying
in themselves. Not even the snow-capped tops.
What made my hair stand on end was the sight
of those terrifying crests falling, sending avalanches of
frothing, hissing water into their valleys.*

**Robert Manry**

*Tinkerbelle*

# CHAPTER 16

## [SATURDAY, AUGUST 21, 1926, 3:35 A.M.]

*The water was finally calming and the sky was showing hints of dawn. Wagerman knew that he was still alive, but his mind was laboring and he was having a difficult time discerning between dreams and reality. When he fell asleep, he knew why he was finding Suzanne in his dreams. He was searching for her and her image was entirely understandable since it was clearly of Wagerman's own making. But Suzanne was somehow also coming to him when he was awake and these waking visions of her were disturbing. They seemed to have their own motivations and to speak to him in ways that he knew were not constructions of his own imagination.*

*In her reassuring voice, Suzanne (or at least Wagerman's image of her) seemed to want to calm his fears. She interrupted Wagerman's inner-dialogue when she came, convincing him to have confidence and remain optimistic. For a time he had decided that he was doomed because he couldn't see the* Maitland *any more.*

*"If the ship isn't even within sight, there can be no hope of rescue," he thought to himself.*

*Wagerman's pessimistic, wet, and cold self was trying to make him believe that the car ferry captain had given up and returned to his regular run. But in the midst of terrible doubts, with Wagerman's mind suspended between dreaming and reality, Suzanne appeared again, and this time she seemed absolutely real.*

*Dressed in jeans and a cotton blouse, she walked across the surface of the lake, then stepped into the water with him. She* crawled inside his life jacket, held him gently and whispered reassuringly into his ear.

"Herman," she implored, "there is nothing to worry about. I know that the captain of the car ferry will never give up looking for you. You have to have faith," she added. "Lots of people are praying for you so don't disappoint them!"

Suzanne's image seemed to respond to his inner thoughts. He didn't have to consciously think about her or try to make his dreams bring him to her. She came automatically. So the optimistic part of him accepted her advice at face value. Wagerman decided, internally, that the car ferry captain was inevitably going to find him. All he had to do was wait patiently!

With his faith in a rescue restored, Wagerman began to relax once more and tumble toward sleep. As he drifted in the water, he wondered what was happening aboard the Maitland.

# Maitland Braves the Lake

## [FRIDAY, AUGUST 20, 1926, 11:00 P.M.]

They sat quietly, staring through *Maitland*'s wheelhouse windows: Acting Captain Thomas Heyman, First Mate William Burke, and Watchman Pete Brinley. As Heyman watched in amazement, an endless row of twenty-five foot waves paraded toward *Maitland*'s beam. For as far as he could see to the south, monster waves were relentlessly pushing their way across the lake's surface. Each arriving crest seemed to have only slight variations, mainly the size of the frothing white beard perched perilously at its peak. As successive waves struck, the car ferry would rise slowly, yawing ever so slightly to starboard. The big ship would pause for a split second at the top of each wave, then pulsate back to port as it sank into the depression between crests.

"Jesus!" muttered Heyman. "I've never seen anything like this before. Have you, Pete?"

"Devil Wind waves," responded Brinley. "The old-timers used to tell stories, but to be honest it's my first time caught in them. Happens when the wind blows like hell off the American shore. They're short and steep, and they don't blow apart when they hit. Hell on the boat, and if it keeps up much longer," continued Brinley, "they'll get even steeper. Pity the poor bastards who get stuck along the south shore of Long Point. These southeasterly waves bounce off the beach and grow twice as big on their way back!"

"At least the ship's motion is easier," added Burke. "Since we put the wheel to starboard the ride has smoothed out."

"I'll say," added Heyman. "And we can thank Pete for the suggestion to run for Long Point," he added. "It was the right move!"

"Thanks, captain," muttered Brinley, "and the crew appreciates it too. The motion is a lot easier down below."

So the car ferry *Maitland* wallowed along toward Long Point that night as the rain slowed and stars slowly began to appear. Heyman tweaked the wheel, trying to smooth the ship's motion while Brinley and Burke worked out a dead reckoning position on the wheelhouse chart table. Heyman was thankful that Brinley had accepted the invitation to stay in the wheelhouse. He had never attempted to go behind Long Point's north beaches as he would tonight. Heyman's growing concern, after hearing Brinley's description of the probable size and shape of the waves on the south side of the point, was that he might pass to the south side of the tip by mistake. If this happened, he would have to bring *Maitland* about in the very waves that Brinley had just described. He was also more than a bit nervous about running aground on the shoals near the tip. While Brinley and Burke worked on the charts, he alternated his attention between driving the ship through the waves and scouring the horizon for a glimpse of the Long Point Lighthouse.

"We're right about here," Burke announced, holding up a chart of Lake Erie. "Ten, maybe twelve miles due east of the tip of the point."

"Then why can't we see it?" asked Heyman. "It's getting clear enough that we should be able to spot the light from this distance."

"Because its off to starboard, Cap," replied Brinley, who had moved from the chart table to the wheelhouse windows. "We're way off the rhumb line to port, probably from correcting through the waves. See it, Cap," he repeated. "It's 15 degrees to starboard."

"Shit!" muttered Heyman. "I was sure that I had been taking us starboard of the rhumb line, and I was looking for the light on the port side. You're right again, Pete."

Heyman was feeling like a junior captain, as Pete Brinley continued to interpret for him.

"Where should we aim, Pete?" he asked.

"Head a mile to starboard of the light, Captain," responded Brinley. "That way we'll miss the shoals. When we get close, we'll be able to see the breakers on the tip of the point. From there it will be easy to work our way around. If we miss the shoals at the tip we're in good shape. There's 100 feet of water behind the north beaches."

Heyman eased the wheel another 15 degrees and handed the helm over to Burke. The motion was made even easier by the steering maneuver and Thomas Heyman was finally beginning to feel secure in his navigation. He knew that the men below would support his decision to run for shelter and he was confident that the ship's owners in Ashtabula would know that he had done the right thing as well. He was also grateful that Pete Brinley had been with him that night. He planned to recommend a promotion and commendation for him when they returned. In any event, there was one thing Heyman knew for sure as he gazed toward the clearing American shore: Brinley would be staying with him on the bridge until *Maitland* was anchored securely behind Long Point. As Heyman gazed south across the lake, still mesmerized by the parade of waves, he noted the clearing skies. A glow was beginning to appear along the U.S. shoreline.

Suddenly, Heyman's contemplative mood was shattered by Bill Burke.

"Jesus, look at that!" Burke shouted, pointing toward the clearing south shore.

The three stared out the port window in disbelief, watching a huge wall of flames literally burst from the southern horizon.

"What could it be?" asked Heyman aloud.

"A light from shore?" offered Burke.

"No way!" responded Brinley. "That's a fire coming from somewhere between the south shore and us."

"A fire?" asked Heyman.

"Must be a ship in trouble," added Brinley. "What else could it possibly be?"

## [FRIDAY, AUGUST 20, 1926, 11:21 P.M.]

Without hesitation, Acting Captain Heyman took the wheel and swung *Maitland* to port. Before the flame, which seemed to dominate the horizon, slowly subsided, Heyman lined the ship up on it, bringing her bow uncomfortably back into the waves.

"Get a bearing on that flame before it goes out," barked Heyman.

"Already got it, Cap," responded Brinley, "one hundred eighty-two degrees magnetic."

"Dead upwind again," muttered Burke.

"We have no choice," added Heyman. "We have to see if they need help."

"If they didn't they wouldn't have sent up a signal like that," added Brinley. "A flame that size either means that a ship is on fire, or that its crew is burning stuff to attract attention."

"How far away, Pete?" asked Heyman.

"Hard to say," responded Brinley. "We can't see the outline of the ship, so it must be below the horizon. Maybe ten miles or so."

With *Maitland* plowing up and through rather than across the waves, they set out to cross the lake and come to the assistance of an unknown ship in distress. As the motion changed, the ship's cook came through the wheelhouse door with coffee and biscuits.

"Noticed a change in the motion," he grumbled. "The men down below are wondering what's up."

"Take a look," Brinley said, pointing to the horizon and the now-faltering flame.

"Sweet Jesus!" responded the Cook. "Somebody's in trouble out there. I'll tell the crew!"

"Better get them up on deck," added Heyman. "We're going to need all the eyes we can get up here. If that's a ship on fire, there are going to be people in the water." Thomas Heyman was now clearly the captain of the ship. Any remnants of the insecurity Heyman had felt disappeared as *Maitland* plodded through the waves on a bearing of 182 degrees. While he pushed the ship forward, the entire crew gathered on deck, preparing to help fellow sailors who might be in trouble.

# CHAPTER 17

## [SATURDAY, AUGUST 21, 1926, 3:40 A.M.]

*Wagerman awoke again to nothing. Cold water, a predawn sky, shivering and no signs of rescue. He was growing despondent again: exhausted, freezing cold and depressed. Sleep seemed to be his only friend now and wakefulness felt like a mortal enemy. While tired eyes searched the horizon, his internal negativity kicked up once more. He realized that his chances of being spotted by a single rescue ship were minimal. The longer he floated and the further he drifted from the site of* Gerken's *sinking, the worse his odds were. Slipping into his most morose state of the night, he began to wonder why Suzanne hadn't appeared to him for reassurance this time as he harbored renewed negative thoughts. After all, she had just told him a few seconds ago that he was going to be rescued. Or was it hours ago? Wagerman was growing increasingly confused as his body cooled.*

*With nothing else to do, he returned his gaze to the horizon in the vague hope of spotting a rescue ship. Suddenly, he thought that he saw something.*

*"Could it be Suzanne?" he wondered to himself. "And if it is," he mused, "who is that with her?"*

*As he watched, two figures slowly moved across the surface of the lake toward him. Wagerman opened and closed his eyes, checking to see if he was really awake, but before he could decide he recognized a voice. It was Bill Logan.*

*"Herman," the voice said in a clear tone, "are you ready to come with us yet?"*

*"Is that really you, Bill?" Wagerman asked, trying to see who Logan was with.*

*"You might as well call it a night, Herm," Logan continued. "There's no way anybody is going to find us out here, so I decided to give up! Why don't you just give it up and come with us?" he urged.*

*"What do you mean, us. Who's your friend?" asked Herman Wagerman. As he spoke, he struggled to make out the facial features of the man who stood quietly with Logan on the water not twenty feet away.*

*"I don't know his name," answered Logan, "but he came to get me a few minutes ago. We're going to a place where it's warm and dry."*

*"But who is he?" asked Wagerman again insistently.*

*"Come on, Herm! You must know him, he's been with you all your life, just waiting," answered Bill Logan.*

*Wagerman knew who Logan's friend was. It was Death. And Logan was right. Death had been with Wagerman since he first learned about him as a young boy. But then, as now, Wagerman had struggled to ignore him. There had been moments through the years when he found himself wondering about Death but he always rushed nervously away from these thoughts, finding such ideas far too frightening to deal with. Why should a strong young man think about such things, he reasoned?*

*Wagerman had always conceived of death as terrifying; something that he would rail against. But now that Death was a real person who stood in front of him with his friend Bill Logan, he didn't seem frightening at all. In fact, Death seemed almost reassuring.*

"If you're going to come with us, Herman, you have to leave right now," Logan noted. "You could just untie your life jacket again and let yourself sink," he added.

But just as Wagerman was about to give in, Suzanne returned. She walked across the surface of the water toward him hurrying, almost running across the water. Seeing her, Logan and his friend set off quickly in the opposite direction.

"See you soon, Herman," Logan yelled over his shoulder as he walked away.

When Suzanne reached him, she slid into his life jacket again, warming him as she spoke gently into his ear. "You can't give up, Herman," she implored. The Coast Guard is out looking for you, too. There's more than one rescue ship! So it's only a matter of time until they find you. Please try to stay awake."

Wagerman was torn. He wanted to stay awake with Suzanne, and yet he realized that if he succumbed to sleep, she would be there too.

"How could he lose?" he wondered to himself.

# The Coast Guard Beach Patrol

## [FRIDAY, AUGUST 20, 1926, 6:00 P.M.]

It was change of watch at the Erie Coast Guard Station. Petty Officer Joseph Baker spoke in a monotone without looking up from his clipboard toward the duty crew.

"Good afternoon, men," he barked. "Let me get through today's special announcements and we'll get to work," he added.

As Baker spoke, the crew suspected that they were about to hear something they didn't want to know: that tonight was going to be a "beach walk" night. Wind was howling through the cottonwood trees on Presque Isle Peninsula, and rain was pelting the side of the stationhouse. These were the kinds of evenings when the Erie Coast Guard Station seemed completely isolated from civilization, even though it was just a few miles from town on the channel leading to the lake.

"Tonight's first announcement concerns the station communication system," Baker noted. "The land lines are down, so we're cut off from town and from the downtown cutter. More important, our antennas are down too, so we have no way of listening to ships at sea. So it's back to the old days tonight, men! We're going to walk the beaches and keep a weather eye on any shipping that's out there. You know the procedure," he continued. "If you see a ship, no matter what she seems to be doing, note its position, description and direction and then report it to the control center when you come back in. We'll maintain a continuous observation and monitor the position and direction of each vessel until it's out of range."

"Now for the schedule," Baker continued. "A new beach patrol will leave every hour on the half-hour, beginning with 18:30 hours. Two men per patrol. Be sure to check the locations of any ships observed by the previous shift before you go out. By the way, first shift reports five vessels. Two fish tugs from Erie: *Rocket* and *Uranus* outbound through the channel at 16:05 hours, a commercial sailing vessel, reaching east along shore (first spotted by the 16:30 beach patrol), an up-bound steamer almost out of sight to the west, and a sandsucker. The sandsucker is the *Gerken* registered out of Buffalo. She cleared the channel today at 13:30 hours and the 16:30 patrol reported her working three miles offshore. Cramer and Johnsten will walk the first patrol. Keep your eyes open men, and fall out!"

Baker walked to his desk at the station's main lookout site while Cramer and Johnsten headed for the locker room to prepare for their patrol. Johnsten was a first-year Coast Guard reservist and he had never gone on a beach patrol before. Carter, a career seaman, seemed irritated to be walking the beaches that night. As they headed for their lockers, Johnsten was looking forward to the new experience.

"So what do we do?" asked Johnsten. "How do we dress for this?"

"It's August," responded Cramer. "So at least we won't be freezing our asses off. Most of these goddamn beach patrols happen in November or March when it's blowing like stink and snowing. This will be a piece of cake. A walk on the beach!"

They took light jackets, to protect themselves from the rain, changed into soft-soled shoes and returned to Baker's desk. There, they met the earlier patrol. The 17:30 patrol indicated that there was no change from the 16:30 report. Cramer and Johnsten stepped through the stationhouse door at precisely 18:30 hours and began their walk.

"Every goddamn time it blows from the south or the north, the lines go down out here," complained Cramer on the way down the concrete walkway toward the beach. "This whole operation is designed for the prevailing winds. Struts, braces, poles, the whole shooting match goes to hell in a handbag as soon as the wind shifts. You can count on it every fall and spring, but usually not in the summer."

"So exactly what is our job?" queried Johnsten as he followed Cramer toward the beach. The two were on sand now, walking the hard wet sweep between the soft dry beach and the water.

"We get to keep an eye on the five ships that the chief reported. It's babysitting duty. We keep track of them until they're out of sight. And look!" he added. "Two of them are coming back right now. Only three left to keep tabs on."

Johnsten looked up to see two fish tugs churning toward the channel.

"Make a note on your clipboard," noted Cramer. "It's *Rocket* and *Uranus*. Those guys wouldn't be stupid enough to go offshore in a big southeast wind like this. They probably set their nets within a few miles of the beach."

"Lucky guys," added Johnsten. "They're probably heading back to town to drink illegal beer tonight while we walk the beach."

"Yup," added Cramer, "commercial fishermen always seem to know how to find a drink."

By 18:50, the pair had reached the northernmost point on Presque Isle's beaches. They stood there for a few moments surveying the horizon. Even though it was more than an hour before sunset, the deep gray sky and low lying clouds made it possible to see running lights.

"Two vessels," noted Cramer. "See the sailing ship off to the east?"

Johnsten strained to pick up a green running light and a white stern light to his right, and nodded agreement.

"Just like the chief said," added Cramer, "she's heading east and doing fine. She will probably stay close to the south shore tonight and get a nice ride on these offshore winds."

Looking almost due north, the pair noted two running lights. A red and a green, close enough to indicate that they were from the same ship.

"How do you explain that?" asked Johnsten. "We can see both running lights!"

"Must be the sandsucker the chief mentioned. The *Gerken*," answered Cramer. "She's either headed back toward us, or she's working, sucking sand off the bottom with her bow to weather."

They watched *Gerken* for a full five minutes and the running lights didn't seem to be getting any bigger.

"Must be working!" noted Cramer. "She'll probably fill up, then head for Buffalo. She won't have any trouble, either, if she stays under the shelter of the bluffs along shore. Come on we're done, let's get back to the station."

As Cramer and Johnsten entered the station house at 19:15 hours, *Rocket* and *Uranus* powered past them through the channel.

"Only two ships still out there," Cramer reported to Chief Baker. "The sandsucker *Gerken* working offshore and the eastbound schooner we've been following. She'll be out of sight when we go back out for the 20:30 patrol. No sign of the westbound steamer, Chief," he added. "She must be in Ohio by now."

Cramer placed pencil marks on the chart to designate *Gerken* and the schooner while the 19:30 patrol readied itself.

At 20:15 Cramer and Johnsten tore themselves away from a card game and put their gear on. By 20:25, they were in the control room checking the previous shift's report. As Cramer had suspected, the schooner they had spotted on the eastern horizon two hours earlier had passed out of view. The *Gerken* was still working offshore, according to the 19:30 shift report that noted a white stern light instead of the red and green running lights which Cramer and Johnsten had reported an hour earlier.

"Let's go," Cramer said, nudging Johnsten through the door and into the cool evening air. "There's probably just one little lamb out there for us shepherds to watch over. And unless I guessed wrong, they'll either be steaming back into the channel right now or headed for Buffalo."

"How do you figure that?" asked Johnsten.

"Only takes a few hours to fill up a sandsucker," answered Cramer, "and she's been out there for about the right amount of time.

Besides," he added, "the white running light means that *Gerken* was moving, not dredging. She's probably pulling away from the dredging grounds and making a swing north to get organized. By now she'll be on her way to dump the load in either Erie or Buffalo."

Cramer and Johnsten reached the northernmost beach point at 20:50, the spot from which they had seen *Gerken*'s lights in the twilight two hours earlier. It was almost dark, with any leftover sun obliterated by clouds on the western horizon. But as they strained to find *Gerken*'s lights, they could see nothing. She wasn't steaming toward the channel and she wasn't visible to the east.

"Strange," commented Cramer, "we should still be able to see her. Come on," he muttered as he turned toward the station, "we should report this to the chief."

Back at the station, Cramer mentioned his concern to Chief Baker.

"*Gerken* is nowhere to be seen, chief," he reported. "She should have either steamed back into town or headed east for Buffalo, but there's no sign of her."

"Probably steamed out of sight to the east already," remarked Baker, looking at the position report from the 19:30 beach patrol.

"How?" asked Cramer. "If she was northwest of the peninsula at 19:50, how could she be out of sight to the east already? She couldn't possibly move that fast."

"Maybe her lights were off, or you just missed her," offered Baker. "Don't worry about it! I'll have the 21:30 boys make a careful check of the eastern horizon when they go back out."

## [FRIDAY, AUGUST 20, 1926, 11:45 P.M.]

Captain Nelson Seymore was commanding officer of Erie's Coast Guard Station. Life at the station was remarkably pleasant for Seymore and his family, except for the isolation. Sometimes his wife Mary missed having a regular life on shore and normal social interactions with friends other than "Coasties." Seymore had not spent much time with her over the past weeks, being busy with the station's summertime rush. There were pleasure boaters to be "rescued" and other interminable duties, all of which involved report writing and government forms. So Seymore had excused himself from the station that evening to take his wife to Erie for dinner at a downtown hotel.

Driving on or off the peninsula was an adventure. The state was just beginning to develop a roadway system on the park. Coast Guard personnel usually moved people and supplies to the stationhouse by boat, crossing the channel to Erie's East Side. It was unusual for them, or anyone else, to use the rugged dirt and gravel roads that paralleled the beaches for seven miles, connecting the station with the mainland. Because of the high winds that evening, however, Seymore had chosen to drive rather than row across the channel.

Midnight found Seymore and his wife returning to the station, picking their way along roads littered with fallen branches caused by the high winds. Nearing the halfway spot on the peninsula, he heard the unmistakable sound of a siren approaching from the rear. Seymore pulled to the side of the road where he watched in amazement as a City of Erie police car sped past him and continued east. Fearing an emergency at the station he followed the police car, at times driving almost forty miles an hour. When the cruiser pulled up to the stationhouse, Seymore parked behind it and intercepted the two officers who were racing for the station's front door.

"There's some kind of emergency offshore," reported the older of the two officers. "A ham radio operator in Hamilton, Ontario intercepted a radio distress signal from Lake Erie. A ship named the *Gerken* is sending an SOS. The ham operator said that the *Gerken* is in imminent danger of sinking."

"Where is this ship supposed to be and how did you get the message?" asked Seymore as he stepped through the door and hurried to the control room.

"The radio operator in Hamilton called the Buffalo Police Department. They phoned the Coast Guard Station in Dunkirk. The Dunkirk Station couldn't raise you, so they called us. They reported that the *Gerken* is somewhere off Erie, approximately three to four miles offshore and east of town," noted the police officer.

"Baker! Do you have a sighting of the *Gerken* from tonight's beach patrols?" Seymore asked entering the control room with the officers in tow.

Cramer and Johnsten looked up from preparations to leave on the 00:30 patrol and answered before Baker could get organized. "Yes, sir," responded Cramer, "she was off the Peninsula working at 18:50 hours and again at 19:50 hours. But she was gone with no trace at 20:50."

"Where the hell did she go," asked Seymore, "and has anyone seen a distress signal? We have a report from these officers that the *Gerken* is sinking just offshore and east of Erie."

With that, Baker bolted toward the station door. "Come on," he said, "if she's really there we'll be able to see her from the channel wall!"

# CHAPTER 18

[SATURDAY, AUGUST 21, 1926, 3:45 A.M.]

*He had been trying to avoid it, but in his delirium, Wagerman's thoughts finally turned to his mother and how she would feel if he did not survive the night. He recalled her reaction to his working career on the docks. Unlike his father, she didn't seem at all disappointed when Herman told his family he would not be going to college. In her own way, Wagerman's mother was pleased that her son would be staying home and working locally. She packed lunches for him as her son continued life in the Wagerman home, leaving for the docks every morning rather than school. But when Wagerman told her that he had given up his job as a stevedore to become a sailor, she excused herself from the dinner table, went to her room and cried.*

*Wagerman tried for years to console his mother; to explain that the Gerken job was relatively safe and that as a sandsucker sailor he would not really be exposed to the dangers of being offshore. But she was not comforted. Instead, she became obsessed with his departures and arrivals and mulled obsessively over news of shipwrecks and sailors lost in the Great Lakes. She never missed an opportunity to suggest that her son change jobs. She was forever dropping newspaper clippings about shore-based job opportunities in places where Herman would find them. As Wagerman gained sailing experience he began to realize that his mother's repulsion of the sea was not unique. It was, in fact, shared by the wives and mothers of all sailors. He decided that women's distrust of the sea must somehow be instinctive.*

*Wagerman pondered the nature of women and the sea as he floated, wondering exactly where this genetic fear came from.*

# Life On-Shore

## [MID-NINETEENTH CENTURY SAILING FAMILIES]

Ask the wife or family of a sailor and they'll tell you that waiting helplessly on shore is far more difficult than braving the elements at sea. For the sailor, whose entire work life is clouded by danger, day-to-day activities aboard ship create thousands of numbing distractions. The men generally don't have time to think about it. And it's not just the work. The jokes, the camaraderie and the endless banter seem psychologically designed to deflect attention from the ever-present, low grade danger. This process of denial may represent a kind of magical thinking, or it may be an overdose of sailor testosterone. But when they are at sea in difficult weather, the sailors at least know where they are and what is happening to them. For the women who have traditionally waited, watched and hoped, however, having a sailor for a husband or a son is a terrible cross to bear. Like seaport women everywhere, the wives and mothers of Erie fully participated in the tradition of worrying over loved ones at sea.

Erie's most visible monument to the plight of its shore-bound women has always been the 1846 homestead of Charles Reed, the Great Lakes "Steamboat King." Charles was the third generation of Erie Reeds. His grandfather Seth, Erie's first settler, established the Reeds' commercial power and presence on the waterfront. Later, Charles' father Rufus propelled the family business into shipping by commissioning the first sailing vessels in the harbor. But it was young Charles who made the biggest mark on local, regional and national shipping. He could foresee the commercial potential of steamships for moving passengers and goods throughout the lakes. And when he returned to Erie, after being educated in the east, Charles talked his father out of his bias for sailing ships and began to build a major fleet of steam vessels. Unlike his father, Charles spent little time aboard his own ships, preferring to engage in business dealings instead.

When Charles Reed built his mansion near the downtown waterfront, he had his gang of ship's carpenters create a widow's walk atop the imposing structure. But his wife didn't spend much time there. The walk was primarily for Charles himself. His sojourns to the rooftop walkway were usually in the company of business associates after the opulent dinners he hosted at the mansion.

Even though there were few, if any, anxiety-filled widow's walks on the Reed mansion roof, the structure serves as a timeless reminder of the sea and its perils. It reminds locals of sailors who never came home. And indeed, there were many who lost their lives on the lakes, both local boys and others whose stories were brought to Great Lakes citizens by newspapers. The local dailies featured maritime disasters as front-page items, and it was the rare local family which could not list a relative or friend lost at sea. Even the wealthy and privileged Reed family, itself, suffered a significant loss. Charles Reed's brother-in-law, who served as ship's bursar on the Reed Line's flagship *City of Erie*, was lost at sea in 1841 when that grand old side-wheeler caught fire and sank off the bluffs fifty miles east of Erie. Generally, however, losses at sea were the burden of Erie's working class. During the nineteenth century it was the poorly-paid sailors aboard older steamers who were most at risk.

By the early twentieth century, a new breed of sailor emerged to encounter the perils of Lake Erie, the commercial fisherman. In the late 1800s, Erie's commercial fishermen perfected the use of the gill net, a deadly fish harvesting technology. Gill nets allowed fishermen in small boats (tugs) to ply the entire lake, setting nets in places where they knew they would harvest the most fish. Mild-tasting Lake Erie whitefish, pickerel and blue pike were in demand in cities as far away as New York and Chicago. By 1920, there were 120 fish tugs registered in Erie's harbor. Each boat utilized a crew of five, and most worked seven days a week, two shifts per day. This placed approximately 1,500 fishermen in daily contact with the potentially deadly waters of the lake's central basin. It was only by the grace of God, and the prayers of wives and mothers, that there were not more losses.

While the descendents of the Reeds walked their ornamental widow's walk thinking about long-gone adventures of the steamboating era, thousands of wives, mothers and children from Erie's bayfront neighborhoods walked their own widow's walks. They walked, worried and waited for the fishermen to come home. But their widow's walks were not glorious wooden structures perched atop grand downtown mansions. Instead, they were paths and overlooks along the bluffs that stood silent guard over Erie's Presque Isle Bay. Suzanne Franzesi's mother, grandmother, aunts and neighbors had all walked the bluffs waiting for their men.

As a young girl, Suzanne became painfully aware of the relationship between the weather and her mother's anxiety levels. Cold temperatures, high winds, storms, or snow were automatic thermostatic devices in Erie's waterfront neighborhoods. When the weather got dirty, the women went to the water. And when they arrived they greeted each other in quiet consoling tones, reassuring themselves that all would be well. They knew in their minds that there was nothing they could do, but in their hearts they could

worry. And they could pray. When the men were out on the tugs in a
nor'easter, Suzanne's mother would leave the house after lunch with
rosaries in hand. Her grandmother, whose friends had lost many
husbands and sons, would sit quietly in her stuffed chair with lips
moving and ancient worn rosaries flying through crippled, arthritic
fingers. She couldn't walk to the bluffs anymore, so she prayed faster.

The fish tugs were better now and the losses less frequent. But
memories of tragedy are long. A Canadian fish tug, the *Angler,* was
lost the previous year and accounts in the local press reminded the
women that danger still existed. In fact, they had all prayed for the
men of the *Angler* and their families in church that year on Trinity
Sunday. Grama Franzesi had friends whose husbands died on
the fish tugs *Trinter* and *Mischler* in 1916 and on the *Charles Reed*
in 1921.

The 1926 shipping season held special concern for Erieites.
In addition to the sinking of the *Angler,* the city of Erie had lost its
beloved excursion steamer, *Colonial,* the previous season. The 284-
foot *Colonial* was originally launched as a luxury passenger steamer
in 1885. By the early 1900s, when passenger steamer business waned,
she was brought to Erie and retrofitted for the excursion business.
The *Colonial* became a harbor fixture, sitting at the downtown Public
Dock in new coats of gleaming white paint. Admittedly, she was far
less opulent than the newer luxury liners which took summer
excursion passengers to the northern lakes, but the citizens of Erie
had grown used to her presence at the town's Public Dock and they
had evolved a true affection for the grand old lady.

*Colonial*'s owners had a busy summer excursion schedule.
They took passengers back and forth across the lake to Port Dover,
Ontario, several times per week. In addition, the *Colonial* was

available for charters, offering a variety of trips on Lake Erie. *Colonial* also offered weekend moonlight cruises featuring their own on-board orchestra and dancing. By the end of the 1925 season, most of the citizens of Erie had taken cruises aboard *Colonial* and the town had begun to think of her as their own. The daily papers would report her comings and goings, and simple ship's alterations such as a new coat of trim paint would inspire front-page news.

When headlines on September 1, 1925, announced the sinking of the *Colonial* thirty miles east of town, shock waves reverberated through Erie. *Colonial* had completed a round trip to Port Dover on Saturday, August 31, before departing on her moonlight cruise with 800 passengers. Her moonlight cruises were immensely popular and that particular August evening had been perfect. Glistening stars and a gentle offshore breeze made the night seem magical. As soon as the ship discharged her passengers, she left the harbor and steamed east to pick up an excursion charter in Dunkirk, New York. Her itinerary was to take her from Dunkirk to Crystal Beach, Ontario early the next morning after which she was to stop at Port Dover to return weekending excursioners to Erie on Sunday evening. *Colonial* cleared Erie's channel at 11:30 p.m.. As she did, Captain Robert Parsons handed the wheel to the first mate and went to bed. He was exhausted from being on the bridge since early that morning.

At 1:55 a.m., the crew reported a fire near the ship's bow. The first mate left the bridge to investigate and his inspection revealed a major fire. Flames were spreading rapidly, and to make matters worse, life jackets stored forward over the decks were beginning to spontaneously ignite. The first mate raced back to the wheelhouse where he simultaneously ordered the fire detail to the bow and wheeled *Colonial* hard to starboard so he could head *Colonial* toward the safety of shore. As he steamed for the beach, the first mate began ringing the ship's alarm bell to signal off-duty crew to come on deck. Unfortunately, however, the chief engineer misunderstood the alarm signal and shut down the ship's engines. By the time a bleary-eyed Captain Parsons reached the bridge, *Colonial* was doomed. Without power, the crew was unable to operate the firehoses. Dead in the water, with a rapidly escalating fire, captain and crew watched helplessly as fire relentlessly consumed the flammables aboard the metal ship. When flames reached the after-section, the crew went overboard to avoid being burned to death. The Coast Guard reached the ship quickly, but three crew members had already died in the water. Two days later, firemen extinguished the last of the flames from shore.

On Trinity Sunday 1926, the traditional first day of commercial fishing for Erie's Portuguese Community, Suzanne Franzesi and her family went to 9:00 Mass at St. Andrew's Church. They prayed for the deceased crew of the *Colonial* and their families that day. They also prayed that no sailors would die during the 1926 season.

# PART SEVEN

# Widow's Walks

*I received a card from a man in Scotland*

*who said he prayed every day for sailors at sea.*

*I have since joined him in this practice.*

*Few people realize that they have this wonderful power.*

*It's like turning on an electric light.*

*You don't know the source of the power,*

*you just need faith that it will go on!*

**Sheila Chichester**
*Gipsy Moth Circles the World*

# Chapter 19

[Saturday, August 21, 1926, 3:50 a.m.]

*Wagerman was sleeping more now. The reality that greeted him when he awoke stood in stark and frightening contrast to the places where his mind had taken him. So he spent most of his time dreaming about Suzanne, and finding himself totally seduced by his internal images of her. He was far more comfortable with her in his sleeping visions than he had been in real life; able to share his feelings and tell her just how much he loved her. In dreaming Wagerman was self-assured, confident and clever rather than the bumbling person that he had been when he first met her. And in his dreams she spoke back to him, offering reassurance and telling him how much she loved him.*

*When his eyes were open, Wagerman saw nothing but the horrific sights of waves and darkness. But when he closed them, he was whisked to wonderfully warm places where he could meet Suzanne. So he closed his eyes once more, taking refuge in the warmth of his imagination. This time, however, his dream was more vivid than ever. Suzanne didn't join him in the water. Instead she was standing in front of him and beckoning for him to follow her. The clarity of her image confused Wagerman and he opened his eyes to see if he was really dreaming. As his vision cleared, Wagerman was shocked to see Suzanne actually standing in front of him, suspended on the waves and calling him.*

*He stared at this apparition in disbelief, while she motioned to him, saying, "This way, Herman! Hurry! Follow me!"*

*He tried to make his eyes focus on the image of Suzanne, but just as he was organizing his senses, he dropped off the crest of a wave and fell into a dark trough.*

*Wagerman shook his head. "God," he thought. "I'm starting to hallucinate."*

*He rode to the top of the next wave trying to decide if his eyes had actually been open when he saw Suzanne. Even though he was a practical man by nature, he strained to look toward the place where he had just seen her as he rose to next wave crest. Cupping his hands around his eyes, he stared intently to the north.*

*"Damn it," he exclaimed to himself, "there is something out there!"*

*He didn't see it on every wave, but when two crests were just right, with Wagerman and the apparition both suspended on wave tops, he could make out a standing silhouette.*

*"How could she be out here in the waves?" he mused, as he strained to see more clearly. He watched in amazement while the silhouette began to move closer. In an instant, Wagerman began to realize that the shape he was seeing wasn't Suzanne Franzesi at all. It was a pair of sailboat masts.*

*"Why would a sailboat be out in this kind of weather?" he wondered to himself.*

*In any event it was a boat, and anything was better than floating in a life jacket and waiting to freeze to death. Motivated by Suzanne's beckoning call, Wagerman swam for all he was worth toward two masts that were somehow heading right toward him in the center of the desolate lake. He wasn't going to question why they were there. He was swimming for his life.*

*With only a hundred yards to go, he stopped to get his bearings and try to attract the attention of the people on the small sailboat. Just as he organized himself, however, a rattling sound erupted from the boat. Wagerman watched in horror while the two masts popped straight into the air, abandoning the angle at which they had been attacking the wind. Then with a slow spin, the sailboat turned its beam toward Wagerman and tacked away. Wagerman could see the outline of a man on the foredeck, gathering a headsail as the sailboat continued its spin onto a new tack. When the boat's stern came into view, Wagerman could read* Pterodactyl, EYC. *He screamed for help, but the din of the waves drowned out his voice. He could barely hear himself!*

*"What was Suzanne trying to tell him?" he wondered. "Surely she couldn't have been aboard* Pterodactyl *that night, so what psychic connection brought me so close to the sailboat?" He knew that it had to be more than a coincidence, but in his exhausted and confused state, Wagerman didn't have the energy to contemplate such matters as chance. Exhausted from the effort of swimming, he began to slip toward sleep once more. This time his imagination drove him back toward memories of* Pterodactyl *and its owner, Ben Cooley.*

# Swimming for Long Point

## [FRIDAY, AUGUST 20, 1926, 12:00 NOON]

Ben Cooley and George Stickle sat in *Pterodactyl*'s cockpit, anchored off Long Point's north beach. As they sat, they watched cottonwood trees a half mile away on the south beach bend in the wind. They both realized that the impending return trip was not likely to be pleasant. It was raining and the sky was a deep, ominous gray. Stickle was reluctant to leave but Cooley was convinced that they should go.

"If we don't start soon there's no way we'll be back before midnight," he grumbled, "and if we miss tomorrow night's dinner party we'll both be in the dog house at work."

Reluctantly, Stickle moved forward to pull *Pterodactyl*'s anchor. Even in the shelter of the north beach, the wind was strong enough to make the job of lifting the anchor extremely difficult. Eventually, Cooley went forward to help with the anchor and by 12:30 p.m., *Pterodactyl* was underway. Even with shortened sail, Pterodactyl was literally screaming along the north side of Long Point. The little yawl cut through the water making a gurgling sound as she moved at hull speed.

"Nice ride, eh?" remarked Cooley, emulating the expressions of their Canadian friends from the previous evening's card game.

Still skeptical, Stickle worked his way into a cockpit corner and muttered something about how the waves in the middle of the lake might be a little bit rougher than the flat water behind the point. True to his prediction, *Pterodactyl* was laid over on her side the moment she emerged from the protection of Long Point. Without saying anything, Stickle climbed to his feet and put a second reef in the mainsail, easing the motion.

"Nice ride, eh?" Stickle repeated sarcastically as he returned to his cockpit niche.

Cooley looked down at the compass and had his first misgivings as he noted that the best course *Pterodactyl* could manage was 130 degrees. The course to Erie was 190.

"Tell me the bad news," Stickle grumbled, as he watched his friend study the compass. "What's our course?"

"We can hold 130 degrees," noted Cooley in a sarcastically cheerful voice while *Pterodactyl* blasted through the waves.

"Are you kidding?" asked Stickle. "That's 60 degrees off the rhumb line course to Erie, we'll never get home at that rate!"

"Let's get away from the tip of the point and try bringing her about," suggested Stickle. "If we can do 220 or 230 degrees on the port tack, we'll be better off."

"Good idea," noted Cooley. "We'll sail for an hour, then try a tack."

At 2:00 p.m. Stickle and Cooley prepared for the first tack of the day. Yawls are generally difficult to bring about, a general characteristic of the design. But *Pterodactyl* was even more cantankerous than other yawls her size because of her short keel and long water line, so Cooley and Stickle took care to wait for the right moment. With Stickle glued to the jib lines, Cooley picked a spot atop a particularly short, non-breaking wave and pushed the tiller to starboard. The wooden yawl reluctantly climbed to the top of the wave, then descended into its trough without completing the tack.

Instead of sliding gently from starboard to port tack, *Pterodactyl* came head to wind with sails flapping, then stopped dead in the water.

"Shit!" muttered Stickle as he struggled to hold both jib sheets at the same time. Gritting his teeth, he waited as *Pterodactyl* rounded back up on its original tack near the top of the next wave. At the top of the crest, the wind hit the sails like a sledgehammer and dumped *Pterodactyl* onto her side where she sat motionless for almost a minute. Gradually, the wind caught her mainsail, lifting her back up and she slowly began to move through the water again.

"Great tack," noted Cooley with a sardonic smile. "Maybe we'll adjust our strategy and stay on starboard for a while," he added

"Why not," noted Stickle, "I always wanted to sail to Buffalo."

"Think of it this way," chuckled Cooley, "even if we stay on this tack and head for Buffalo, we'll get closer and closer to the American shore. Eventually we'll get some protection from the waves. When the water calms down, we'll try the port tack again."

"Okay," muttered Stickle, "I guess I really didn't want to try tacking again right now anyway!"

*Pterodactyl* and her crew carried on for six hours, sailing generally east and struggling to make southerly headway. But as the day wore on and the sky began to signal nightfall, Cooley and Stickle grew concerned that they were not making southerly progress. Between 2:00 and 8:00 p.m. the waves and winds continued to build, reaching velocities which the two judged to be between forty and fifty miles per hour. Instead of pointing higher into the building waves, *Pterodactyl* was forced to run off to the north while the wind was literally blowing whitecaps off the tops of the crests.

# [FRIDAY, AUGUST 20, 1926, 8:30 P.M.]

The skies darkened prematurely that night. As they did, Cooley and Stickle began to realize that they had very little idea of their position on the lake. They had been sailing easterly, alternating between 120 and 140 degrees for much of the day on a continuous starboard tack. But they still couldn't see the southern shoreline. The waves were not calming as they had hoped. Instead, they were growing in size and breaking intensity, with vicious whitecaps knocking *Pterodactyl* off the top of each successive wave. The motion was extremely tiring and the two, who started out alternating one-hour shifts at the tiller, were now changing place every twenty minutes.

"We're not getting anywhere," muttered Cooley, as *Pterodactyl* was blasted off the top of a particularly nasty wave.

"I agree," added Stickle, "let's do something different. What if we take the mizzen sail down?" he continued. "Do you think we could put her on another tack?"

"Let's give it a try," added Cooley.

So the two set to work reducing *Pterodactyl*'s sail.

"We'll put her on a port tack and sail back to the west. Maybe the sky will clear as it gets dark so we can see where we are," added Stickle.

"Good idea," answered Cooley. "If we're still in the middle of the lake, I'm ready to call it an evening. Dinner party or not we'll sail back to Long Point and anchor in Gravely Bay again."

"Let's go!" cried Stickle.

Cooley put *Pterodactyl*'s rudder over, but this time, even though the waves and winds were stronger than before, the little yawl responded well, coming about under shortened sail and snapping to attention on the opposite tack.

"Great tack," yelled Cooley. "Let's head for Erie!"

"She's pointing west for sure," noted Stickle, "but with our leeway I doubt that we'll be anywhere near Erie. My guess is that we'll be at least ten miles offshore when we get back to the original rhumb line."

The two pressed on, pounding through southerly winds and waves until Cooley's watch indicated that it was 10:00 p.m.

"So where are we?" asked Cooley rhetorically, watching Stickle scour both the north and south horizons for lights.

*Pterodactyl* had settled down with her reefed sail and was making a steady three or four knots as she plodded westward on a bearing of 235 degrees.

"Damned if I know," answered Stickle, glancing at his watch, "but I think we're making better progress on this tack."

"My guess is that we passed the Long Point–Erie rhumb line, and that we're heading for Cleveland. Great night, eh! Tack toward Buffalo for a while, then head toward Cleveland. At this rate they'll be having that dinner party tomorrow night and we'll still be tacking back and forth in thirty-foot waves."

"You were right," muttered Cooley. "If we had stayed in Gravely Bay at least we'd be having fun." At that, he began to retch for the third time that night, spilling the last traces of the breakfast he had eaten twelve hours earlier.

## [FRIDAY, AUGUST 20, 1926, 10:30 P.M.]

"Look at that," exclaimed Ben Cooley, pointing astern. "Lights!"

"Couldn't be land," answered Stickle from the tiller. "It's too far north."

"Almost looks due east of us. It must be a ship," answered Cooley. "Come on let's tack back and head toward it. At least we'll feel better if we have company."

Without a second encouragement, Stickle put the tiller across the cockpit and brought *Pterodactyl* smartly about onto a starboard tack. Perhaps too smartly, since Cooley wasn't quite ready on the jib sheets. *Pterodactyl* came around with her jib tied off on the windward side and a breaking wave picked the boat up and rolled it almost horizontally onto her beam.

"Shit!" exclaimed Cooley, grabbing for the winch as he fell across the cockpit.

There was a loud tearing sound that indicated trouble on the foredeck. *Pterodactyl*'s sail had fouled on a whisker pole and in an instant there was chaos. Sounds of splintering wood, tearing cloth and grinding deck hardware punctuated the dull roar of breaking waves.

"Sorry. I guess I screwed up," muttered Stickle from the helm.

"Not your fault," offered Cooley as he inched his way onto the foredeck to survey the damage. "Fall off a little!" Cooley yelled from the bow.

"Be careful up there," answered Stickle as he brought the helm to port and eased *Pterodactyl*'s motion.

Ten minutes later Cooley was back in the cockpit and the noise had quieted down.

"Ripped the bottom of the jib, blew up a block and sl
the whisker pole," he commented. "Nothing too serious."

"Did you fix it?" asked Stickle.

"Shortened the jib and tied the clew to a new block. The
whisker pole is finished, so I lashed it down," Cooley answered. "Now
let's see if we can get her back up on the wind," he added, taking over
the helm.

It was 10:45 p.m. and both men could clearly see the lights of a
second ship. The first ship that they had spotted was three or four
miles east of them and slightly south. The second was well off to the
north and heading west. As they gazed at the lights of the two ships,
flares suddenly illuminated the waters from the ship that was east of
them.

"What do you think it means?" asked Stickle.

"They must be in trouble," answered Cooley as the pair watched
dozens of flares go off over a fifteen minute period.

The flares stopped and the two architects watched running
lights reappear from the muddy red glow of flares on the eastern
horizon. Then, without warning, a monstrous wall of fire erupted
from the ship. Flames totally illuminated the night sky, making the
waves seem even more ominous. As fire lit the night sky, they could
see glimpses of Long Point across the port side of the bow.

"Jesus!" Cooley muttered. "What was that?"

"I don't know," answered Stickle. "Either that ship is on fire, or
it's another distress signal."

The two watched the flame for several minutes until it went
out. After the fire subsided, the lights of the ship were clearly visible
but they weren't running lights. Instead, the ship seemed to be
emitting a strange glow.

Darkness returned and Cooley and Stickle began to recognize and take stock of their own circumstances.

"We've been sailing for more than twelve hours and we're still within sight of Long Point," Stickle muttered in obvious disappointment. "How far are we from Erie?" he continued, almost afraid to hear the answer.

"Maybe twelve or fifteen miles," answered Cooley. "We've been sailing back and forth almost parallel to the tip of Long Point," he added. "The leeway in these waves is killing us!"

"Since we can see the lighthouse, maybe we should give up and head back for Gravely Bay," muttered Stickle. "Tomorrow has to be a better day."

"Let's press on toward the ship's lights ahead of us. Perhaps there is trouble over there and we can be of assistance," he added. "If we're not making southerly progress by the time we get there we'll give up and head downwind for Long Point," offered Cooley.

"Okay," added Stickle, "but I wonder how we could be of any help. We probably need to be rescued ourselves."

As *Pterodactyl* sailed east toward the mystery lights, they noticed that the ship which was north of them changed course and seemed to be coming directly toward them.

"They must be heading for the fire, too," noted Stickle as he watched the lights come closer.

*Pterodactyl* plodded on, heading toward the location of the mystery vessel, but the closer they came to the fading glow from the ship, the more the southerly waves seemed to push them north. Using the lights as a benchmark, Cooley could finally measure the immense leeway that was keeping *Pterodactyl* from closing on the American shore. Over the next hour, the yawl slid well to the north of the ship that had been sending off flares, missing it by more than a mile. While they continued east, the second ship, which had changed course and headed south toward them, crossed their stern and headed directly for the ship which seemed to be in distress. At 1:00 a.m., the glowing light that had been radiating from the mystery ship quite suddenly went out. It was as though someone had switched the lights off. Cooley and Stickle were puzzled and disturbed by the sudden disappearance. Refusing to believe that it had happened, Cooley stood in the cockpit, held onto the boom and scanned the horizon. The running lights of the big ship that had crossed their bow were still visible and seemed to be closing on the location of the mystery ship.

"That's crazy," he stated. "Five minutes ago we were watching those lights. They couldn't have been more than a few miles away! How could that happen? And look! The other ship is almost at the place where the lights were! Could it be rumrunners signaling each other?" he mused.

"Are you kidding?" offered Stickle. "Only crazy people would be out in this kind of stuff."

"I think it must be a sign," continued Stickle. "A sign from God that we should get the hell off this lake! Come on, Ben, let's head back for Long Point, I'm just about out of energy."

Cooley knew his friend was right, but something was compelling him to continue on starboard tack. As he sailed east, his thoughts drifted to Suzanne Franzesi. Ben Cooley knew that he had used terrible judgement in trying to sail to Erie that night but he somehow reasoned that he had done it because of Suzanne. He wanted to make this trip up to her; to promise that there would be another opportunity to sail to Long Point. He just couldn't stop thinking about her as *Pterodactyl* pounded along toward the east. In his tired, semi-groggy state, he began to think that he could hear Suzanne's voice imploring him to change to a port tack.

Cooley stayed on starboard tack for another ninety minutes, wondering why his thoughts of Suzanne were compelling him not to do the obvious: to give up and turn for Long Point. He couldn't shake the intuitive feeling that he should tack back toward the west.

"Let's try just one more tack," he muttered to Stickle. "We'll try heading as close to the wind as possible and use that big ship as a guide. If we're not making southerly progress after a half hour we'll give up."

"Okay," answered Stickle, "one more try!"

*Pterodactyl* came about and Cooley headed the yawl on a close port tack, aiming for the navigational lights that were now southwest of him. As he fought to bring *Pterodactyl* higher on the wind, the ship's motion became more difficult and their progress through the waves slowed noticeably. They were sailing at almost 60 degrees to the wind and moving through the water at only two or three knots. The ship that had crossed their stern seemed to be circling near the place where the lights of the first ship had been. By using it as a benchmark to judge *Pterodactyl*'s leeway, Cooley could see that Pterodactyl was slipping steadily away to the north. Cooley was conflicted. Watching the expression on his friend's face, he realized that he should give up this struggle to the south and head for Long Point. But his thoughts of Suzanne compelled him to continue on the port tack. Finally, the intellectual side of his brain overruled his emotions and Cooley made the logical decision.

"Come on, George," he said to his friend, "let's fall off and get back to Gravely Bay. There's no way that we're going to get to Erie in these waves."

"I wondered when you would come to your senses," muttered George Stickle. "Let's head north before we're beat to a pulp!"

At 3:52 a.m. Cooley moved *Pterodactyl* through a slow tack to starboard. As he did, George Stickle pulled the damaged headsail to the deck, holding on for his life as the yawl snapped to attention on a starboard run for Long Point. Ben Cooley eased the tiller and brought *Pterodactyl* to a course of 15 degrees.

"We're right on line for the lighthouse," said Coolly. "Ease the sheets and let's go!"

## [SATURDAY, AUGUST 21, 1926, 4:00 A.M.]

Running downwind in the big waves, even with reduced sail, was substantially faster than plodding upwind through them. In fact it was so much faster that it was frightening. *Pterodactyl* would rise to the top of each big curling crest, then perch there for seconds, surfing along at speeds that neither Coolly nor Stickle had ever experienced. When the little yawl finally fell from a wave crest, her stern would sink first, falling like a stone into the depression that preceded the next white-capped monster. Then, just as it seemed that the yawl was standing almost upright on her stern, the next wave would straighten her and lift her into the air again. *Pterodactyl's* sails would fill one more time and she would surf up to the top of the next wave.

By 5:00 a.m. *Pterodactyl* was within five miles of Long Point's south beach and sailing at more than eight knots. But Cooley was noticing that her course through the waves was bringing her alarmingly close to jibing as she fell into the depressions between waves. Cooley steered his way through the waves and struggled to keep the boat headed for the tip of Long Point, which was clearly visible from the wave tops. Steering carefully and trying not to jibe, he realized that when *Pterodactyl* got to the end of the point he would have to put her onto a port tack again to get around the tip. But he wasn't anxious to do so until he was closer to the beach. Cooley fully realized that these waves would put *Pterodactyl* in peril during a tack, and he was reluctant to try tacking so far offshore.

In addition to being south of Long Point's beaches, *Pterodactyl* was a mile west of the tip of the point, so Cooley brought her even lower on the wind heading as far to the east as he dared without risking an accidental jibe. With the yawl running almost directly downwind, her motion changed dramatically. *Pterodactyl* began to roll severely as she dove into the depressions between waves.

Stickle looked over his shoulder at the wave crests and questioned the change of course.

"I hate to mention this," he said, "but it seems like the closer we get to the beaches, the steeper these waves become!"

The words were hardly out of his mouth when disaster struck. *Pterodactyl* slipped into a trough between two particularly steep waves and the crest of the following sea was so large that it blocked the wind. The sails collapsed, and *Pterodactyl* immediately broached and rolled sideways. Instead of rising up and over the next wave as it hit, the breaking crest filled the cockpit, weighing the yawl down in the water, stern first. Ben Cooley frantically pushed the tiller to straighten the boat out and head back toward the direction of the waves, but *Pterodactyl's* response was agonizingly slow. She was pooped, with water pouring into her cabin from the cockpit. The next wave filled the cockpit a second time, and while Cooley continued his struggle to straighten *Pterodactyl* out, the gradual turn to port accelerated. No matter what he did with the tiller, the yawl kept rolling to the left.

"We're going to jibe!" yelled Stickle.

"I can't hold her back," answered Cooley. "She won't respond to the tiller!"

The two sat in waist-deep water watching helplessly while the little wooden yawl slowly rolled from starboard to a port tack. Rising to the crest of a wave as she jibed, a blast of wind hit her sails and brought the rig down with a sound that was louder than the crack of a rifle. In an instant, broken bits of spars, wire rigging, sheets and sailcloth covered everything. It looked as though a bomb had exploded on deck. Both main and mizzenmasts were draped across the topsides and dragging through the water. Cooley sprang into action first, racing below for a knife. He worked frantically to cut away the tangled lines, Stickle dragged *Pterodactyl's* sea anchor out of a cockpit locker and deployed it. To do so, he had to crawl slowly to the bow along the starboard rail and tie its 100-foot line to a cleat. The moment the sea anchor opened itself in the water, *Pterodactyl* began to turn so that her bow headed into the waves. Instantaneously, her motion eased. *Pterodactyl* was lying quietly, bow to weather, a momentary oasis of tranquility.

"Whew," remarked Cooley, "for a minute there I thought we were in trouble."

"Great!" noted Stickle. "I'm glad to hear that we aren't really in any trouble. We're just five miles offshore, in twenty-five foot waves on a dismasted boat. That's not a problem, is it?" he muttered sardonically.

"It's going to be all right," answered Cooley. "We're going to sit here and wait while we wash right up on the south beach at Long Point. When the weather calms down tomorrow we'll rescue the boat and tow her back around the tip of Long Point to Gravely Bay."

Stickle surveyed the scene and reluctantly decided that Cooley might be right. *Pterodactyl*'s rig was down, but the sea anchor had eased her motion and she was drifting rapidly through the waves toward Long Point. Stickle knelt quietly in the cockpit with Cooley, bailing water and watching *Pterodactyl*'s drift-course.

"Not to disappoint you, Ben," he offered after several moments, "but I don't think we're going to drift onto the beach. Take a look at our course. We're going to slide by, to the east of the point. And what do you propose that we do then?" he asked. "If we drift past the tip of Long Point at this angle, it's at least fifteen or twenty more miles to the mainland!"

Cooley stopped bailing and studied *Pterodactyl*'s progress. "Damn it, you're right!" he noted. "We do have a problem."

Cooley began tweaking *Pterodactyl*'s sea anchor rig. First he lashed the tiller hard to port which brought the angle of the yawl closer to the desired course. Then he moved the sea anchor line to the starboard rail and tied it down.

"Let's see if that helps," he noted, seemingly pleased with his adjustments.

"Makes the motion harder," Stickle noted as *Pterodactyl* began yawing violently against the sea anchor, "but it looks like it might work."

They watched the new motion nervously, wondering if it was going to be too hard on *Pterodactyl*. Their unstated questions were abruptly answered when the sea anchor burst violently, disintegrating into tiny pieces. Instantly, *Pterodactyl* was back in trouble, rolling ponderously to port.

"What next?" asked Stickle.

"Get some blankets from down below," yelled Cooley, as he crawled to the rail for the sea anchor line.

Working frantically, Stickle and Cooley tied a blanket to the sea anchor line. Using a knife to puncture the corners they tied it into a crude replacement sea anchor. By the time they had thrown the blanket-sea anchor over the side, *Pterodactyl* was filled with water again. All of their bailing had been for nothing. The makeshift sea anchor lasted less than ten minutes and exploded in the same manner as the original one.

"This is a waste of time," yelled Cooley. "Let's try dropping the regular anchor."

Stickle retrieved *Pterodactyl*'s fifteen-pound naval anchor and laid it, with its 200 feet of line, on the stern. Then he took the bitter end and crawled along the starboard rail to tie it to *Pterodactyl*'s bow cleat. As he inched his way forward, a breaking wave enveloped the yawl, filling the cockpit and rolling *Pterodactyl* hard to starboard. As *Pterodactyl* dipped, the anchor went overboard. Cooley grabbed the running anchor line and secured it to the starboard winch so the bitter end would not be yanked from Stickle's hand. *Pterodactyl* was in more than 100 feet of water, but when the anchor hit the sandy, shoaling bottom it caught and held for a brief second. And that was all it took. The line tightened, momentarily holding *Pterodactyl*'s stern to the bottom and exposing her cockpit to the waves. A huge crest crashed into her. And then another.

*Pterodactyl* made a moaning sound, probably not unlike the cry emitted by her namesake creatures, as they were dying million of years earlier. As she groaned in agony, the varnished white sailboat stood almost vertically on her stern with the anchor successively nipping at, then holding her to the lake bottom. All of the water that had collected in the cabin rushed into her below-deck aft sections and she sank, stern first.

In shocked horror, Cooley and Stickle floated upward past the cockpit, to the foredeck and finally, past the bow. Cooley made an instinctive effort to grab the bow pulpit, but in an instant he realized that *Pterodactyl* was taking him under with her, so he released his death grip and struggled to the surface. An instant later, Cooley and Stickle were alone in the blackness of Lake Erie, swimming for Long Point and for their lives.

# CHAPTER 20

## [SATURDAY, AUGUST 21, 1926, 4:00 A.M.]

*Pterodactyl was gone and Wagerman was alone again with his dreams. With dawn so close, he began to worry about falling into a final sleep. Desperate, he began to play mental games, trying not to be seduced by sleep. But he was so cold that all of his attempts at intellectual gymnastics inevitably seemed to make him fall asleep rather than stay alert. Times tables, spelling games, attempts to recall the names of the children from his first grade class. The repetitious thoughts all seemed to be mantras that sent him careening toward sleep. And he knew that he must resist the temptation to sleep, at least until dawn when he might be spotted by a rescue ship.*

*He had been in the water for more than three hours now and he could no longer feel or move his legs. They felt like someone else's legs, lead weights dangling lifelessly below the surface of the water. Wagerman painfully turned himself to the east so that he was facing Buffalo. Gazing at the horizon, he strained wishfully, hoping to see the skyline of his hometown.*

*"Wouldn't it be wonderful," he mused, "if I could be magically transported to the downtown docks. I would just climb out of the water and walk home."*

*As his imagination painted images of Buffalo, a bolt of green light suddenly flashed across the horizon. Like St. Elmo's Fire, the flash seemed to come right at him. Its intensity and clarity caused Wagerman to instinctively duck, splashing water on his face as he twisted in his life jacket. The shock of the experience awakened him.*

*"God," he thought to himself, "did I really see the green flash?" Sailors always talked about the infamous green flash, a supposed good luck omen, but few had ever seen it. Or at least, admitted so.*

*Just as he was thinking about how lucky he was, he returned to his reality and laughed at himself. "Good luck, bad luck," he muttered.*

*He caught himself wondering if what he had seen was real or imaginary. Obsessively puzzling over this problem, he decided that it would be better to do something useful. So Wagerman began to scan the horizon again, hoping to spot a rescue ship. He scoured the edges of his world while he paddled himself slowly through a 360-degree circle.*

*Wagerman was less than halfway around when he saw it. A large ship was heading right toward him. Wagerman stared in disbelief and watched the ship approach. The green flash might have been imaginary, but this ship certainly wasn't. Wagerman began to wonder how he could signal them and if they might have already spotted him when the ship made a long slow turn to the north and began to steam away. For the second time, a rescue ship was leaving him. Wagerman didn't recognize the ship as it turned. He couldn't be sure if it was the car ferry* Maitland, *but he hoped that it was.*

*"At least someone is still out here looking for us," he thought to himself.*

*Pleased that the rescuers had not given up, Wagerman decided that whoever it had been, they were probably making systematic runs, searching for him and his friends. All he had to do was to stay awake until it came back on its next pass. With any luck it might be daylight by then.*

*Wagerman thought about luck and about how he and his friends had come so close to being saved that night. He wondered what the vision of the green flash had to do with the* Maitland *and the rope that broke, sending him into the water.*

# *Rescue*

## [SATURDAY, AUGUST 21, 1926, 12:06 A.M.]

"How long since we changed course, Pete?" asked Captain Heyman who was peering intently through *Maitland*'s wheelhouse window.

"Almost fifty minutes since we came about for the signal flame," noted Brinley.

"If we're making eight knots through these waves, we've come about seven miles," added Burke.

"So if the flame we spotted was ten miles away when we first saw it, we could be within two or three miles of whatever it was," noted Heyman.

"Yup, Cap," added Brinley, "almost close enough to see something if it's out there."

"Look at that!" exclaimed Bill Burke. "The anemometer just hit eighty-two miles an hour! I'm not sure we can even estimate our speed in this kind of stuff," he added.

"Whatever is out there should be dead on the bow," added Heyman while studying Brinley's nods of agreement. "If it's a ship in distress and it is disabled, it will be sliding down the waves toward us since we're heading upwind," noted Heyman. "I think we should get a watchman on top of the wheelhouse," added Heyman. "I hate to post a man outside in this weather, but if we get someone up high, he might be able to spot something."

"Good idea," added Brinley.

In an instant, Pete was on deck talking to the crew. Even though commercial sailors tease each other incessantly about their ships, no other occupation has such a long history of coming to each other's assistance during emergencies. The very sailors who had been beating each other's brains out in a bar fight a day earlier were willing to risk life and limb in a disaster. *Maitland*'s full complement of crew was on deck, dressed in foul weather gear and waiting. Brinley's request was eagerly followed by three crew members who scrambled up the steel ladder to the roof of the wheelhouse. Brinley reentered the wheelhouse and not a full minute later, a crew member descended from the rooftop lookout. He burst through the door and blurted out the bad news.

"Dead ahead about two miles, sir," he said. "And maybe just a point or two to port! It's a big ship. She's turning turtle and lying just barely above the surface of the water."

"What else can you see?" asked Heyman.

"Nothing much," responded the seaman. "It's too far away."

"I'll go up there and keep an eye on our course," offered Brinley, heading for the wheelhouse roof.

The next half hour saw what has been described as one of the Great Lakes most remarkable acts of seamanship. And by an "acting" captain! First, Thomas Heyman ordered *Maitland*'s engineer to increase speed to an uncomfortable level. He knew that if crew members went into the water and began to float away on a night like this, it would be next to impossible to find them. Heyman worried that if a ship turned turtle in these seas, the crew might not have had time to deploy lifeboats. And even if they were able to launch the lifeboats, in these conditions it would be only a matter of time until sailors aboard open boats would be soaking wet and suffering from hypothermia. As *Maitland* crashed south through the waves, Brinley stepped into the wheelhouse.

"Captain!" he yelled. "She's about to go down! We can see her clearly now from the roof. The hull is overturned but the magnetos must still be running, because there are lights glowing from under the water. She's sliding under real fast. In ten minutes it will be gone!"

"Can you see any people?" asked Heyman.

"Not a soul," answered Brinley, "they must have gotten off already."

"Or else they're trapped inside," offered Burke.

## [SATURDAY, AUGUST 21, 1926, 12:50 A.M.]

"How much farther?" asked Heyman.

"No more than a half mile," answered Brinley. "We can't see them yet because of the waves and the fact that the ship is somehow lying just below the surface. It seems to be floating just a few feet below the water! Waves are breaking right across the tops of the upside down hull."

Heyman swung *Maitland*'s wheel 20 degrees to starboard and slowed the ship.

"But she's almost dead ahead," questioned Brinley.

"I know," answered Heyman. "I don't want to hit anybody in the water! I'm going to swing around in a circle to starboard and then come up behind the ship. That will give anybody in the water some protection in the lee of our hull. If there's anyone around here they will have seen our lights by now. I'm going to park and hope that they can get to us somehow. You keep an eye on the position where the ship is going down, Pete, and watch for sailors in the water, " Heyman added, "while I round up to weather."

Silently, *Maitland* powered past the site where the stricken ship had been, passing a few hundred yards to the south. Then Heyman allowed the car ferry to come to a full stop and slowly drift down the wreckage field.

"Look, Cap!" yelled Bill Burke a few moments later. "A lifeboat three hundred yards ahead and just to port."

"Okay," replied Heyman. "I'm going to come up behind them. Pete, you get up on deck and get some lines ready. We'll drift down on them."

"Got it, Cap," answered Brinley.

"Bill! You stay with me and watch to see how I'm doing when we get them in our sights," added Heyman.

Thomas Heyman guided the big car ferry around behind the first lifeboat, and the men aboard the tiny craft cheered. They could see what the captain of the car ferry was doing and they began to help with the maneuver by rowing into the swath of calmed water in *Maitland*'s lee. Slowly but surely, Captain Thomas Heyman brought the big car ferry beam-to-wind, two hundred yards upwind of the first lifeboat. Heyman slipped *Maitland*'s propellers into reverse as he made the turn. Even though the car ferry reacted violently to the cross momentum of the wind on her beam and the reversing engines, *Maitland* came to a virtual standstill less than one hundred yards upwind from the lifeboat. Heyman held the big ship in place in the churning waters while the calming effect of its wall of steel allowed the men in the lifeboat to bring their rowing dory within yards of the car ferry. With the lifeboat moving ever closer to the *Maitland*, the southeast winds pushed the car ferry down to meet it. Eventually the two boats came within a few feet of each other and Pete Brinley tossed a line to the lifeboat.

Now the problem was getting the men out of the lifeboat, which rode the waves almost twelve feet below the deck of the car ferry. *Gerken*'s engineer, Jesse Gerken, helped solve this problem from his position in the front of the lifeboat by allowing the dory to drift away from *Maitland* so that its pitching in the waves did not exactly match that of the car ferry. Using his considerable size and strength to hold the lifeboat steady, he and Brinley worked together timing the motion of the two ships. When the wave action was just right and the lifeboat rose while the car ferry fell, a crew member could be plucked out of the small boat and lifted aboard *Maitland* with a rope harness. It was laborious work, especially for Jesse Gerken, who stood at the gunnel of the lifeboat for twenty minutes, controlling the motion until each crew member was lifted to safety. When Jesse Gerken, the last to be saved, was finally dragged aboard, he hit the deck with a terrible thump. Even in his nearly exhausted state he quickly climbed to his feet and asked to see the captain of the car ferry. Brinley took Jesse Gerken to the wheelhouse to meet Thomas Heyman.

"Please don't move from here, captain," he pleaded before he was even introduced. "There are two more lifeboats out here somewhere."

Even as Jesse Gerken spoke, Bill Burke spotted a second lifeboat. It was much smaller than the first, and rowing steadily toward *Maitland*. "There's one of them now," he cried out, pointing to the northeast.

"They're rowing right up the patch of calm water in our lee," added Pete Brinley. "Hold her steady and I'll go down and get them," Brinley added.

Heyman turned the wheel over to William Burke and followed Brinley down to the rail. Jesse Gerken went with them, even though Heyman offered him his own cabin so that he could rest.

"Doesn't that figure," muttered Jesse Gerken as he studied the small lifeboat. "It's Wagerman and Logan!"

"Who?" asked Heyman.

"Our terrible twosome. They're always figuring out some new way to cheat death," Gerken added.

The rowing dory approached *Maitland*'s rail and Brinley tossed them a line. At the same time, crew members along the rail started shouting and pointing east where they had spotted the third lifeboat. "Lifeboat number three, a quarter mile to starboard," a crew member yelled.

"Is that all of them?" asked Heyman.

"Yes," answered Jesse Gerken, "and thank God, that's the boat with my brothers on it and the cook's son!"

"Okay," added Heyman, "we'll get this crew aboard, then go get the third lifeboat. Get someone to keep a watch on the third lifeboat, Pete, while we secure this bunch."

"I'm on it, Cap," added Pete Brinley as he cleated the line that connected *Maitland* to the lifeboat.

The line, which tethered the little dory and its crew of four to the big ship, was passed to the big man who had been rowing the dory. He, in turn, stood bracing himself against the bow of the dinghy, using his strength to hold the little boat against the waves. Every time a swell ran under the two boats, the tiny dinghy would rocket toward the sky with a terribly unsettling motion. But the man on the line was keeping it tight and steadying the motion, even though there were times when the dory would lean directly away from the *Maitland* at an alarming angle. The sailors in the lifeboat held on for dear life while the car ferry crew prepared a second line to use in plucking them off the small lifeboat.

"I still don't know why they took the captain's small rowing dory," Jesse Gerken mused, "it's only half as big as the regular lifeboats." As the two commiserated, Brinley suddenly noticed that the line connecting the two vessels was parting at the rail. The ship's motion had been severing the cotton line at the place where it passed over *Maitland*'s metal deck.

"Watch it!" Brinley yelled.

But it was too late. As Heyman dove for the line, it parted. Then in a moment of horror which seemed to last an eternity, the small dory stood vertically at the top of a particularly nasty swell. It stood straight on its stern, suspended in mid-air for a brief moment, then walked on its beam-ends away from the *Maitland* until it landed upside down on the water. Once it hit, it began to blow away at a rapid rate.

"Where did those men go?" yelled Heyman.

"No sign of them. They went under," responded Jesse Gerken.

"Let's go get the lifeboat, maybe they're underneath it," suggested Brinley.

"No," responded Heyman. "They have life vests so they'll float. If we leave the lifeboat in the water, they might be able to get to it. We have to go get the men in the third lifeboat right now. If we spend time looking for the four in the water, we could miss the opportunity to rescue the men we can see."

"And look," added Brinley, "the third lifeboat is swamped and in danger of going down."

# [SATURDAY, AUGUST 21, 1926, 1:48 A.M.]

Heyman raced back to the bridge where he carefully began to power *Maitland* toward the third lifeboat. As he did, he told Burke to take a bearing on the place where they had lost the four men in the water.

"As soon as we have those guys aboard we'll go back and look for the others," he added. "They'll be able to see our lights and maybe they'll manage to swim to us if we go in slow circles." Burke sat at his charts and began developing a dead reckoning position so that they could come back and resume their hunt for the four lost crew members.

The third rescue went without a hitch. Repeating his previous navigational magic, Heyman took *Maitland* to weather of the third swamped lifeboat and let the big car ferry drift down onto it. In less than twenty minutes, Pete Brinley and Jesse Gerken had secured the remaining crew, including Howard Gerken Senior, Chief Engineer John Gerken and Captain Gamble aboard the car ferry.

# CHAPTER 21

### [SATURDAY, AUGUST 21, 1926, 7:00 A.M.]

*Wagerman was startled back to reality after his longest sleep of the night. At first he had no idea what had awakened him, but he soon decided that it must have been the light of dawn. He felt like he had been sleeping for hours. Even though it was light now and the waves had calmed to an almost normal state, he was not able to appreciate the dawn. He was colder than ever and terribly concerned that he might never wake up again if he were to fall asleep another time. He scanned the horizon, looking for signs of the ship that had come so close a few hours ago and wondered why he could see no signs of it.*

*"I hope that it didn't pass by while I was asleep," he thought to himself. "If it did," he mulled, "and it's gone for good, I'm probably going to die out here." The thought had barely registered in his mind when he began to receive a flood of slow motion mental images. There were pictures of his family with his mother telling him that he should never have become a sailor, Fr. Mitchell (his high school science teacher) commenting on Lake Erie and Mr. Leonardi (his seventh grade teacher) expounding on Lake Erie and its dangers. And there were vivid images of Captain Wall's lecture on Lake Erie shipwrecks. Wagerman could see himself so clearly that it seemed as if he were watching a movie. He was a child, sitting in the front row at Captain Robert Wall's lecture and asking the first question from the audience.*

*Herman Wagerman was shocked that the lecturer would even take a question from such a young boy, much less allow it to be the first.*

"Sir," he asked, "how many sailors have actually died on Lake Erie?"

Captain Wall paused thoughtfully and scratched his white hair for a few seconds, then seemed to begin a new topic; a mini-lecture on sailing casualties. Floating along almost twenty-three years later, Wagerman could still remember the answer that the sea captain had given.

# Lake Erie Casualties

## [DECEMBER, 1903 BUFFALO: A LECTURE ON LAKE ERIE SHIPWRECKS]

Historians disagree over the precise number of maritime casualties on Lake Erie, but official estimates generally place the total near 2,500. The greatest contributions to that staggering number came from just two shipwrecks: the sinking of the steamers *City of Erie* in 1841 and *Atlantic* in 1851. Depending upon accounts, between 200 and 250 perished in the burning of *City of Erie* and another 300 to 325 lost their lives in Central Lake Erie's most stunning tragedy, the sinking of the steamer *Atlantic*. The majority of Lake Erie's shipwreck casualties resulted in smaller death tolls; totals which generally represented the typical size of the crew on a commercial ship.

As years passed, the average number of casualties per sinking fell, since the typical complement of crew was reduced. Great Lakes ships, like their ocean-going counterparts, became mechanized and efficient over time, reflecting the overall trend of the Industrial Revolution. Thus, the typical casualty numbers were usually in the range of ten to thirty. Casualty totals grew steadily as shipping volume increased prior to the Civil War. The wartime reduction in Great Lakes shipping resulted in a dramatic drop in deaths. But as soon as north–south hostilities ended, there was a frenetic return to Great Lakes shipping, and the number of wrecks increased again.

By the late 1800s, navigational improvements, accurate charts, improved weather forecasting and structural advances in ships had led to marked reductions in both shipwrecks and casualties. But there were still many maritime disasters. Between 1880 and 1900, for example, there were 85 shipwrecks in Central Lake Erie.

## [MODERN SHIPWRECK CASUALTIES]

But for Wagerman, those were the old days. Modern times did not really begin until he started working on the docks in June of 1909, and by then, he was confident that the days of shipwrecks and dead sailors were distant memories. His first summer on the docks, however, there was a marine disaster. The schooner *Sir C. T. Van Straubenzie,* sailing under her own power, collided off Erie with the steamer *City of Erie.* The old wooden schooner was badly holed and sank within minutes, taking three crew members with her.

A young Wagerman was shaken by that tragedy but put it off to owners who were trying to keep an old schooner working long past her prime. This rationalization failed him later that winter with the sinking of the *Marquette & Bessemer #2.* The car ferry *Marquette & Bessemer #2* was Lake Erie's major twentieth century disaster, taking its crew and one passenger (a total of thirty-three) with her in 1909.

There were many more losses during Wagerman's career. In 1916, the Black Friday storm accounted for two major losses on Lake Erie; the steamer *Merida* with its crew of twenty-three and the whaleback steamer *James B. Colegate* with its crew of twenty-six.

There were other modern tragedies, as well. The wooden steam barge *Tempest* sunk within feet of Erie's channel entrance in 1918 taking its engineer with it, and the *City of Dresden* foundered off the base of Long Point in 1922, resulting in the drowning of the captain's young son. There was the 1925 burning of Erie's beloved excursion ship, the *Colonial,* in which three crew members drowned, and finally, the sinking of the Canadian fish tug, *Angler.*

For every sailor who didn't come home there were wives, mothers, sisters, daughters and friends who never fully recovered from the losses. And sometimes the tragedies were made even more terrifying when the bodies were not immediately recovered. It was not unusual for a sailor lost during late fall months to float up on shore the following spring or summer, sometimes miles from where he had been presumed lost. There were thousands of lost sailors but tens of thousands of psychic connections to loved ones on shore. A sailor's life could be terribly cruel.

While Wagerman's body floated in its near-comatose state, his mind revisited the terror he had felt when he read newspaper accounts of the loved ones of the *Marquette & Bessemer* crew. One particular story had haunted him since he first read it. On December 5, 1909, Sarah Clancey woke up with a start. She was bathed in cold perspiration from a terrifying dream of a storm on Lake Erie. In her dream she could hear wind shrieking through cottonwood trees on shore and she could see waves. Monstrous waves! She was somehow afloat in the middle of Lake Erie and horrified to see white-capped waves as big as mountains. Wave crests were lifting her into the air, throwing her down into the troughs between them. Each wave smashed her so hard into the following depression that she was thrust underwater and had to fight her way to the surface, gasping for air. There she would be lifted skyward and thrown into the sea again. But it wasn't the howling wind or crashing waves which had awakened Sarah. It was the voice of her brother John, wheelsman aboard the car ferry *Marquette and Bessemer #2*. John's terrified voice was calling for help, begging Sarah to come for him.

The voice was so real that Sarah presumed, when she woke up soaked with perspiration, that her brother had come home during the night, and that he was in the house calling her. In a dazed, semi-awakened state, she got out of bed and began searching the house for her brother. Sarah's frenetic middle-of-the-night behavior awoke her family. Her parents and sisters tried to calm her. They assured her that she was having a bad dream and that John was all right. But Sarah knew that what she had experienced was more than a bad dream. She was so convinced it was real that she went outside to see if it was storming. But the winds that night were calm. Still agitated, she resolved to try to reach her brother in Conneaut, Ohio the next day to warn him of her dream. But her parents and sisters convinced her that this would simply worry John, so she never contacted him.

When December winds rose to near-hurricane proportions two nights later, Sarah knew that her dream had been an omen. She rushed to the waterfront, looked at the waves and experienced déjà vu. It was the exact sound that she had heard in her dream! Sarah knew in her heart that her beloved brother John was in trouble that night somewhere on Lake Erie. The news the next morning confirmed her intuition. *Marquette & Bessemer #2* was lost at sea. Sarah lived the rest of her life racked with guilt for not having warned her brother of the dream. Her pain, and that of her entire family, was shared by the families of all the crew who perished the night of December 7, 1909 in Lake Erie. Sarah was experiencing her personal share of the pain that regularly visits the families of Lake Erie's sailors.

Wagerman had never been able to clear his mind of the frightening account of Sarah Clancey's dream. As he slipped into his own dreams, his memory of the *Marquette & Bessemer* made him sick with concern over the people who would be worrying about him that night. He cursed his memories!

# PART EIGHT

# Salvation

*I couldn't tell you any special prayer*
*I used when I was afloat on the lake,*
*the mysteries of religion are beyond me.*
*You've got to believe and that's all there is to it!*
*They say my wife's prayers were answers,*
  *but what about the other wives?*
*Those wives prayed all night long too.*

**Watchman Frank Mays**

*Survivor of the sinking of the*
*Steamship Bradley*

# CHAPTER 22

### [SATURDAY, AUGUST 21, 8:00 A.M.]

*"Herman! Herman Wagerman! Please pay attention to me at once! I don't know what is wrong with you, Herman," the woman said in a stern voice. "You are always daydreaming."*

*Wagerman struggled to understand who this woman was and what she was saying to him. He had been sleeping soundly and the voice that was beckoning him seemed terribly irritating. As he tried to focus his eyes on the darkened image before him, the shape of a catholic nun in a formal black habit slowly materialized. She was standing on the water talking to him. Then he recognized her! It was Sister Marie Renée from his first grade class.*

*"How did I get so far back in time?" he wondered aloud, trying to clear his mind and make an intelligent response.*

*Looking around him in the water, he saw his friends Logan, Freeman and McMinn. They were sitting next to him in tiny desks, working on school assignments.*

*"They weren't paying attention either, Sister," he objected, "we're all busy swimming right now."*

*"I'm not talking to them," Sister Marie Renée responded. "They're not in my class today, Herman, you are."*

*Wagerman was getting more disoriented by the minute. He could see that all of them were submerged in water and that they were shivering. Logan looked gray and as Wagerman tried to talk to him, he could see that his eyes were frozen shut.*

*"Don't talk to them, Herman," Sister Marie Renée admonished. "They can't help you now, only I can."*

*"What should I do, Sister?" Wagerman asked. "I'm cold and I'm afraid," he blurted out, somehow embarrassed by such a self-disclosure*

*"Do you remember what I taught you?" she asked.*

*"I'm not sure," answered Wagerman. "Will you help me remember?"*

*"Take your crucifix out and hold it up, Herman," she answered. "You have to pray."*

*Wagerman fumbled frantically through his pockets until he found a metal object. He pulled it out and held it up for Sister Marie Renée to see.*

*"That's not a crucifix, Herman, it's a jack knife," she said.*

*"But I don't think I brought my crucifix," Wagerman responded sheepishly.*

*With that, Sister Marie Renée moved toward him. Wagerman stiffened, expecting to be chastised for forgetting his rosary beads again. Sister Marie Renée expected students to carry their rosary beads with them at all times. Instead of being angry, however, Sister Marie Renée put her arm around Herman and comforted him.*

*"It's all right," she said in a gentle voice. "I understand. I would forget my rosaries too, but they're a part of my habit. Why don't we pretend that your knife is a crucifix," she suggested. "God doesn't care about details. It's what you dream that counts. So open your knife, Herman," she added. "Hold it up in the air and pretend that it's a crucifix. Then if you pray," she said reassuringly, "God will send an angel to help you."*

*With frozen and swollen fingers, Wagerman struggled to open his knife. Finally he released the shiny steel blade and held it toward the sky.*

"Like this, Sister?" he asked, looking at her for approval.

"Yes, Herman, just like that," she answered.

Wagerman studied her face while he held the knife up. He was puzzled that she looked so much younger than he remembered. "It's amazing," he thought. "She looks so much like Suzanne." Wagerman was completely confused. "Who is this woman?" he mused.

As he wondered, she placed her arms around his shoulders and hugged him.

"Go to sleep, Herman. Everything will be all right," she whispered.

For the first time since he had entered the water more than six hours earlier, Wagerman relaxed as he fell asleep.

# The Coast Guard Search

## [SATURDAY, AUGUST 21, 1926, 2:00 A.M.]

Captain Nelson Seymore stood on the northern tip of the channel wall, scanning the eastern horizon for signs of a ship in distress. The rain had stopped and the night skies were clearing.

"I don't see a thing," he commented.

Cramer, Johnsten and the two Erie policemen stood with him staring into the darkness.

"Whatever is out there must be at least seven or eight miles away, sir," added Cramer, "or we would see it from here."

"Let's get the picket boat and take a run out there," barked Seymore. "You guys suit up. Get me two more crew members and we'll get out there and have a look. On the double!" he added.

At that, Nelson Seymore broke into a sprint for the station house.

"Wait, sir, look toward town," shouted Cramer, pointing toward the west end of the channel. "It's the downtown cutter heading our way," he offered.

Seymore and his party paused in front of the stationhouse, while Lieutenant Albert Coppine roared into the channel at hull speed, throwing a huge wake across the relatively calm waterway.

"He must be in a hell of a hurry," noted Cramer. There was a strict no-wake policy within the channel.

Cramer and Johnsten received dock lines from the cutter and Coppine jumped ashore.

"What's up, Al?" asked Seymore.

"Just got a message from the police in town, sir," he responded. "Seems that a car ferry called the *Maitland* has been radioing its home base in Ashtabula that they are at a shipwreck site searching for survivors. They're in twenty foot waves approximately ten miles north of here, hunting for crew members lost from a lifeboat."

"North? The report that we received put them east of here," noted Seymore. "No wonder we can't see them!" "Let's go inside and develop a plan," added Nelson Seymore as he led the way to the stationhouse chart table.

"Al," he said, "I hate to send you out into these waves in the cutter, but we have to get out there if there are men in the water."

Seymore placed a mark on a chart of Lake Erie in the approximate spot where the *Maitland* was reported to be. Then he drew a long elliptical circle to the east.

"Take the cutter, go about five miles east, then swing out into the middle of the lake. Run parallel to the shoreline and stay about four or five miles from the bluffs. That should give you some shelter from these southeasterlys. I'll take the picket boat north toward Long Point. If I don't see anything, I'll circle east and meet you. By the time we rendezvous about here," he noted, making a second mark on the chart, "one of us should have spotted something. *Maitland* is a big car ferry and they'll have lots of lights on. They should be easy to spot."

"Yes, sir," answered Al Coppine as he rushed back to *Cutter #142* to cast off.

By this time, Seymore's crew of four had donned foul weather gear and brought U.S. Coast Guard *Picket Boat CG3122* into the channel. Seymore grabbed his oilskins and ran to join them.

By 2:15 a.m., two vessels from the Erie Station were in Lake Erie joining the search for the sailors from the *Gerken.*

Coppine's thirty-five-foot cutter was heading east along the bluffs.

The cutter, while faster than Seymore's picket boat, was eighteen years old and narrow, making it vulnerable to the high seas that Seymore knew they would encounter in mid-lake. In fact, the old cutter was so small that it rarely saw duty on the open lake. In the summer, it was stationed at Erie's downtown docks where it was available for calls within the protected bay. Under ordinary circumstances the downtown cutter was in telephone communication with the main station at the peninsula, but the storm had knocked the phone lines down.

Seymore's fifty-three foot *Picket Boat CG3122*, was brand new and built for heavy seas. Coast Guard picket boats were designed for offshore duty in response to prohibition and rum running. The "picket" designation was derived from a plan to create a fence, a picket fence, down the middle of Lake Erie so that Canadian commercial fishermen would not have free access to the middle of the lake as they hauled illegal whiskey to the American market. Picket boats were large, heavy and seaworthy. Each carried a substantial fuel payload, allowing it to patrol the lake for days at a time. Since Seymore's picket boat was far better than the cutter for offshore work, he took the northerly route into the churning center of the lake while Coppine powered east along the shelter of the bluffs.

By the time the two Coast Guard vessels began their search, the winds were dropping and turning west. At their peak, near 1:00 a.m., they had been recorded at the station as southeast with sustained velocities of fifty-five to sixty miles per hour. Gusts had reached the mid-seventies. A "southeasterly" blew perpendicular to the lakeshore and was generally considered by weather forecasters to be a temporary lake-effect wind. It was ordinarily the by-product of a low-pressure system passing north of the lake. While the system passed, the wind direction would ordinarily clock to the west, shifting south then southwest (the prevailing direction) before calming. Seymore powered down the wave-backs toward the center of the lake, feeling the change in weather. The winds were decreasing and heading southwest. He was pleased by the changes but concerned for Al Coppine in the cutter. When the wind shifted, Coppine would be fighting new southwesterly waves on his return to Erie.

At 3:05 a.m., Seymore spotted running lights almost dead ahead. "There they are," he yelled, bringing the picket boat 20 degrees to port. "Further west than I expected."

"Look sir," added Cramer, peering east, "there's another set of running lights over that way."

"We'll head for the closer lights first," noted Seymore.

*CG3122* powered toward the running lights and Seymore carefully studied the profiles of both vessels. "The ship directly ahead of us is a car ferry for sure," he noted. "It must be the *Maitland*! But the second set of lights seems to belong to a passenger liner. What would they be doing out here in this kind of stuff?" he wondered aloud.

Seymore pulled within hailing range of the car ferry at 3:45 a.m., and *Maitland* signaled that they wanted to put a man aboard the picket boat. Seymore nodded agreement and brought *CG3122* into the lee of the big car ferry. In an instant, Captain Thomas Heyman was aboard the picket boat with an arm full of charts.

"Morning, captain," he muttered hurriedly. "Let's get to your bridge so I can show you what's going on."

"Good," answered Seymore as he led Heyman to *CG3122*'s wheelhouse. Heyman quickly recounted the evening's events and estimated the location where the four sailors had gone overboard. He then indicated the search pattern that *Maitland* had been following for the past two hours.

"We've been steaming in slow circles," he noted, "trying to go a bit farther east on each swing."

"What's that other ship doing out here?" Seymore asked.

"It's the passenger liner *North American*," replied Heyman. "They intercepted our radio communications and came out to help with the search. They told us they have a deck full of seasick passengers, but that they are more than willing to stay out here and help for as long as we need them!"

"Okay," said Seymore. "You and your crew have done a great job so far. But I think that the best thing would be for you to take the survivors back to shore so they can be cared for. I have two boats out here myself. Between the *North American* and my two vessels, we can carry on while you take those men back to land."

"Captain Seymore, I have a slightly different suggestion," replied Heyman. "If you could use the help I would rather stay aboard with you. Maybe an extra pair of hands and eyes will come in handy," he added. "Searching for men in the water in these waves is like looking for a needle in a haystack," offered Heyman. "And besides, I feel personally responsible," Heyman added, "since I had a rope on the third lifeboat and lost them."

"What about your ship?" questioned Seymore.

"It's in good hands," Heyman replied. "My first mate and crew can take it home."

"In that case I'd love to have you aboard," replied Seymore. "Our best hope is for the sailors to stay awake until dawn so that they can signal us if we come close to them. The more watchman's eyes we have with us the better. Do they have life vests on?" Seymore asked.

"Affirmative," replied Heyman.

"Good, there's hope," responded Seymore.

Heyman went on deck where he signaled *Maitland*'s crew to head west for Ashtabula. Then he joined Seymore at the chart table in *CG3122* where they began estimating the drift pattern of four men in life jackets.

"They're floating in breaking seas and the wind has been shifting from southeast to southwest," Seymore mumbled as he drew lines on a chart. At 4:10 a.m., he completed his work and took over the wheel heading his picket boat directly for the *North American*. By 4:35 a.m., Seymore was within hailing distance of the passenger liner. He used a megaphone to communicate his search plan to the captain. Remarkably, passengers lined the decks. They had volunteered to stand outside in the rain and rough seas to scan the lake's surface for survivors. Seymore had copied the estimated drift pattern of the lost sailors onto two extra charts. The resultant shape resembled a four-mile wide cornucopia-shaped swath, arching east from the estimated point where the men were originally lost. He drew three course lines through the drift pattern. Two lines formed the northerly and southerly perimeters. A third was drawn down the center of the cornucopia shape.

Seymore sent one chart on a carrier line to the *North American* with an instruction suggesting that the captain take the northern-most perimeter of the drift pattern and run back and forth from west to east. Seymore planned to drive his picket boat up and down the centerline of the drift pattern and to send Al Coppine in *Cutter #142* to work the southern perimeter where the waves might be smaller. The captain and crew of the *North American* immediately understood Seymore's request.

They steamed off to begin their northern perimeter search pattern, and Seymore headed southeast to rendezvous with Coppine. Seymore spotted Coppine's cutter dead ahead at 5:00 a.m. It was running extra lights as it scanned the water ahead of it. At 5:20 a.m., he brought his picket boat alongside.

"What's up?" asked Coppine. "We haven't seen a thing!"

Quickly, Seymore briefed Coppine on the situation, introduced him to Captain Heyman and asked if he could run the southern perimeter of the search pattern.

"Yes, sir," answered Coppine. "We're getting the shit kicked out of us out here in these waves but we're doing all right. We wouldn't consider giving up now. Not with four men in the water," he added.

"How's your fuel?" asked Seymore.

"We're eating it up in these waves," responded Coppine. "But we're good for another seven or eight hours," he added.

"Be careful," admonished Seymore. "We don't want to have to rescue you guys out here tonight! Make sure you get back before you run empty!"

"Yes, sir," Coppine answered, and headed *Cutter #142* away to begin his search.

By 5:50 a.m., the light of pre-dawn was breaking on the lake and three ships were making parallel east–west runs along the drift course calculated by Seymore. The wind had dropped substantially, clocking at fifteen to twenty miles per hour on *Picket Boat CG3122*'s bridge instruments. And it had shifted all the way southwest. The waves were confused with the new southwest breeze blowing the tops off of swells from the earlier wind. In fact, the new breeze was blowing at a 90 degree angle to the old one.

"These waves are really ugly," noted Heyman as he peered through the bridge windows. "Spotting anyone in this stuff is going to be next to impossible!"

"If we go slow," Seymore responded, "and maintain this search pattern, our best hope is that the men in the water will see us. It's getting light, so visibility will improve. Maybe they will be able to signal us somehow. Keep your eyes wide open," he added. "These men have been in the water for almost five hours," he continued, "so we have to hope that they stayed awake!"

"It would take a hell of a man not to give up and go to sleep in these conditions," noted Heyman.

"I know," answered Seymore. "We'll just have to hope and pray."

All three vessels were at the western extremity of the search pattern at 7:00 a.m. As Seymore prepared to turn east, Coppine brought *Cutter #142* north to meet him.

"We're low on fuel," he yelled from outside the bridge as the two boats came within hailing range. "I'm going to make a half run east then head back to the station."

"Good," responded Seymore. "Don't risk running out!"

With that, Coppine circled south. As *Cutter #142* powered away, the *North American* closed on the picket boat and signaled that they also wanted a conference with Seymore.

"We're six hours overdue in Buffalo and running low on fuel," yelled the captain through his megaphone. "We'll make one more run to the east, but then I'm afraid we should retire."

"Okay," answered Seymore, "thanks for your help!"

*Picket Boat CG3122* began its 7:10 a.m. easterly run with Seymore realizing that the chances for the lost sailors were growing slimmer by the moment. Growing increasingly concerned, he went back to his original chart calculations and asked Heyman to check them over. He had assumed that the sailors went into the water just west of the rhumb line between Erie and Long Point. They would, he reasoned, have been sent northward in southerly gale winds, then east as the winds shifted. More determined than ever, Seymore decided to search further to the east. In these waves, he noted to himself, a man in a life jacket could easily have floated ten miles, especially if he was sitting high in the water in a big life vest. Heyman nodded agreement.

"Let's slow down and make a long run east," he muttered to Heyman.

## [SATURDAY, AUGUST 21, 1926, 8:00 A.M.]

The sun was up and glistening on the waves. In fact, the morning brightness was making it difficult to see clearly ahead. Seymore had four men on deck watching in different directions. Two were gazing forward while the others watched over the stern. Powering at three knots, Seymore rolled through the waves, thinking about what it must be like to have been adrift for so long, and about what the families of the lost sailors must be going through.

Coppine was gone and the *North American* was rapidly disappearing to the east. *Picket Boat CG3122* was now the last hope for the missing. At 8:15 a.m., Seymore was about to bring his ship around and turn west, when Heyman thought he saw a flash of light to the north.

"What was that?" Heyman yelled.

"What? I didn't see anything," responded Seymore.

"There! Look to port!" continued Heyman. "I saw a flash of light."

"Probably the sun hitting a wave," offered Seymore.

"No, it isn't! There it is again," replied Heyman. "Let's get a compass heading on that direction," he added.

Slowly, not wanting to lose the bearing, Seymore brought *CG3122* to port and put the bow right on the spot where Heyman had seen the glimmer of light.

"There it is!" yelled Seymore. "I see it, too."

Moments later, a cry went up on deck. "Sir, there's a man out there dead ahead," a watchman yelled from the foredeck.

"Thank God," murmured Seymore.

At 8:20 a.m., *Picket Boat CG3122* pulled alongside a person in a life jacket. He was a big man, riding high in a life vest and holding a shiny knife in a deathgrip. It was a reflection from the knife that Heyman had seen from the bridge. By 8:30 a.m., the crew had attached a line to the floating sailor. Seymore and Heyman left the bridge to help with the retrieval. When they pulled him onto the deck, they could read the name Wagerman on his life jacket. Seymore leaned over to see if he was still breathing.

"He's alive," he yelled to the crew. "Get him down below and let's see if we can warm him up."

Seymore rushed back to the bridge and took over the wheel.

Moments later, Heyman joined him. "He's in really bad shape," noted Heyman. "A big guy! We had a hell of a time getting him down below and wrapped up in blankets. Especially since he wouldn't let go of that knife. Kept muttering something about how it was Suzanne's and that he had to see her."

"He's probably delirious," offered Seymore. "The poor guy is shivering like crazy and obviously near frozen to death. Let's get him back to the Coast Guard Station right now before we lose him," noted Seymore as he aimed *CG3122* for Erie.

# CHAPTER 23
# The Swimmers are Saved

[SATURDAY, AUGUST 21, 1926, 5:30 A.M.]

"I don't believe this!" exclaimed George Stickle while he treaded water. Stickle gazed in shocked disbelief at his friend who was just a few feet away and coughing up water.

"Believe it," grumbled Ben Cooley. "We're now officially in trouble!"

"It might help if we had put our life jackets on," muttered Stickle.

"Look over there," yelled Cooley, pointing to a spot on the water twenty feet behind them.

The two watched in disbelief while jetsam was breaking the surface near the spot where *Pterodactyl* had gone down. A life ring. Then bits of wood and other assorted gear. Without saying a thing both men struggled to the debris pool and grabbed at anything big enough to support them. Cooley passed a life ring to his friend and then grabbed the long section of wooden whisker-pole that had broken earlier in the evening.

"Lucky my knots failed," he muttered, placing the wooden pole under his shoulder.

"What's next?" asked Stickle.

"Offhand, I would say swimming," answered Cooley. "And we can do it, George," he added. "Look," he said, pointing toward Long

Point's beaches from the top of a wave, "we can't be more than two or three miles offshore."

So the two began swimming, alternatively stroking through the water and peeling off layers of clothing. Within moments both men, who were good swimmers, had stripped down to shorts and T-shirts, leaving shoes, trousers, sweaters and other apparel to the lake. At first, Cooley had a vague hope of hanging onto his wallet, but he soon gave the idea up as he found himself spending more energy keeping track of it than swimming.

After thirty minutes, the pair stopped to take their bearings. They were approximately two miles from Long Point's beaches and they could clearly see the lighthouse with its blinking beacon, dead ahead. Treading water, they judged that they were about a half mile west of the tip of the point.

True to Long Point legend, the south beach waves near the tip of the point were frightening. Not only were they monstrously high, but they carried huge breaking crests. Each wave top carried an avalanche of tumbling water that danced precariously on its crest. Now that Cooley and Stickle were in the water, rather than riding *Pterodactyl*, the waves seemed to be a part of them. They rode automatically up each wave, then plummeted into the depression behind it. When they were lifted toward the top of the next wave, they were rudely buffeted by the breaking water at its crest. They soon learned to hold their breath while the breaking water consumed them. It was like being little children on a beach in storm waves. But there was no reassuring parent to hold their hands or to save them from the continuous dumping of wave-borne water. Swimming was exhausting work in these wave conditions and both men realized that their only hope was to reach the beach as quickly as possible.

"How are you doing?" sputtered Cooley as he kept an eye on his friend.

Stickle had seemed tired and depressed before *Pterodactyl* went down, and Ben Cooley was worried that he might run out of energy on the swim to the beach.

"I'm fine, Ben," his friend responded, "but I'm not sure if I'll be sailing to Long Point with you any more."

"Are you getting cold?" asked Cooley.

"No, I'm not getting cold, goddamn it," he added, " I've been cold for the last ten hours!"

"Me, too," replied Cooley, "but if we can last another hour we should be able to make it to shore. Come on, let's go!"

With that, Cooley struck off to the north again with his friend following.

## [SATURDAY, AUGUST 21, 1926, 6:30 A.M.]

"Let's take a break and get our bearings," suggested Cooley after another prolonged swim.

George Stickle stopped kicking and rested in the water, still clutching *Pterodactyl*'s life ring. The wind was noticeably calmer now but the waves seemed steeper and more confused. As they rose to the crest of the next wave, however, an alarming reality suddenly became evident to them.

"Ben, look at where the Long Point Light is now!" exclaimed Stickle.

It was obvious that as they had been swimming north they were also being swept east. The waves had shifted from southeast to southwest with the wind and they were propelling the two swimmers east along the beaches faster than Cooley and Stickle could make progress to the north. The Long Point Light was moving to their left and they could now see open water beyond the tip of the point.

"George, we're in serious trouble," said Cooley in a voice that had suddenly lost much of its confidence and optimism. "We're going to be swept past the tip of the point and into the open bay behind Long Point. If that happens, we'll never get back to land in these waves," he continued.

"Your ass," countered Stickle as he came to life and took command of the situation. "Look, Ben!" he implored. "This is a trigonometry problem and we're architects. We have to swim west for all we're worth. If we aim west instead of north, we might land right on the shore."

"Come on, let's try it!" yelled Cooley.

So the two architects swam like men possessed, stroking and kicking for their very lives. As difficult as it was to swim away from the beach, they realized that it was their only hope. A half-hour later, Cooley stopped for another look.

"We're going to miss it," he said in a defeated voice.

Looking down the tops of the breaking waves that were carrying them relentlessly northeast, Cooley could see that the crests ahead of them were rolling past the tip of the point. The row of waves which held them hostage was passing well east of Long Point's tip, missing the beach by a half-mile.

"Keep swimming!" yelled Stickle. "What choice do we have?"

At 7:00 a.m. the navigational currents, which had spelled doom for hundreds of sailing ships, miraculously conspired to save two young architects. As the newly-forming southwesterly waves rolled along the beach, parallel to Long Point, the waveforms were captured by the shoaling waters and took on a new directional shape. Each wave gradually hooked north, away from the prevailing current and back toward the beach. This curving action had captured many ships over the years, driving them onto the sandy shoal that extended for more than a mile beyond the tip of the big peninsula.

The old time sailing schooners that ran aground here often did so in March or December storms. And they foundered in waters that were six to ten feet deep, putting the sailors who attempted to abandon ship at serious peril. But for Cooley and Stickle, the lee shore currents proved friendly. They were propelling the swimmers in a large arc-shaped semicircle with each successive wave twisting back toward the tip of the point. Just when it had seemed that all was lost, Cooley and Stickle could see that the waves were changing in their favor and they swam even harder.

Stickle's hand touched sand at 7:25 a.m. Even though he was more than a quarter mile from the tip of Long Point, he scraped the ground in less than three feet of water. He had rediscovered Long Point's infamous sandbar. Unlike the old-time schooners foundering in November storms, however, the sandbar was a welcome sight to the swimmers. For two exhausted men in danger of being swept beyond Long Point's rugged tip, nothing could have been more welcome!

"Ben, we've done it!" Stickle yelled, as he stood and walked toward his friend who was still swimming. "Come on, let's get ashore!"

Remarkably, the pair was greeted by a voice while they struggled along the sandbar through breaking waves. Lighthouse keeper Lorne Brown was standing on the beach watching in astonishment.

"Kind of a rough day for an early morning swim, isn't it boys?" Brown commented sardonically.

Brown was even more confused when he watched Ben Cooley fall on the beach, kiss the sand, then stand up and hug his friend George Stickle. After the swimmers had explained their plight, Brown took them to his keeper's cottage where he offered the frozen and exhausted men clothing, warmth and breakfast. Ben Cooley and George Stickle were barely able to express their thanks before falling asleep.

Cooley and Stickle awoke to the sounds of dishes clattering in Lorne Brown's cottage. The smell of apple pie permeated the small cabin. Stickle dragged himself out of bed, momentarily confused by his surroundings. And then in an instant he remembered what had happened the night before and where he was. Cooley glanced at him with a knowing look.

"I woke up in a cold sweat, George," noted Ben Cooley, "I think we're pretty lucky to be here."

"What time is it?" asked Sickle.

"About 7:00," answered his friend.

"In the morning?" asked Stickle.

"No, it's 7:00 p.m.," answered Cooley. "We slept all day."

Brown stuck his head into the spare bedroom. "I see that you guys are up," he noted. "That's good because I was going to have to wake you up in a few minutes if you were still asleep. I placed a call to Port Rowan," Brown continued, "and it seems as though you guys have a ride home if I can get you there by this evening."

"With who?" asked Ben Cooley.

"There's a sailboat from Erie at the city dock." Brown responded. "A yacht called the *Eagle*. The owner says that you're welcome to sail back with him if you're up to it!"

"What do you think, George," asked Ben Cooley of his friend. "Are you ready to go out there on the lake again?"

"Absolutely!" answered Stickle.

Lorne Brown led the pair into his kitchen where he and his wife served them a lighthouse style meal including fresh fish, vegetables grown in the garden behind the keeper's cottage and huge slabs of fresh apple pie. After dinner, he loaned them spare clothing from his closet. Lighthouse keepers didn't usually keep a huge wardrobe, but he was somehow able to find pants, sweaters and boots to fit both Cooley and Stickle. By 8:00 p.m., Brown was driving them along the network of crude roads that the lighthouse keepers used to commute to Port Rowan. The ride through the interior of Long Point in Brown's ancient truck was an exciting trek in itself, and ended at The Cut, a small channel which connected the open lake to Long Point's Inner Bay. The trio transferred to a dingy which Brown kept locked to a tree, then rowed across the Inner Bay to Port Rowan. The winds were almost dead calm that night, a dramatic contrast to the day before. As Brown rowed the two architects to the public pier at Port Rowan, the crew of *Eagle* stood at the dock and cheered for their friends!

# CHAPTER 24

[SATURDAY, AUGUST 21, 1926, 8:05 A.M.]

*Wagerman wasn't sure if he was sleeping or awake. There seemed to be no difference now. He had shifted to a new state of foggy distance from reality, a place from which it seemed to make no difference if he were awake or asleep. It was almost as if he could be in both places at once. Remarkably, Wagerman didn't feel cold anymore. In this emerging state of consciousness he floated effortlessly in a large field of slate gray.*

*He was deciding to accept this new reality when he suddenly thought that he heard a real noise rather than one from his dreaming imagination. Wagerman struggled to look up. To his shock something seemed to be moving through the water toward him. But no matter how hard he tried, he simply couldn't focus on whatever it was.*

*Through frozen eyes he stared at this strange new misty shape and watched it with suspicion as it seemed to approach. Then he recognized it. It was a church. Somehow, a gray church with numbers on its walls was drifting through the water toward him. Someone was standing on the front of the church yelling. While Wagerman watched in gray slow motion, others joined the person who had been standing alone on the porch of the church.*

*The church grew larger as it approached, finally obliterating the entire horizon. It looked to Wagerman as though the church was about to run him down. The people on the church leaned over the porch as it approached and began to grab at him. Frightened and confused by this apparition, Wagerman went back to sleep, trying not to think about churches or about how he had not gone to Mass regularly during the past several years.*

# The Churches

## [Maritime Church Communities]

Churches have been an integral part of North America's maritime development since the earliest days of sailing. As ethnic communities formed along the Atlantic and Great Lakes coasts, churches sprang up to offer spiritual support and pastoral care for sailors and their families. Long after coastal cities had matured and spread inland, the churches nearest the water often retained special missions to sailors and fishermen.

Erie was no exception. A number of churches emerged along its early bayfront, helping anchor the lives of the men who worked on the lake. Since Erie was primarily a Roman Catholic town, two waterfront Catholic churches emerged. St. Patrick's provided a spiritual home for the eastside's Irish fishermen and sailors, while St. Andrew's became a community center for the westside Italian, Portuguese, and Scandinavian communities.

Ethnic fishing and sailing church traditions continued into the twentieth century while the city was turning its attention toward an emerging manufacturing economy. At St. Andrew's, for example, Trinity Sunday marked an annual celebration for the parish Portuguese community. The Portuguese would parade en masse from their neighborhood social club, playing traditional musical instruments as they filed into church for 9:00 a.m. High Mass. The parade, in which women and children dutifully followed the men into the church, was a major celebration in honor of the commercial fishermen. Trinity Sunday traditionally marked the day when the fishing fleet was officially permitted to begin operations and when the boats were blessed. It was the only day of the year that so many men attended Mass. As sailors and fishermen, they were away on the boats almost every other morning.

Fr. Daniel Sheehan wasn't much of a sailor. But as St. Andrew's pastor he had quickly learned the importance of weather to the mood of the parish. In fact, he had learned to tell the weather just by counting the number of women standing on the church steps when he got up to prepare for 6:00 a.m. Mass. On a balmy day there might be three or four ladies patiently waiting. On stormy days, however, there would be five times that number. The fair weather regulars were the parishes' elderly Italian and Portuguese ladies; women who were perennially dressed in black because their husbands had passed away. Good weather or bad, summer, winter or fall, they were always there when Fr. Sheehan arose to prepare for Mass. The stormy-day women were much younger. They were the wives and lovers of men who were out on the lake. And they came to pray specifically for the safety of their loved ones. Fr. Sheehan's compassion for the women always compelled him to throw something on, descend the rectory steps and open the church doors, especially if it was raining or cold. It was not as though the women expected him to let them into the church. The sign on the door clearly stated that the church would be locked from midnight until 5:45 a.m. But when Fr. Sheehan arose, he automatically looked out his bedroom window to see how many were there. On nasty days he got up earlier to be sure that the elderly ladies didn't have to stand in the elements.

## {FRIDAY, AUGUST 20, 1926, 6:00 P.M.]

Suzanne Franzesi sat at the kitchen table of her home just two blocks from St. Andrew's Church. She sat with a blank expression, staring at her dinner rather than eating it. Ever since she had watched the *Gerken* disappear into the lake that afternoon, she had been uneasy. She felt the strength of the wind at her back as she waved good-bye to Herman Wagerman and as she watched the ship disappear her waterfront savvy aroused her instincts to worry. Her father and grandfather had often talked about the offshore Devil Winds when they sat at the dinner table telling their stories. In fact, their best stories always involved storms that blew from the southeast. Tonight's meal was no exception. In honor of the roaring winds that accompanied dinner, Suzanne's father began telling his all-time favorite story, the adventure of Solomon Sweatland from Conneaut, Ohio.

In 1847, Sweatland was participating in Conneaut's annual town deer hunt. Each fall, the townsmen would cooperate in a massive effort to push through the woods east of Conneaut driving deer toward the beach. As deer were herded toward the edge of the lake, the men would circle, then close ranks, forcing the deer closer and closer to the beach. The desperate deer would instinctively enter the water to swim for safety. Once in the lake, the deer were easy prey for men waiting in canoes. The canoeists would lasso the deer, then kill them with guns and clubs. On a productive year, the townsmen would harvest as many as twenty deer during the fall hunt. Then they would spend the afternoon cleaning and dressing meat for the winter. The fall deer hunt was both a festive annual tradition and an important source of food for the village.

Solomon Sweatland had volunteered to be one of the canoeists that year. It was his job to chase and lasso a deer once it entered the water. Sweatland, who was using a particularly clumsy dugout canoe that Saturday, went into the water with his sights set on a big buck with a huge rack of antlers. Not realizing that an off-shore wind was brewing, Sweatland (who had fortified himself with a few nips of liquor) leapt into his canoe and chased the buck for more than a mile as the frightened deer swam directly away from the beach for all he was worth. Then, with what onlookers claimed was a sardonic smile on its face, the wily animal made a starboard tack and began swimming in a wide arc to the east. When Sweatland struggled to turn his canoe and give chase, the gravity of his error of judgement quickly became apparent. He had mindlessly paddled a mile offshore in a Devil Wind. When he tried to follow the deer east, the canoe kept heading north. Sweatland maneuvered the canoe so that it was parallel and then facing the shore. But no matter how hard he paddled, he was steadily swept farther offshore by the wind and waves. He had been seduced by the Iroquois Devil Wind and now he was trapped.

Friends on shore watched in horror while Sweatland desperately tried to get back to the beach. He attempted to paddle straight back to shore, with no success. Even though he paddled south for all he was worth, Sweatland's canoe was being pushed backwards and moving farther and farther offshore. He turned to an easterly course for a while, thinking that he might be able to tack the canoe toward Erie and get to shore there. But the farther out he was swept, the more it became obvious that he was doomed. The winds and waves were far too strong to paddle against. Three hours after he had launched the dugout canoe, the deer was safely back in the forest, but Solomon Sweatland was out of sight of land in a swamped canoe thinking about how to save his own life.

Examining his options, Sweatland decided that the Canadian shore was his only hope. So he decided to try for Long Point which he calculated to be roughly fifty miles downwind. He took off his boots, used them to bail out the canoe and began paddling north instead of south. As he paddled he used the waves as a northerly directional guide, aiming his dugout canoe down their backs and trying to keep from turning sideways. Thirty hours later, a tired and hungry Solomon Sweatland guided his canoe through Long Point's infamous on-shore breaking waves and came to a grinding halt six miles west of the eastern tip of the point. From there, he walked the south beach to Port Rowan, a formidable distance of twenty miles. By the time Sweatland reached town, where he received food, dry clothing and a place to sleep, he had been gone for more than two days. It was another five days until he got himself to Buffalo. There, he purchased a ticket on a steamship heading for Conneaut. Sweatland arrived at the Conneaut town dock just in time to see his own funeral procession pass by. At the rear of the funeral cortege, he recognized his wife in mourning clothing.

Even after the ritual retelling of the Sweatland story, dinner was peppered by Suzanne's father's observations about the wind, and by his stories of maritime tragedies that had been triggered by the wind.

"At least we don't have anyone out in the lake tonight," commented Grama Franzesi during dessert.

Suzanne excused herself and went to bed early. She didn't want to mention to her family that she, indeed, had several people out there: Cooley, Stickle, and most importantly, Herman Wagerman. She didn't want to discuss her feelings about Wagerman since she was confused by them, herself. She had just met this man but somehow she found herself thinking about him constantly. He was different from anyone than she had ever known. She wasn't sure how to interpret her feelings toward Herman but she knew that she needed to see him again.

Suzanne fell asleep trying not to think about the lake or the adventures of Solomon Sweatland. Instead, she directed her pre-sleep dreaming to Herman and replayed the events of the last few days over and over again. In the last showing of her dream, Suzanne kissed Herman Wagerman on the lips and even in her sleep, the kiss sent an electric shock through her body.

Suzanne awoke with a start at 2:00 a.m.. She was bathed in cold sweat, a feeling remarkably different from the warm glow she had experienced as she fell asleep. As she gathered herself, she realized that she had been dreaming. But it wasn't a pleasant picnic dream. It was a horrific vision in which she had been watching Solomon Sweatland paddle his dugout canoe through monstrous waves in the pitch-black center of the lake. In her dream, a particularly huge breaking wave swamped the canoe and sunk it, leaving Sweatland alone and swimming. He turned and looked directly at Suzanne, but to her horror, it wasn't Sweatland at all. It was Herman Wagerman. Herman looked helplessly at her as the canoe disappeared beneath the waves.

"Suzanne!" he cried. "I need you. Please help me!"

Her dream of this wonderfully gentle but strong man crying for help was so real and so disarming that she had awakened instantaneously. She got up and went to the window to look at the wind in the trees. The wind was even stronger than it had been earlier. It was bending the old apple tree behind her window almost to the ground. At first she reasoned that it must have been the wind that startled her, but the dream was so vivid that she couldn't put it out of her mind. She pulled on jeans and a sweater and went to the kitchen to get a glass of milk.

Suzanne tiptoed through the living room where she was startled to see her grandmother sitting in the stuffed chair with her rosary beads.

"Gram, why are you up?" she asked.

"I always get up to pray when it's storming," Grama Franzesi replied.

"Who do you pray for?" Suzanne asked.

"Whoever is on the lake," she replied. "There are always fishermen and sailors out there, and someone has to look after them!"

"You pray for all of them?" asked Suzanne, realizing the rhetorical nature of her question.

Ever since she was little, Grama Franzesi had prayed for everything. And she prayed with a faith that Suzanne could only wish for. As a modern woman of the 1920s, Suzanne was more apt to shape her personal destiny through action than prayer. But she recognized the simplicity and beauty of her grandmother's faith and often wished that she could share it.

"Yes, dear," her grandmother answered. "I pray and God does the work. You should try it!"

If Grama Franzesi had one instinct that surpassed her inclination for prayer, however, it was faith in the power of food. When Suzanne wandered into the kitchen, her grandmother stepped past her, opened the icebox and began setting a snack on the table.

Suzanne wasn't hungry, but she drank milk and nibbled at one of her grandmother's cookies.

"What's the matter, honey?" Grama Franzesi asked. "You seemed so quiet at dinner and now you're white as a sheet."

Slowly, she told her grandmother about Herman and about the strangely powerful feelings she was having for this man whom she had just met. She related the story of her times with Herman and her anger toward Ben Cooley, and her grandmother listened carefully. Suzanne had always been able to pour her heart out to her grandmother. Unlike her parents, Grama Franzesi listened to everything she had to say before offering an opinion. Then, if Grama offered any advice at all, it was kinder and far less direct than the impatient opinions of her mother or father.

"Follow your heart, dear," offered Grama Franzesi after listening. "Life is far too short to worry about doing the proper thing. And I think that your young man will be fine out on the lake tonight. My prayers will be especially for him. I'm going to bed now," she added. "An old lady needs her sleep!"

With that, Grama Franzesi left the kitchen and Suzanne was alone with her thoughts.

"Follow my heart?" she thought. She put on a jacket and quietly left her house to go for a walk. "My parents wouldn't approve of my being out by myself in the middle of the night," she mused, but then Suzanne had spent her entire life doing things differently.

It was almost 3:00 a.m. as she headed down the street toward the bayfront, but the neighborhood wasn't particularly quiet or peaceful. The rain had stopped, but the winds were howling through the trees as she headed north along a darkened, moist street. Wind-borne bits of paper tumbled down the road around her, casting an eerie tone to the early morning. Suzanne found herself drawn to the edge of the bluffs overlooking the water; the working class widow's walk of her grandmother's generation. As she walked she hoped that seeing the water would somehow be reassuring. But the perspective from the edge of the bluffs was not at all comforting. White caps were clearly visible through the dark early-morning sky. The wind was howling and Suzanne could feel the power of the sustained blow as it painted streaks of foam on the water's surface. These were exactly the conditions which her father described during the most horrific of his stories.

She had hoped to see the *Gerken* tied to the pier below the bluffs. She wondered if they might have given up the notion of running to Buffalo in the storm and returned to Erie for shelter. She even fantasized about climbing down the bluffs to the ship where she had hoped to see Herman sitting on deck, waiting for her. In her mind, she had almost convinced herself that his pleas during her dream had been a psychic request to join him on the ship that morning. But the *Gerken* was nowhere to be seen.

Disappointed, Suzanne turned to walk home. But as she grew nearer to her house, she decided that she didn't feel like stopping. Instead, she passed her house and continued her pre-dawn walk. She wasn't sure where she was headed or why she was still walking until she spotted St. Andrew's Church. Then she knew how to follow her heart. She broke into a trot and headed directly for the front steps of the church. Out of breath as she climbed the last stair, she grabbed at the massive brass handle of the church door only to pull and find it locked.

"Shit!" she muttered to herself. "This is what I get for missing Mass, I don't even know the damn church schedule."

Disappointed, tired and confused, Suzanne sat on the top of the steps and began to cry. She sobbed uncontrollably, wondering what to do next. It was so unlike her not to know exactly what to do in any situation that she was emotionally devastated by her own confusion.

"Suzanne, what's wrong?" asked a gentle voice from just a few feet away. It was Fr. Sheehan, dressed in a robe and slippers.

"It's complicated, Father," she responded between sobs. "I just needed to go to church and pray."

"Well, we can't have you locked out here if you want to pray, can we?" answered Fr. Sheehan, moving to the door to unlock it. "Help yourself! Can I be of assistance?" he offered.

"No, Father," replied Suzanne, "but thank you so much for letting me in. I really appreciate it."

"It's okay," he replied. "I couldn't sleep with all this wind anyway. Why don't you stay for 6:00 Mass?" he added, heading back to the rectory.

Even though she had no money, Suzanne lit four candles; one each for Cooley and Stickle, and two for Herman Wagerman. Then she sat in the pew next to the flickering candle stand and prayed. For the first time in years, she prayed fervently, asking God to take care of Herman that night.

Suzanne was awakened at 5:50 a.m. Her grandmother had entered church for Mass and was nudging her shoulder.

"Honey, how long have you been here?" her grandmother asked.

"I'm following my heart," Suzanne responded. "I've been in church all night!"

Suzanne's grandmother put her arms around her and gave her a hug. "Good girl," she added. "After Mass I'll buy you breakfast."

During Mass that morning, Fr. Sheehan offered a special prayer for all the sailors who were on the lakes during the evening storm. As he blessed the small, mostly female, congregation after mass, Suzanne and her grandmother were already walking through the church doors and heading for the restaurant a block from church.

"My God!" said Suzanne's grandmother as she stepped through the door.

A morning paper on the counter featured headlines about the *Gerken*: "Local Ship Sinks: Four Men Missing." Suzanne grabbed the paper and poured through the copy until she came to the paragraph which confirmed her worst fears. "The missing include Bill Logan, Richard Freeman, George McMinn and Herman Wagerman." With tears streaming from her eyes, Suzanne Franzesi bolted through the door of the restaurant and ran toward her home.

# PART NINE

# Reunion

*Jesus was a sailor,*
*when he walked upon the water*
*and he spent a long time watching*
*from his lonely wooden tower.*
*And when he knew for certain,*
*only drowning men could see him*
*he said all men will be sailors,*
*then, until the sea shall free them.*

**Leonard Cohen**
*Suzanne*

# CHAPTER 25
# Returning to Erie

## [SATURDAY, AUGUST 21, 1926, 7:15 A.M.]

Suzanne Franzesi crashed through the front door of her house. She was sobbing uncontrollably and panting for breath after running home. Her mother was in the kitchen making breakfast and the sight of her daughter in such a state startled her.

"Suzanne, what is it?" she asked.

"I can't explain right now, Grama will tell you in a few minutes. But I need to borrow the truck," she answered.

"Are you sure you can drive?" asked her mother, concerned that Suzanne might have an accident.

"I can drive, Mom," she answered, "and I really need the truck. Please!"

"Go ahead and take it, but be careful," her mother begged.

For the second time in twenty-four hours, Suzanne found herself driving her father's Ford truck toward the waterfront and thinking about Herman Wagerman. But this time she was not feeling the romantic high she had experienced the day before. She was frightened, confused, and unsure of where to drive. Something compelled her to turn west and head toward the peninsula and the Coast Guard Station. By 7:45 a.m., she was on Presque Isle, following rough inland roads toward the eastern end of the sand spit. She drove too fast, swerving to avoid fallen branches and other debris from the storm. Halfway to the stationhouse, a fallen tree blocked her way. A huge cottonwood had dropped across the road, leaving no room to drive around it.

Suzanne pulled the truck to the side of the road, got out and climbed over the tree. Once on the other side, she broke into a run, heading for the Coast Guard Station on foot. After a half mile, her throat ached. She was gasping for breath and gagging on blood which had trickled into her throat from the exertion. She slowed to a trot, then walked until she regained her breath. Then she alternatively ran and walked, conserving energy. The terrain was difficult and she slipped several times, but by 9:00 a.m. she was nearing the channel. When she approached the concrete pier, which ran the length of the channel, Suzanne could see a Coast Guard vessel heading in from the lake.

"Oh, God," she thought, "please let them tell me that they found Herman."

She sprinted down the walkway, watching the stationhouse crew as they hurried to the channel's edge to meet the arriving boat. Letters on the big gray boat read *CG3122*.

The sight of a lone female running toward the Coast Guard Station was quite a shock for the men on the pier. Suzanne raced up to them and blurted out her question.

"Did you find anyone from the *Gerken*?" she asked breathlessly.

Al Coppine studied the young woman, wondering how she had gotten to the peninsula and why she was asking.

"We don't know yet," he answered, "but there's a good chance that they found someone or Captain Seymore wouldn't be coming back just yet. He's been on the lake all night searching."

"I'm looking for a man named Herman Wagerman," Suzanne added. "Please tell me if you know anything about him!"

"Try to be patient, Miss," Coppine answered. "We'll have to wait until the boat ties up."

As Coppine spoke, the picket boat's bowman began hailing. "Prepare for a survivor," he shouted. "We have one man aboard and he is half frozen to death!"

At that, Suzanne Franzesi sunk to the ground in exhaustion and despair.

"What's wrong?" asked Coppine, trying to help her to her feet.

"What if it isn't Herman?" she answered.

Suzanne sat on the wet ground in a daze, watching as the boat pulled up to the pier. Quickly, lines were thrown to the men on shore and the picket boat was secured to the channel wall.

"Help us unload this man!" yelled Captain Seymore. "We have to get him inside and warm him immediately."

While she watched, four men climbed aboard, went below and emerged with a stretcher.

"Careful there!" Seymore barked, as he and Heyman helped the crew carry the stretcher from the boat.

Suzanne rose and ran to the side of the boat.

"Sorry, Miss," cautioned Seymore, "but this man needs medical attention right away."

Undaunted, she moved to the side of the stretcher and pulled back the blankets.

"Herman!" she cried. "Thank God it's him."

Wagerman's lips moved in response to Suzanne's voice but they made no sounds. Then with a twist of his body Herman Wagerman pulled his hand above the blanket. He was still clutching the knife that Suzanne had given him just days before. She bent to kiss him and took his frozen hand in hers.

"My God!" she said. "He's so cold!"

"So you're Suzanne," chuckled Seymore. "That's all he could say when we fished him out of the water. He's been clutching that knife and repeating your name over and over."

"Can I please go with him into the stationhouse?" she begged.

"Of course," answered Seymore, "you're probably the best medicine we have for him right now."

With Suzanne's assistance, the crew took Wagerman inside. Seymore led the way to a small room near the rear of the station and directed the crew to carry Wagerman inside.

"It's the closest thing we have to a sick bay," he noted. "Not too fancy, but there's a warm bed with plenty of wool blankets. We have to warm him up as fast as we can."

She helped the men peel off Herman's wet clothing. Wagerman's lips were white and his skin was almost gray, but he was breathing steadily and Suzanne thought that he was responding to her. They took all of his clothing off, then covered him with wool blankets.

"What's next?" asked Suzanne, after everyone but she and Seymore had left the room.

"We could put him in warm water," replied Seymore, "but that's risky. Bringing a man back from freezing needs to be done slowly and carefully," he added. "I don't mean to pry, Miss, but just how well do you know him?" asked Seymore.

"We're almost engaged to be married," blurted out Suzanne. As soon as she had said it, she wondered what had compelled her to say such a thing.

"Well, Miss," added Seymore thoughtfully, "there is something that you could do for him if you're up to it. The very best thing would be to have you lie next to him. He could use your body heat to warm up. It could even save his life!"

Without hesitating Suzanne agreed. "Of course I'll do it," she replied. "Should I leave all of my clothing on?" she asked. As she questioned Seymore, her embarrassment was growing.

"I don't know your relationship with him," answered Captain Seymore, "but this man needs warmth and he needs it fast. We won't get a doctor out here for hours," he added, "so whatever we do for him has to be done by us and done right away."

Sensing both her willingness and discomfort, Seymore opened the door to leave.

"I can guarantee that you will be left alone with him in this room. No one will disturb you. Now having said that," Seymore continued, "the closer you get to him and the more you share your body warmth, the better his chances for coming out of this."

Nelson Seymore leaned down for a last look at Wagerman.

Glancing at Suzanne he said, "You're a lucky man sailor, an angel really did come for you!" With that, he left the room and closed the door. "Call if you need anything," he added, walking down the hallway. "Someone will bring hot food at noon."

Seymore left the station, returned to his picket boat and headed back out into the lake to search for the missing crew members.

Alone with Herman, Suzanne looked at herself in the mirror on the door. Her clothing was muddy and wet from perspiration and her hair was a mess from the wind and rain. She was embarrassed and nervous as she pondered Captain Seymore's words. Then she looked at Wagerman again. His eyes were closed tight and he was trembling uncontrollably, even though it was warm in the room and he was covered with woolen blankets. As she watched him shake, her reservations melted. She pulled her wet sweater over her head and put it on the table next to his bed. Then she untied her shoes, removed them and took her muddy jeans off.

Slowly, gently, she pulled back Herman's blankets and gazed at him. He seemed thinner than before. Pale. He looked like a little boy, trembling in fear and bunched into a near-fetal position. It was an amazing contrast, this strong, handsome man looking like a frightened, cold little boy.

Suzanne Franzesi slid into bed next to Herman and pulled him to her, flinching when his icy body met hers. As Herman's skin touched hers, he seemed to relax and roll toward her. His head fell naturally into the crook between her shoulder and chin. When their bodies met, she felt the full electric shock of cold stabbing at her. In moments she was shivering too, but she pulled the covers around the two of them and drew him to her. Suzanne grew colder and colder. Soon, she was shivering almost as hard as Herman, but she didn't move away from him. At first she didn't know if she could stand the piercing cold, but after several minutes she began to warm up. At the same time, she could tell that Herman's shivering was lessening. She responded by holding him even tighter and wrapping her arms and legs around him.

# CHAPTER 26

# Redemption: Wagerman's Last Dream

[SATURDAY, AUGUST 21, 1926, 10:00 A.M.]

*Herman Wagerman was having another dream and it was a vivid one. He had finally given up and fallen asleep. The water was far too cold for him to go on swimming and he fully understood that he was freezing to death. He said his final sailor's prayers and fell into a deep sleep, realizing that the next time he awakened he would be in the hereafter.*

*Herman drifted, shifting his attention from the cold Lake Erie water to the waves of peacefulness that came with deep sleep. He wondered how things would be in the next world. Had he done enough good deeds to tip the cosmic balance in his favor? Would he be meeting people from the good side or the bad? He waited patiently for his new friend Death to return and take him to Logan. As he pondered eternal destiny, he felt himself lifted from the sea and turned in circles by strong hands. He heard voices talking about him and wondered who these beings were. They didn't look like Death!*

*Wagerman was still cold, but at least he didn't feel wet anymore as they lifted him. Then a comforting face appeared.*

*"It must be St. Peter," Herman decided, "and he's talking to me about something."*

*But as hard as Herman Wagerman struggled, he couldn't pay attention. He didn't understand what St. Peter was telling him, but he was comforted by the fact that the guardian of heaven's gates seemed to be wearing a naval officer's uniform.*

*"That's going to work to my advantage up here," he thought to himself, remembering that St. Peter was a fisherman. "How ironic," he mused, "the Great Fisherman has just pulled me out of Lake Erie!"*

*Suddenly, Wagerman thought about Suzanne and the fact that he was still clutching her knife. He knew that he had to return it to her, so the next time St. Peter stopped to talk with him Herman tried to tell him that it was Suzanne's knife and that he had to return it.*

*"Maybe he'll let me go back," he thought.*

*Suspended in this strange place, Wagerman listened while St. Peter told his assistants to put him down below so he could warm up.*

*"No! Not down below!" he thought in a panic.*

*"Don't worry," St. Peter said in a reassuring voice, "it's just for a few moments until we can take you back."*

*"Back where?" he thought.*

*St. Peter left and his assistants wrapped Wagerman in something and took him to a warmer place.*

*"This must be purgatory," he decided, as he drifted into a sleep that had no dreams.*

*Sometime later, Wagerman was aroused again by St. Peter's voice. It sounded as though he was giving instructions.*

*"Oh, great," he thought to himself, "they're deciding if I should go to heaven or hell and I'm not going to be able to get in a word edgewise."*

*He tried to open his eyes and speak but he was still too cold. As he waited there, trying to get his bearings, St. Peter moved closer* to him and said, *"You're a lucky man, sailor, an angel has come for you!"*

*"An angel? Does that mean that I'm going upstairs?" he wondered.*

*A moment later, Herman could feel the angel. She was holding him, pulling him close to her and stroking his head. The angel kept repeating his name, telling him that she loved him. Herman moved closer and closer to his angel as she warmed him, feeling heat from her body radiate through his. As he warmed, he stopped shivering and gradually opened his eyes.*

*"Are you really my angel?" he asked, looking through blurry eyes at the being who was taking him to heaven.*

*The angel leaned away from him for a moment and looked into his eyes.*

*"St. Peter sent an angel who looks exactly like Suzanne," he thought to himself. Herman tried to speak once more. "I know you're an angel, but do you know a beautiful woman named Suzanne Franzesi who lives on earth?" he asked.*

*With that, his angel removed her bra and pressed Herman's face to her breasts.*

*"Yes, Herman, I do," she answered, "and she loves you very much."*

*Confused by a flood of new feelings Herman mustered a final question. "I'm not sure if I should do this," he whispered, "what would Suzanne think? I really love her," he added.*

*The angel answered Herman's query by pressing herself against him even more tightly. Wagerman was drowning again. But this time, he was drowning in the warmth of a dream woman.*

# CHAPTER 27
## Life Continues

[SUNDAY, AUGUST 22, 1926, 7:30 P.M.]

Bedraggled and tired, but otherwise unharmed, Ben Cooley and George Stickle sailed into Erie's harbor with the crew of the yacht *Eagle*. Reporters, fresh from stories about the weekend sinking of the *Gerken*, flocked to the Erie Yacht Club to interview the pair. Cooley and Stickle noted their extreme good fortune in not being swept beyond the tip of Long Point and their appreciation for the generosity of Long Point lighthouse keeper Lorne Brown. Monday's headlines in the *Erie DailyTimes* read: "Local Architects Narrowly Escape The Wrath of August Gale."

After gathering strength the next week, Cooley and Stickle prepared a shipment of gifts and clothing for lighthouse keeper Lorne Brown that they sent via railroad express. Cooley didn't understand why Suzanne Franzesi never called to ask about his adventures on the lake. He phoned several times to express his apologies for what he had done, but his calls were never answered.

Lighthouse keeper Lorne Brown, who continued at the Long Point light for another ten years, added the names of the two Erie architects to the long list of sailors who had been assisted over the years since the lighthouse was built in 1830. The list persists to this day, even though the last lighthouse keeper was relieved of duty when the Long Point Station Light was automated in 1989.

# [TUESDAY, AUGUST 24, 1926]

Headlines in the *Erie Daily Times* announced the death of silent film actor Rudolph Valentino. Valentino had taken terribly ill several weeks earlier. Doctors in Los Angeles attempted exploratory abdominal surgery, but finding nothing apparently wrong they sent the actor home to die. The paper predicted a hopeful day in the not-too-distant future when science and technology would provide marvelous new inventions that would save people from premature deaths.

In the shipping news section at the bottom of the front page, it was noted that a fish tug from Erie had found the body of First Mate George McMinn, lost in the weekend sinking of the *Gerken*. McMinn was spotted floating in his life vest, five miles off Dunkirk, New York.

Watchman Dick Freemen washed ashore on a beach near Dunkirk the following day. His body, also clad in an orange life jacket, was found by two young boys walking the beach. Later that day, the fish tug *Venus*, working out of Erie, found the missing lifeboat floating near the New York–Pennsylvania state line. On Wednesday, August 25, the Erie fish tug *Toledo* found the body of Bill Logan in the water ten miles north of Dunkirk.

Saturday, the shipping news column reported its weekly list of Coast Guard activities. Captain Nelson Seymore was credited with a second life saved for the week when his beach patrol spotted a privately owned fishing boat burning four miles north of Erie's peninsula beaches. William Damon, a St. Andrew's parishioner, was forced into the water when his 16-foot boat caught fire and burned to the waterline. Seymore's crew launched the picket boat and rushed to his assistance, returning him unharmed to the stationhouse at

10:00 p.m. According to the same report, Al Coppine was involved in a high-speed chase with a rumrunner over the weekend. The smugglers, who had eluded Seymore's picket boat in the open lake, came roaring into the harbor looking for a place to dock and unload. Revving his old wooden cutter to its top speed, Coppine chased the Canadian gray ghost across Erie's bay, forcing it away from the town docks and back toward the peninsula. Once clear of the city, Coppine's crew fired thirty rounds of ammunition at the high-speed rumrunners. The smugglers gave up and were taken into custody. It was noted in the article that the U.S. Coast Guard was willing to pay a reward to anyone providing a tip leading to the apprehension of rumrunners.

## [NOVEMBER, 1926]

Thanksgiving was a festive time for St. Andrew's Portuguese community. By late November, fishing was almost over for the year and the men were home after a long summer season. Their inclusion in the holiday generally marked the first time since Trinity Sunday that families were intact. And for Portuguese people, family and children meant everything. But this Thanksgiving holiday was an especially festive occasion. In addition to the traditional turkey eating and celebrating, a Saturday wedding punctuated the 1926 holiday. Suzanne Franzesi stood at the altar and exchanged vows with the Buffalo boy she had met the summer before. Suzanne and her fiancé had been inseparable since August when the gale brought them together. In fact, the story of their romance had been repeated thousands of times that fall as Herman recuperated in a spare bedroom at the Franzesi house under the watchful eye of Suzanne's grandmother. Suzanne's family took Herman in and treated him like a long-lost son, giving him a job on one of their fish tugs.

Since early September, Wagerman had become a mainstay at St. Andrew's Church and a familiar sight in the neighborhood. He and Suzanne spent every moment together. They walked aimlessly through the neighborhood, hand in hand, and sat on the edge of the bluffs watching sunrises and sunsets almost every day. When Fr. Sheehan pronounced Herman and Suzanne man-and-wife and sent them down the aisle toward the rear of the church and a reception at the Holy Trinity Portuguese Society, friends and family literally cheered for St. Andrew's favorite newlyweds.

Herman had become familiar with Suzanne's family and friends so he was taken aback when he noted a vaguely familiar man in an aisle seat toward the rear of the church. He was thin and weathered looking, like a fisherman or sailor, but obviously not a member of Suzanne's Portuguese family. Herman knew that he had met him before but he couldn't remember where. Then the strangely familiar man showed up at the reception, helping himself to food and especially to the "unofficial" drinks which were available at the bar. Herman studied him during the reception. It was obvious that Suzanne's father and brothers knew him. In fact, all of the men seemed to know him and treat him in a deferential way. Finally, Herman asked Suzanne if she knew who he was.

She responded affirmatively. "He's an old waterfront character named Joe Divell. Everybody knows him!"

Part of the tradition at every Portuguese wedding reception was the "money dance." The best man and maid of honor, carrying decorated white boxes, invited everyone to dance with the bride and groom. All of the men lined up for turns dancing with the bride. As they did, they placed money in the box held by the maid of honor. At the same time, the women and young girls lined up to dance with the groom. Traditionally, the money is used for the honeymoon. Dozens of women danced with Herman that afternoon, hugging him and wishing him luck.

His second from last dance partner was Grama Franzesi.

"I know you'll take good care of my little girl," she whispered in his ear, "and I'll be praying for both of you."

As Herman danced with the woman whose prayers may have been responsible for saving his life, Grama Franzesi continued whispering in his ear, letting him know that she had been Suzanne's confidant throughout the troubled night of the Devil Wind. "I'm so glad she went to be with you at the Coast Guard Station," Grama Franzesi told him, "and that she was there with you when you recovered." She winked knowingly.

Grama Franzesi's spell was shattered when a big hand tapped Herman's shoulder for the last wedding dance. Turning, Herman came eye to eye with Joe Divell.

"You want to dance?" Herman asked.

He had become uneasy since Suzanne told him who Divell was. He barely recognized Joe cleaned up and in a suit, and wondered if he was there to extract some kind of payment or to press Herman to continue with their aborted treasure scheme.

"Damn it, Herman," responded Joe Divell, "don't make me start talkin' like a sailor. It's not easy being in church and hanging around with all these nice ladies," he continued. "I came because I wanted to give you this, goddamn it."

Divell reached inside his jacket, pulled out an envelope and handed it to Wagerman.

"I've been feeling guilty for my part in what happened to you and your friends," Divell continued. "So I rounded up everything that you and Logan brought to me and sold it for top buck. I'm giving the proceeds to you and your wife. Use it to start a new life!" he added. "And I don't want to hear any arguments either! Just take it," he said as he turned and walked away.

When the reception was over, Suzanne's father drove the newlyweds to the railroad station where they boarded the night train for Niagara Falls. Secure in their first class compartment, a gift from Grama Franzesi, Herman and Suzanne began to sort through their things and inspect the contents of the wedding dance boxes. Suzanne eventually opened the envelope that Joe Divell had given them.

"My God, Herman, there's more than two thousand dollars here!" she said.

Herman was more interested in the fact that the seat in their compartment folded into a double bed.

"Two thousand dollars," Suzanne mumbled as Wagerman pulled her onto the unfolded mattress. "Why would he give us so much money?"

"Does your Grandmother know absolutely everything about us?" Wagerman asked.

Before she could answer, he turned off the light.

## [EARLY DECEMBER, 1926]

Right after their honeymoon, Herman and Suzanne Wagerman used the money that Divell had given them to make two down payments. First they purchased a five-year-old fish tug. Even though there was a superstition about changing a boat's name, Herman immediately

took a bucket of maroon paint and renamed it *Suzanne Marie*.
Wagerman wasn't worried about Lake Erie anymore. He would have
an angel working with him on the tug that summer. They used the
rest of the money to make a deposit on a house that was on the same
block as the Franzesi family homestead. Herman was pleased that the
house had four bedrooms, lots of room in case Grama Franzesi ever
needed a place to stay.

# EPILOGUE
# Maritime Litigation & Salvage

## [LATE DECEMBER, 1926]

The early Great Lakes ship owners were entrepreneurs. Technology changed during the twentieth century, however, and the complexion of ship ownership changed. Individual owner/captains were joined in the business by giant corporate fleet owners. Organizations such as Ford and Bethlehem Steel entered the world of Great Lakes shipping, operating fleets of large, modern freight-hauling vessels. But well into the early 1900s, the majority of ships were still owned by small businessmen whose livelihoods depended entirely upon the efficiency of their vessels.

A shipping disaster was such a threat to economic prosperity that many owners took out insurance on ships and cargoes. Others, especially the operators of the small older vessels, preferred to take their chances. They reasoned that the ships, themselves, and their bulk cargoes were not worth insuring. Maritime disasters, especially those that did not lead to significant losses of lives, often turned into protracted legal disputes. The contestants were usually owners, anxious to be compensated for their business losses, and the "official entity" which could most logically be held accountable. Suits were regularly launched against other ship owners (maritime accidents), insurance companies (which were often reluctant to pay), and government agencies. Since the Coast Guard seemed to bear responsibility for safety at sea, they were a regular litigation target.

Desperate owners would spare no end of creativity in seeking payment for the loss of a ship or its cargo. The owners were also clever enough to orchestrate their claims in court jurisdictions that promised to be most sympathetic. When the steamers *Atlantic* and *Ogdensburg* collided off Erie in 1852, for example, *Atlantic*'s owners filed their suit in an Erie Court. They knew that the survivors had been brought to Erie after the disaster and that the local press had featured front-page coverage of the collision for weeks on end. The three daily papers had followed the plights of survivors, the sorrow of their families and the attempts to salvage the safe from the great ship. As deep-sea salvage diver Johnnie B. Green worked to recover the *Atlantic*'s safe, Erieites followed the newspaper accounts of his adventures with bated breath. And they shared in Green's disappointment when he was stricken with the bends during his attempts. The people of Erie had adopted the *Atlantic* as their own and vilified the *Ogdensburg* for her part in the collision.

*Ogdensburg*'s owners, realizing that they were at risk of paying a small fortune in damages, launched a countersuit in Ohio where the ship was officially registered. As might have been predicted, Erie courts found the captain of the *Ogdensburg* negligent for not having avoided the *Atlantic*, while Ohio courts ruled the opposite. The opposing judgements sent the aggrieved parties to higher courts. The legal matter simmered for years before it was determined that both captains shared responsibility.

There was another major controversial case in 1893 surrounding the burning of the steamer *Oneida* just east of Erie. *Oneida* mysteriously caught fire a few miles offshore and was driven aground before the fire could present a danger to captain or crew. Lifeboats were launched only a few hundred yards from the beach on a calm summer evening and the captain and crew rowed to shore. Meanwhile, the ship burned to its water line. *Oneida*'s owner presented a claim for the loss of the steamer and her cargo that was contested by his insurance company. The insurer questioned the "convenience" of the fire, noting that the owner had a reputation for not insuring any of his ships. He had often bragged that he was able to totally refit one of his ships each year on money that would have otherwise been "wasted" on insurance premiums. Ironically, the *Oneida* had been the one ship from his fleet that was refitted the previous winter. The owner argued that with advances in safety and navigational aids, insurance was redundant to good maintenance.

In light of this business philosophy it seemed odd that a slow 1892 shipping season, followed by a disastrous business year in 1893, had led *Oneida*'s owner to purchase insurance on the old ship in mid-season. The fact that the *Oneida* was the only ship from its fleet both to be insured and lost that season, seemed far too great a coincidence to the insurance company. A Buffalo court, the *Oneida*'s home jurisdiction, ruled that there was no proof that the fire aboard the steamer had been deliberately set. Consequently, the insurance company was forced to pay the settlement.

The wreck of the *Gerken* represented the third major litigation, set in Central Lake Erie. The loss of the sandsucker presented a huge difficulty for Howard Gerken, Sr. and his Buffalo-based business. The sandsucker was the basic revenue-generating tool of Gerken Sand & Gravel Company. To get into the sand and gravel business in the first place, Howard Gerken, Sr. had spent years hunting for a suitable old steamer that he brought to Buffalo and carefully retrofitted for the dredging business. To repeat this feat, even if another bargain ship could be located, would take years. In the meantime, Senior Gerken's ability to do business was, for all intents and purposes, totally ended. Without an immediate and substantial settlement, the Gerken family and its sixty-three employees would be without work. Once the human tragedy associated with the deaths of the three crew members had partially dissipated from the Gerken family and its Buffalo business office, Senior Gerken became intent upon seeking a financial settlement to save his company.

Howard Gerken, Sr. took the Erie Coast Guard Station to court in Buffalo during the Fall of 1926. Seeking damages in an amount that would ensure the continued operations of his business, he argued that the Coast Guard was derelict in its duty as watchmen for not seeing distress signals launched from the *Gerken* on the evening of August 20. He noted in his argument that his ship originally foundered just a few miles north of the U.S. shore while still in the protection of the bluffs. Continuing his testimony, he reasoned that Coast Guard personnel should have seen the first distress signals. Howard Gerken noted that they should have come to the assistance of the ship, long before gale-force winds and waves drove them into the center of the lake where they were put in peril because of the huge offshore waves.

"Had the Coast Guard responded properly," he stated in the court record, "the ship and its entire crew would have been saved."

Throughout the proceedings, Gerken claimed that his ship had been just east of Erie and well within visual range of Coast Guard watchmen. He argued vehemently that on such a stormy evening, it was the responsibility of the government-funded office to maintain a proper watch. Senior Gerken's counsel noted that, given the intensity of the emergency signals from the deck as the ship went down that night, any reasonably competent watchman should have spotted the ship in distress.

Several of *Gerken*'s crew members attested to the sandsucker's schedule that evening. Unfortunately, first mate McMinn, who was at the wheel while the owner and his engineering officers were having dinner, had drowned and was unable to testify. Both John and Jesse Gerken, the engineering officers, testified that their instructions to McMinn had been to complete a final dredge just east of where they had been sucking sand, then head back toward the bluffs to get out of the mid-lake waves.

The judge expressed interest in hearing testimony from the one man who was lost at sea, but survived. Howard Gerken vehemently insisted that Herman Wagerman had endured enough tragedy already and that he should be excused. Senior pleaded with the court not to bother the unfortunate young man with legal details.

Captain Nelson Seymore's testimony followed that of *Gerken*'s crew. He and his corroborating witnesses brought the evening log from the beach patrol indicating precisely when *Gerken* had steamed out of the channel and moved to the dredging grounds. The beach patrol had spotted the sandsucker working offshore and then reported seeing her move off and disappear to the north, rather than heading east as Howard Gerken had suggested. In their final presentation of evidence, the Coast Guard offered testimony from two City of Erie police officers who noted that they were with Seymore on the Erie channel wall staring east, after they had already heard reports of a ship in distress. Even then, they were not able to spot anything east of the station.

The *Maitland's* newly-appointed full-Captain Thomas Heyman, First Mate William Burke, and recently-promoted Second Mate Pete Brinley were also called to testify. Their testimony was consistent. They said that they were unsure of their own exact position because of the storm but judged that that they were about ten miles from *Gerken's* signal fire when they first spotted it. They were unable to pinpoint *Gerken's* location with certainty in reference to the Erie channel. They could not be sure if the ship was northeast or northwest of the channel entrance. Heyman seemed to play politician and suggest that the size of the waves that night made it difficult to accurately determine position. When the judge pressed him to estimate if the *Gerken's* or the Coast Guard's estimate of position was more correct, he offered a compromise.

"If I had to speculate, Your Honor," Heyman stated in the court stenographer's record, "I would say that the actual position of the *Gerken* was halfway between the two opinions previously presented!"

# [AUGUST, 1996]

The 1980s and 1990s witnessed renewed interest in Great Lakes history and particularly in shipwrecks. Recreational diving grew in popularity and as Lake Erie's waters cleared following decades of pollution and abuse, scuba enthusiasts rediscovered shipwrecks. Even though more and more divers became obsessed with locating Central Lake Erie's long-lost deepwater wrecks, the *Gerken* eluded discovery. The most notable shipwreck discoveries of the era included the steamer *Atlantic*, located in 1983 by Mike Fletcher, and the *Dean Richmond*, found in 1984 by Garry Kozak. Several other schooners and steamers were located in the relatively shallow waters surrounding Long Point and Erie.

Only a few divers had the equipment and dedication required to seek out the elusive deep-water wrecks. To find them they would carefully read the recorded history of the wrecks, newspaper accounts and court testimony (if it existed), then try to retrace the last hours of a fated ship in an attempt to estimate its location. Armed with historical data, they would use underwater side-scan sonar detectors to scour the lake bottom. The car ferry *Marquette & Bessemer #2* was a primary target during the 1990s with most divers convinced that the big ship would be located using modern technology. But even with detailed information regarding a wreck's probable location, finding it in deep water is like hunting for a needle in a haystack.

A number of divers expressed interest in the *Gerken*, but information about its location was confusing and conflicted. While most thought it was east of Erie and substantially offshore, there could be no definitive conclusions about where it actually went down because of the confusion between reports issued by the Coast Guard, the crew of the *Maitland* and Howard Gerken, Sr., himself.

Erie diver, Mary Howard, was fascinated by the story of the *Gerken* and spent four years searching the lake using state-of-the-art sounding equipment. But like other divers, her search was clouded by conflicting reports of where the ship had gone down.

In May 1996, Mary received a call from the Erie Bookstore asking if she was interested in purchasing a log book from an old Erie fish tug called the *Liberty*. Always excited about such artifacts, she interrupted her obsession with the *Gerken* to travel to the bookstore and take a look at the old ship's ledger.

Her first analysis of the document revealed nothing of significance. The book was essentially a business ledger detailing activities, expenses and fish catches. Thumbing through tattered pages, however, her attention was peaked by an entry from October 6, 1928. Captain Harry Boyd, of the tug *Liberty*, noted that he had taken Howard Gerken, Sr., of Buffalo, New York, to the site of his sunken sandsucker and planted anchors around the vessel. Barely able to contain her excitement, she followed the entries for several weeks.

Captain Boyd used the *Liberty* to take divers to the site of the wreck, where they attached lines and prepared an attempt to refloat the *Gerken*. The series of entries ended in late November 1928, when it seemed that the salvage activity ceased. There were no further entries about the *Gerken* and the ledger expired at the end of the 1928 business year. It was impossible to tell if salvage attempts had continued.

Frustrated by coming so close, Mary Howard used this lead to return to the local library and its microfilm newspaper archives. This time, however, she searched the archives for the year 1928, almost 24 months after the sinking of the *Gerken*. And there, she finally struck pay dirt! An *Erie Daily Times* article from the summer of 1928 announced plans to refloat the sandsucker *Gerken*. Divers were supposedly going to attach steel cables to the *Gerken*, after which a number of fish tugs would be used to tow the old sandsucker into the shallow water of the bay. From that vantage point divers would use floats to bring the steamship toward the surface and then pump it out. The newspaper account quoted Mr. Howard Gerken's optimism with respect to the salvage attempt. More importantly, it indicated the precise location of the wreck: Nine miles, 700 feet from the Erie channel entrance on a compass bearing of 40 degrees magnetic.

Following "instructions" from the 1928 *Erie Daily Times* article, Mary and her husband left Erie's channel in late August of 1996 to search for the *Gerken*. It was almost exactly seventy years from the anniversary of her sinking. Amazingly, the newspaper description took them directly to a "hit" on the side-scan screen. Mary quickly donned diving gear and went overboard with a camera and light. There, lying almost on her side, was the steamship *Gerken*. After four years of searching, a fish tug captain's journal and an old newspaper account had, by some mysterious process, taken her right to the site of the shipwreck. It was almost as though the *Gerken* was asking for her story to be told!

The old sandsucker was sleeping peacefully on the floor of Lake Erie, almost as though nothing special had ever happened to her. Mary swam along the sunken hull, barely able to believe that she had finally found the elusive target. As she touched the nameplate, she contemplated the history of the *Gerken* and the lives of the people that the old ship had touched. Peering through underwater haze in that moment of triumph, Mary Howard thought she could hear distant drumming; the mystical sounds of an Iroquois Indian drum.